The Writing Moment

The Writing Moment

A Practical Guide to Creating Poems

Daniel Scott Tysdal

OXFORD
UNIVERSITY PRESS

Oxford University Press is a department of the University of Oxford.
It furthers the University's objective of excellence in research, scholarship,
and education by publishing worldwide. Oxford is a registered trade mark of
Oxford University Press in the UK and in certain other countries.

Published in Canada by Oxford University Press
8 Sampson Mews, Suite 204, Don Mills, Ontario M3C 0H5 Canada

www.oupcanada.com

First Published 2014

Library and Archives Canada Cataloguing in Publication
Tysdal, Daniel Scott, 1978–, author
The writing moment : a practical guide to creating poems
/ Daniel Scott Tysdal.

Includes bibliographical references and index.
ISBN 978-0-19-900236-8 (pbk.)

1. Poetry—Authorship. I. Title.

PN1059.A9T98 2013 808.1 C2013-903555-9

Cover and chapter-opening images: © Petek Arici/iStockphoto,
© Katritch/iStockphoto, and ©zoom-zoom/iStockphoto

Oxford University Press is committed to our environment.
This book is printed on Forest Stewardship Council® certified paper
and comes from responsible sources.

Printed and bound in Canada

1 2 3 4 — 17 16 15 14

For Mr J,
Coach,
and Mike.

Three very different teachers united by their dedication
to the work of teaching
and to the work of what they teach.

Contents

Acknowledgements

I would like to begin by thanking Oxford University Press for the opportunity to write this book. Thank you to Suzanne Clark, Acquisitions Editor, for knocking on my office door and for guiding me with zeal through the proposal process. To my editor, Sarah Carmichael, thank you for your insightfulness, patience, enthusiasm, and wonderful sense of humour. Your discerning eye and sharp mind guided this book through its many restarts, rewrites, and re-orderings, and your enviable capacity to provide astute and practical feedback served as an ideal model in crafting this practical guide for burgeoning poets. *The Writing Moment* would have been a lesser work without you. Thank you, also, to my copy editor, Amy Hick. You went above and beyond in helping me polish up the final draft. I would like to acknowledge and thank the following reviewers, as well as the anonymous reviewers, whose comments and suggestions have helped to shape this text: Melissa Steele (University of Manitoba), Triny Finlay (University of New Brunswick), and Jacqueline Turner (Emily Carr University of Art and Design).

There are many folks at the University of Toronto Scarborough (UTSC) to whom I owe my deepest and most sincere gratitude. Thank you to my brilliant, supportive, and inspiring colleagues in the Department of English. Thank you to the UTSC Dean's Office for its dedication to creative writing in the classroom, on campus, and in the surrounding community. And thank you to the many students who contributed to this book: to those whose poems appear in these pages and also, just as importantly, to the many students whose poems should have appeared in these pages but could not due to the limits of print. I greatly appreciate your invaluable contributions. Thank you, too, to all of the students who participated in my poetry workshops, ENGB60 and ENGC86. This book arose out of our many invigorating discussions, collaborations, and writing adventures.

I have dedicated this book to three teachers, Mr Lyle Johnson (my high school drama teacher), Mr Mark Albert (my high school basketball coach), and Dr Michael Trussler (my professor at the University of Regina). I want to thank them for their incredible mentorship, and again acknowledge their dedication to their respective fields, to their students, and to the work of teaching. I also want to thank all of the excellent teachers and mentors who have guided me as a writer and teacher, including Mrs Marlene McBain, Mrs Julia Waldo, Ms Beverly McIntyre, Mr Dave Cook, Mrs Kathy Wheatley, Ms Kathy Dodds, Dr Jeanne Shami, Dr Alex McDonald, Dr Andy Stubbs, Dr Andrea Schwenke Wyile, Dr Lance La Roque, Dr Rosemary Sullivan, Gary Hyland, Don McKay, Anne Simpson, Tim Bowling, Richard Pass, Jerry Kaiser, and the Rt Reverend James A.J. Cowan.

Having just written a book devoted to the writing process, I feel a deep need to thank two of the venues where much of the process of writing this book took place: the Liberty Village Balzac's Coffee Roastery and the King West and Shaw Starbucks. Thank you to the staff of both establishments for great coffee, a warm environment, and many friendly conversations.

I will conclude by thanking the people who supported the creation of this book, who have supported my previous creative endeavours, and whose own work in this world inspires me to write and live with greater generosity and care. Stewart Cole, thank you for reading the manuscript cover to cover when you had many more pressing duties, and thank you for your friendship, your poetry, your thoughts on poetry, and the many poem-spurring conversations. Thank you to my family—Mom, Dad, Jayne, Nate, Justin, and Jude. I am grateful beyond words for your endless love and unquestioning support, and I am inspired daily by your tireless work ethics, energizing creativity, and continued successes. Finally, I want to thank Andrea Charise, the love of my life, my best friend, and (though I know you deny it) the co-author of everything I write. You are my ground, and the sky into which I reach.

Daniel Scott Tysdal
August 2013

Preface

The Occasions of Poetry and the Writing Moment

> "What would you say to putting together
> a verse or two for the occasion?"
>
> —Uncle Al

One Story about a Poem

My fiancée's Uncle Al asked me this question a few nights back: would I write a poem for the occasion of his son's wedding? You might expect this to be a query that comes right after the wedding invitations have been sent out, or even a few weeks before the big day. Not so. Uncle Al was feeling me out after the ceremony, in the bustling dining hall of the Royal Conservatory of Music, amid the buzz of 200 guests eager to celebrate the arrival of the newlyweds.

I, of course, said, "Yes, I would be honoured."

I was honoured, but also a bit anxious, a feeling that grew as Uncle Al left me—with a grateful handshake and a grin—to the blank page of my suddenly blank mind. I scanned the room for inspiration. Much struck me: the smartly set tables alive with candlelight and bouquets of white tulips, the lively chatter and laughter of the guests, the conservatory's all-glass wall rising two stories high, protecting us from the cold but exposing us to the wonder of one of those slow-mo, snow-globe snowfalls. Yet despite this rich environment, nothing moved me deeply to speak, no image or impression formed the beginnings of a poem.

And that's when it happened.

The bride and groom swept into the hall, took to the dance floor, and we, the guests, rose to our feet, applauding. While my fellow guests continued to cheer, and the newlyweds danced, I pulled out my notebook and started the poem. By the time the first course was served, I had finished an initial draft, which looked like so:

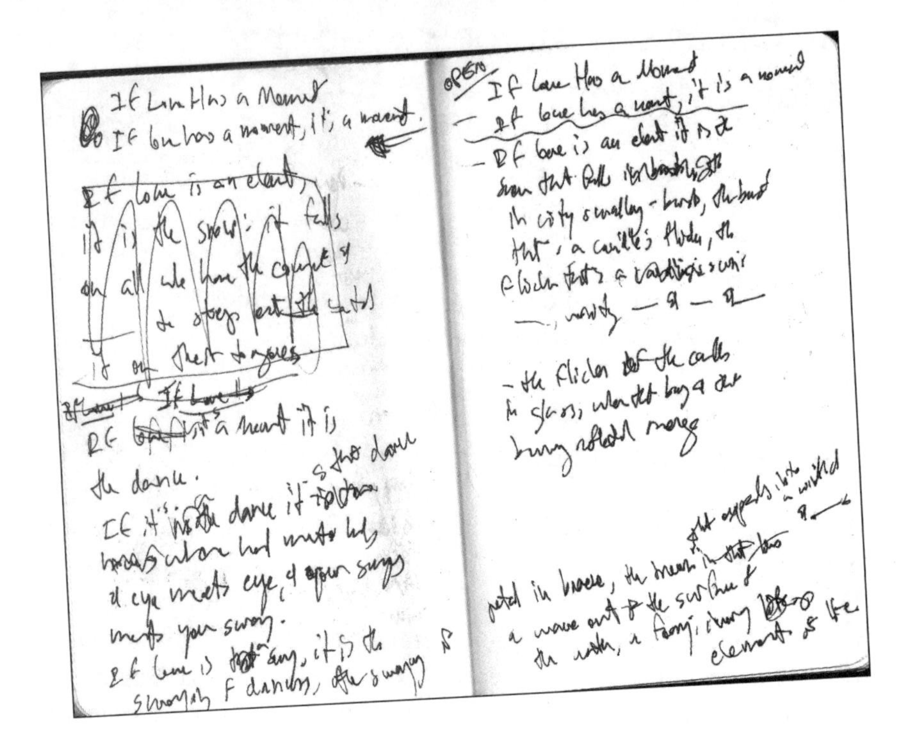

The next morning, I woke, typed up the poem, revising as I went, and emailed the finished work to Uncle Al with the subject line, "Poet Reporting In: A Verse for the Occasion." This is the poem, which, as the notebook draft attests, went through a few title changes: from "Love" to "If Love" to "If Love Is" to, finally, "If Love Has a Moment."

If Love Has a Moment

written on the occasion of Adam and Evanka's first dance,
February 16th, 2013

If love has a moment, it is a movement.
If a movement, it's the dance, the dance
in which hand joins hand, eyes join
eyes, and one sway joins another sway,
and this new swaying doesn't stop

even after the dancers leave the floor.
If love is a sway, it is this swaying
of dancers, the upward sway of petals
toward heat, the swaying of petals in
the breeze, the breeze that births waves
out of the surface of the water, a new
element forming where wind and water
meet. If love is an element, it is the snow
that touches all in a city-swallowing
burst, it is the burst of our applause and joy
as these dancing lovers dip, it is the dancing
light of all these candles in our applause's
breeze. If love is a light, it is the flickering
and dancing of this candle in its glass,
where this burning and this burning reflected
merge.

Not an Occasion, but Occasions

I could have opened this book with any number of anecdotes about the process of composing a poem. This particular story won out because it happened to me recently and was fresh in my mind. I had initially planned to share a story about finally writing my first sestina, a complex and quite old French form (which we will take a look at later in this book). Last term, a number of the students in my poetry course tackled the sestina, inspiring me to do so too. I had also thought about opening with a student anecdote. The writing exercises we undertake in and outside class (adventuring into the woods, say, or to the campus art gallery) often result not only in exciting poems, but also in surprising and instructive stories about how the poems came about.

Any one of these anecdotes could have effectively opened this book because each would have demonstrated the first assumption about the creative process upon which this book is founded: poems are born out of occasions, not a sole occasion.

What do I mean when I say occasions, plural, and not one occasion? I mean that the moment of inspiration, and the ensuing act of creation, arise out of a convergence of the occasions we traditionally think of as stimulating poems: the insight (into love, say, or loss), the emotion (or lack of emotion), the life moment (whether a community celebration or a mundane ride up an escalator), and the artistic motivation (whether to delight or disturb or anything else in between).

We can return to "If Love Has a Moment" as an example. The life moment, of course, is the wedding and Uncle Al's request in general, and more particularly that first, crowd-stirring dance. The insight was a perception of the interconnectedness of things that the poem celebrates. This insight was underpinned by the feeling of love that filled the hall, becoming palpable in the resonating applause and, even more personally, in the closeness of the love of my life as she swung her arm around me with a knowing squeeze when she saw me scribbling. The artistic motivation has an in-depth origin story, but the motivation itself is easily stated. For a few weeks, I had wanted to write a poem that made a series of comparisons by letting one comparison inspire the next. This experience provided the perfect opportunity. Hence, "love as moment" leads to "love as movement" leads to "love as dance," and so on.

This poem, then, might have been written on one occasion, but in it many occasions converge.

The Occasions of Poetry, Writing Moments, and *The Writing Moment*

The second assumption about the creative process upon which this book is founded derives from the first assumption: if poems arise out of a convergence of occasions, then the best way to teach the tools, techniques, and traditions of poetry is to immerse poets in the complex blend of occasions that characterizes the act of writing. This immersion is an effective way to encourage poets to write poems that—to honour the root of the word "verse"—turn, unfold dynamically with ingenuity, imagination, and skill. The following chapters accomplish this immersive introduction to craft by pairing my thoughts on a topic with a series of practical, hands-on writing moments.

These writing moments are micro-writing exercises that invite you to try your hand at the topic under discussion. I call these short exercises writing moments because of the helpful double meaning of moment. These writing moments are "moments" because they will only take a short time to complete and because, when you undertake them, you will be "having a moment," experiencing a break from the day-to-day that may already be common practice for you: turning—from a dinner table conversation or from an obligation at work or from a mindless stroll—to your notebook to scribble down the line or the form or the vision that just struck you.

The writing moments have been designed with two goals in mind. The first is to immerse you in this meeting of life and art, this convergence of occasions, by coupling active practice with abstract explanation; as is the case with all poets, your reading process will also become your writing process. The second is to initiate you into the two extreme poles of the poetic practice: the work—the writing routine, the daily grind, the practice that becomes a habit—and the invigorating experience of inspiration—the burst of insight or feeling with which a poem so often begins (and the experience that can transform the writing habit into an addiction). Writing moments take place within the purview of both of these poles, nurturing your habit and stimulating you to compose new work.

The writing moments, it is worth noting here, have been numbered for ease of reference by chapter and section. For example, the second writing moment in chapter three is labelled, "Writing Moment 3.2."

Each section also ends with a number of writing exercises and a pair of sample poems composed by some of the many talented students with whom I have had the good fortune to work. The writing exercises will give you the opportunity to further expand on the work undertaken during the writing moments, encouraging you to test out the new lessons and techniques as you compose new poems. The sample poems appear under the heading "Poems in Process." I have chosen this title for three reasons. First, all poems are poems in process—open to a tweak or two, or rigorous revision, or outright rewriting. I have heard many poets only half-joke that one of the main incentives for publishing their respective books was so they could work on something new. Second, these sample poems are poems in process insofar as they originated from the processes and practices you will explore in this book. Finally, I like how this designation highlights the fact that when, as a poet, you read any poem, you enter into the processes of the poem, with your way of reading and writing interacting with the poet's compositional strategies, and your vision and the poem's vision mixing, sometimes only to instantly diverge and other times to merge in fertile conversation.

In terms of how you work your way through this book, there is no incorrect approach. You may move through slowly, chapter-by-chapter, section-by-section, writing moment-by-writing moment, exercise-by-exercise. Or you may bounce around, skipping straight to the section-ending exercises or testing out the writing moments built around the tools that are new to you.

Whichever approach you take, there are two connected points to keep in mind. First, the work generated by the writing moments may be combined to create one new poem, kept separate to create a series of different poems, or tossed aside altogether. Second, in the case of this final option, remember that no writing is wasted writing. Just as basketball players—beginners and NBA All-Stars, alike—practice for hours each day to hone their skills, so too do we as poets hone our skills by practicing the "moves" of our favourite poets and getting intimately familiar with our tools by writing, writing, and writing some more.

Originality and the Writing Moment: The Life in Art and the Art in Life

Before wrapping up these prefatory remarks, I want to take the opportunity to answer two questions often raised by burgeoning poets in the context of writing instruction in general and writing exercises in particular.

The first question is: if I use the same writing exercises as other poets, won't I end up composing the same poem as them?

The second question is: if the goal is to compose a new poem, wouldn't I be better off ignoring other poets and focusing on my own experiences?

The easiest way to answer these questions is to consider the life in art and the art in life.

The first questioner is rightfully interested in originality and nervous about cliché. One of the qualities that often links good writing—no matter how different the works are in substance or style—is the absence of, or active reaction against, cliché: the trite phase, hackneyed theme, or commonplace construction. In the context of the writing exercise, which encourages active engagement with tools, traditions, and conventions, originality and difference arise from the life in art:

your particular life, your subjectivity and vision find form in and, in the most moving instances, transform these traditions, conventions, and expectations.

The flipside of this, and the response to the second questioner, is the equally necessary act of discovering the art in life. This means going beyond the mechanical, unreflective documentation of personal experience and feeling; in other words, realizing that experience or emotion alone do not a successful poem make. The tools of the poet allow you to mine the wonder hidden in the mundane, to preserve and explore the profound and stirring experience in a form that is—in its artfulness—equally stirring and profound. These tools allow you to reach outside of yourself to the symbols, structures, and rhythms we share, and with which we think and howl, and by which we are swayed and enthused.

The Writing Moment, then, aims to help you realize both manifestations of originality—the art in life and the life in art—as you compose your poems. It does so by encouraging you to encounter a variety of essential tools, techniques, and traditions through your individual act of writing, allowing you to experience first-hand the fact that *how* you say something in a poem is just as important as what you say. *The Writing Moment* demonstrates the intimate connection between life and art, reminding you that the choices we make on the page—revising this line or changing that word—are choices that extend far beyond the page, transforming the world we perceive and what we feel and how we live.

CHAPTER 1

Image, Music, and Metaphor

Introduction: Beginning at the Beginnings

> "How do poems grow? They grow out of your life."
> —Robert Penn Warren

When did you compose your first poem? What moved you? Where did you write the words and how did you arrange them? Or perhaps you have not yet written your first poem, but you want to. What is it that grabbed you? What moved you to pick up this book?

It started for me in the middle of the night. I was 15. I woke up on the top bunk. My best friend was asleep on the bunk below me. The adolescent meanderings of our late-night conversation had stirred me to reach in the dark for a notebook, fumble for a pen, and write down a pair of lines, a couplet (far too cringe-inducing to share with you here). One poet I spoke to wrote her first poem when she was twelve; it was about a tree she saw growing at a crossroads while on a trip to Montana with her family. Another started writing right after he witnessed his still-favourite poet light the room on fire with her words. One started after an argument with a priest, yet another while falling out of love for the very first time.

As these examples suggest, there are as many particular occasions for inspiring the first **draft** of a poem as there are poets: nature or the night, arguments or awe or anguish. Yet what links these many particular occasions are experiences of being overwhelmed, knocked off-balance, shifted out of the ordinary into the extraordinary, the difficult, the mysterious, the bliss just out of reach. These experiences may, as Robert Frost put it, take the form of "a lump in the throat, a sense of wrong, a homesickness, a lovesickness" (22), or they may arise as "the spontaneous overflow of powerful emotions" that William Wordsworth proposed should be "recollected in tranquillity" (50). "Poetry," as Chris Marker succinctly observes, "is born of insecurity" (*Sans Soleil*). A poem is the child of ambiguity and wonder, the strange and the ignored, whether these states are inspired by strong feeling or a total lack of feeling, by a community's welcome or prohibition, by language effortlessly flowing or stubbornly refusing to say what needs to be said. These are the moments out of which all our ensuing poems grow.

This chapter, then, rather than beginning at the beginning, will begin at the beginnings. The first beginning is three foundational **tools**: image, music, and **metaphor**. The second beginning is these experiences of the lump, the overwhelming, the insecurity, and so on that most often stimulate poems. I hope to stir these experiences by introducing you to your tools in conjunction with fertile life moments—personal experience, nature, and **perception**—and rousing encounters with the forbidden and the transgressed, the beautiful and the ugly, and the unsaid.

We will now begin with the expected—the poetic image—by turning to the not so obvious: the poem you are forbidden to write.

Working with the Image

What is the poem you are forbidden to write?

Before you can answer that question, I suppose, you need to answer other questions first. What, for you, is forbidden? Is it an act you are forbidden to perform? Or is it an object you are forbidden to possess?

Maybe it is an idea about which you are forbidden to think. In that case, what entity or power enforces the forbidding? Why? Does this enforcer exist outside of you or inside? Or is the answer both? Have you ever disobeyed or transgressed this prohibition? If yes, why? If no, why not?

Here is a writing moment that will help you crystallize the answers to these questions, and, in turn, lay the foundations for the poem you are forbidden to write. This writing moment, and the writing moments that follow, will help to clarify and expand on the themes and techniques we encounter throughout this book. Follow the prompts and see where they lead you. At the end of each section, the writing exercises will give you the opportunity to return to your writing moment material and expand it into complete poems—if you haven't already.

Writing Moment 1.1

- Make three columns: Forbidden Object, Forbidden Action, and Forbidden Thought. Take time to reflect on your life and jot down two or three examples in each category. Think carefully, reflecting on your beliefs and assumptions, on the different communities of which you are a member or from which you stand apart, on the variety of categories that define or fail to define you.
- Read and re-read your lists of forbidden objects, actions, and thoughts. Choose and note the one that affects you most deeply, the one that has the strongest memory associated with it.
- Return to this memory. This is a practice encouraged by the comics artist Lynda Barry (and, in turn, promoted by her teacher, Marilyn Frasca) in her excellent book *What It Is*. Situate yourself deeply in that memory; see the space, looking around you in all directions, looking above, behind, and below. Draw on all of your senses. What sounds strike you? What smells mark this moment? What is the taste on your lips? What can you reach out and touch and how does it feel? Look inside, as well: how do these experiences provoke internal sensations? With these questions in mind, close your eyes and explore the sensory environment of this memory.
- Jot down all of the sense memories that you have retrieved from that moment, doing so without filtering or editing.

Sensuous Subjective Imagery

Having completed this writing moment, you have made two gains.

First, you now have one possible beginning for the poem you are forbidden to write. Consider how your sense memories express the mood of this encounter with the forbidden. Perhaps your sense memories could be rearranged in order of intensity to create the impression of moving closer to (or further from) transgression. Another strategy could be to divide the sense memories into different categories, separating, for example, those that for you truly express the mood from those that do not.

Second, you have worked with our first example of the image, the image as **subjective** sensory impression. **Imagery**, most simply, is the material of our senses moved into language to, in turn, influence the senses of our readers. In their indispensable *Perrine's Sound and Sense*, Thomas R. Arp and Greg Johnson isolate seven types of imagery: visual (sight), auditory (sound), olfactory (smell), gustatory (taste), tactile (touch), organic (an internal sensation, e.g., hunger), and kinaesthetic (a movement or tension in muscles or joints) (58).

The benefits of subjective, sensuous imagery are many. The specificity of this imagery infuses your poem with an aura of authenticity. The richness of this imagery can move your readers to feel pleasure, as the hand embraces the stubbly or supple or bony cheek of a returning friend, or to feel pain, as the thumb of that same hand is sliced by the jagged lid of a tin can. Most importantly, when rendered with originality, this imagery will not only pull your readers into the world of your poem, but also offer your readers a new view on their own perceptual worlds.

Sight-Based Objective Imagery and Symbolic Imagery

This description of imagery only tells half the story. As your experience of reading and writing poetry probably indicates, the tools with which we work take a number of forms. For example, two other types of imagery with which we craft are sight-based **objective** imagery and **symbolic** imagery.

Sight-based objective imagery is imagery that aims to create the impression of a detached and emotionally level observer. This effect is achieved through a kind of purification: you do not incorporate your interior thoughts, or the impressions of the other four senses, or overt references to emotion. Often, attending to a single object and documenting its effect on its surroundings can achieve this.

Symbolic imagery is imagery informed by a tradition (for example, a religion), a body of knowledge (for example, a science), or an entity or activity in the world (for example, a type of labour). As poets, we most often employ this type of imagery as a means of exploring and expressing the symbolic richness of an experience or as a means of transforming an experience to reveal an otherwise unnoticed element.

For example, a Christian poet may employ Christian imagery—the cross, lamb, and the trinity—in her description of a landscape to reveal the presence of her God in the world. Or, to take another example, a poet who wants to articulate her experience of being swallowed by the contemporary world may describe her different body parts being transformed into different items that are symbolic of our modern times. In this instance, we can see the fluid quality of symbolic imagery: a poet composing two centuries ago might employ imagery associated with steam engines, a poet composing 100 years ago might employ imagery associated with automobiles, while a poet composing today might employ imagery associated with the Internet.

Here is a simple writing moment that builds on your work with subjective, sensuous imagery, and asks you to investigate these more objective and symbolic regions of the forbidden.

Writing Moment 1.2

- Return to the list you composed during the previous writing moment and choose a specific forbidden object.
- Write a list of descriptions of this object's physical appearance without using "I." The challenge is to suggest the power of the object—as embodied in its colour, shape, size, and so on—while remaining as objective, sight-based, and invisible as you can. Describe the seductive power of the object, the physical, visible qualities that tempt you to reach for and take hold of the object.
- We often associate a box, a safe, or a curtain with the forbidden. Forbidden things are kept in boxes and safes; they are hidden

behind curtains. Employing the same specific forbidden object, describe this object and its forbidden nature via imagery we associate with boxes, safes, and/or curtains.

In Writing Moment 1.1, we considered how the mood generated by the forbidden experience could be expressed through subjective, sensory engagement with the environment. This time, by contrast, we tested our capacity to withdraw and to reveal. With sight-based objective imagery, we erase the "I," focus on one object, and limit the senses to sight. With symbolic imagery, we employ the imagery of a tradition, body of knowledge, or activity as a means of revealing an otherwise unseen or unspoken aspect of our subject.

Both of these writing moments have thus introduced you to one of the poet's most important tools: the unsaid. The power of poetry so often arises from what is left out, from what is suggested, from the shimmering in language of what can only be approached but never fully articulated. Louise Glück is one of many poets to ask that we "harness the power of the unfinished" (74). As Glück observes, "that which we do not know, of the universe, of mortality, is so much more vast than that which we do know. What is unfinished or has been destroyed participates in these mysteries" (74–5). The same can be said for the poem that only gestures and glimpses and suggests. Such a poem enthrals.

The Ideal Image

Our third incarnation of the image, the image as ideal image, is more challenging to elucidate than the three types of imagery we have just explored. Because the ideal image is a more abstract concept than concrete imagery, it is considerably more varied in its manifestations. However, the ideal image figures prominently in a variety of fields of knowledge—from science to the literary arts—and your poems will benefit greatly from pursuing an intimate understanding of this type of image.

The simplest way to begin is with an abstract definition, followed by a specific example. The ideal image is any **figure**—whether mental or physical, whether in language or in picture form—that possesses three traits: first, it establishes a contrast with an apparent reality or "real state of things," second, it acts as a means of giving order to the disparate pieces of this reality, and, finally, it offers a best-case scenario, the model, the idyllic, a vision of this reality perfected.

The word "model" suggests, for me, a somewhat painful but, I hope, helpful example. Those of you who share my combination of poor manual dexterity and a flighty imagination will perhaps be able to relate. At an age I shall leave intentionally unstated, I attempted to build my first model car (a pink Volkswagen Beetle, if memory serves). I diligently snapped the pieces out of their plastic frames (bending and breaking many of them). I carefully applied the glue (leaving long, bubbling threads to harden on the car's exterior). When I finally finished (with my dad's help), I was left with a wreck. My car was to the image on the box what a beetle squished underfoot is to the gold-cast and jewel-encrusted scarab beetle once worn around a Pharaoh's neck. To sum up the analogy, my car was the "real state of things," while the ideal image was the photograph on the box

In works of literature, the ideal image is a dynamic literary tool. One prominent example is the conflict of vision. Works that employ the conflict of vision directly engage this tension between the ideal and the real. This conflict may take the form of fantasy versus reality, the imagined versus the actual, the longed-for versus what actually results. In extreme cases, the ideal can manifest either as a guiding saviour delivering us from the mad, disconnected chaos of reality—or as the rigid, self-enclosed dream blocking us from true access to lived experience. More often than not, writers explore the slipperiness of these supposedly contrasting versions of the ideal, the way in which they bleed into, and depend on, one another.

The following writing moment provides you with the opportunity to compose an example of the conflict of vision and in turn work with the ideal image.

Writing Moment 1.3

- Return to the list you composed during the previous writing moment and choose a specific forbidden action. The action you choose should be one that you know for certain, if you performed it, would have a dire, negative outcome.

- Once you have chosen an action compose a pair of lists, each of which could serve as the beginnings of a **stanza** for a two-stanza poem. For the first list, consider the following question: what could be the ideal, though more than likely impossible, outcome if you committed this forbidden action? What positive outcome could be achieved by committing this action? What would be your ideal emotional state? What would be the ideal transformation of your community or society? Be as imaginative, fantastical, and hyperbolic as you wish.
- For the second list, consider the following question: what, by contrast, would be the more than likely real outcome if you committed this forbidden action? What negative outcome would probably result? What emotional state would you dread? What would be the least desired transformation of your community or society?

The Physical Image

For our fourth incarnation of the image, we turn to the real, physical, visual image—to the image as picture, as photo, painting, drawing, and so on. The image as physical picture has served as a fertile field for poetry in a number of different ways.

The evidence for the physical image's animation of poetry is found most clearly in the **genre** of **ekphrastic** poetry. Ekphrastic poems are, put simply, poems that take works of art as their subject matter. James A.W. Heffernan succinctly defines ekphrasis as "the verbal representation of visual representation" (3). Ekphrastic poems stretch from Homer's famous description of Vulcan crafting the shield of Achilles in *The Iliad* to the present moment, with the most recent example for me being a very fine piece a student emailed me a few days ago on the work of the body modification artist, Orlan.

Within this same contemporary context, and in concert with the growing willingness over the last century by artists of all kinds to break down the boundaries between so-called verbal and visual works, poets have continued to work more directly with the material image, creating **mixed media poetry**. Poets have employed three main strategies, characterized by varying degrees of integration of images into the text. The first strategy involves putting words into dialogue with physical visual images, for example, by printing a poem on one page and an image on the facing page. The second strategy involves integrating images onto the same page of the text, working with design strategies similar to that of a magazine or website. In this same vein, **concrete poets** treat the typographical layout of the poem as an image (for example, composing a poem about a chalice in the shape of a chalice). The third strategy involves total integration of text and image. This may involve integrating images at the level of the poetic line, creating works that are part poem, part comic book, or creating image-word hybrids that defy both the labels visual or verbal art.

This turn to the actual, physical image opens whole new fields for exploration, whether it involves taking as your starting point the pieces at the art gallery or physically working with your words on the page. In Chapter 3, you will have the opportunity to take a more hands-on approach to these new horizons. Thus, rather than leading you to sketch out material for a possible poem, this writing moment will ask you to consider possible new directions for you to take in your poetic explorations.

Writing Moment 1.4

- Considering, one, the material you composed during the previous writing moments, and, two, the reflections you undertook while doing so, jot down some possible poem ideas based on the following questions.
- If you were to compose an ekphrastic poem about your experience of the forbidden, what work of art might you choose to write about? (This work of art can be drawn from more traditional media, such as painting or sculptures, or more contemporary media, such as movies or video games.)
- Which of the three strategies for creating mixed media poetry and integrating visual images would work best for you? Consider possible methods, whether the low-tech (paper, scissors, and glue), or the more technologically enhanced (a laptop with Photoshop). What do these media offer to your consideration of the forbidden? Do they help you to see it better? To expose and unveil it? To further obscure it?

This concludes our exploration of five ways of working with the image: sensuous subjective imagery, sight-based objective imagery, symbolic imagery, the ideal image, and the physical image. I encourage you to develop poems from the materials you composed during your writing moments, or to continue to test out these new insights into the subjective, objective, symbolic, ideal, and real image with the aid of the exercises listed below.

In our next section, we will take a more hands-on approach to the musical qualities of language by stepping outside as we go in search of nature's beauty (and its ugly patches, and where it grows sublime).

Writing Exercises

1. Return to the material you created during your writing moments and compose one or two new poems. For example, drawing on the multi-sensory material from the first writing moment, write a 10- to 20-line narrative poem about being tempted: build to the moment of almost transgressing and then leave your reader on the cusp.
2. Write the poem you are forbidden to write. I realize this is a difficult request. Meeting this difficulty, though, will immerse you in an experience that links many poets: the encounter with boundaries, the boundaries at the edge of what, why, where, when, and how we speak. What you do when you arrive is up to you—pull up short at the border, plunge into the boundary, or break straight through. I only ask that you get there.
3. The old saying, "seeing is believing," sums up our culture's privileging of one sense over the others. What if smelling was believing? Or tasting? Or the work of a sense that we have not discovered? One of your key tasks as a poet is to renew language and perception. One method for accomplishing this is to not only avoid clichés (e.g., "seeing is believing") but to attack them. Two strategies for waging this battle are: first, taking the cliché literally and presenting its lived implications, and, second, turning a cliché on its head. You can attempt both strategies by writing a poem in which you imagine the society that ascribes to the saying, "_______ is believing," with the blank being filled by whichever sense (real or imagined) you wish.

4. While at a butterfly sanctuary, I witnessed a woman covered from head-to-toe in representations of butterflies (printed on her pants and shirt, shaped into earrings, rings, and hairclips) completely lose it when real butterflies swarmed around her head (she was about 30 seconds from needing an ambulance when her family rushed her out). Have you witnessed or experienced a similar encounter with the disjunction between the ideal and the real? Can you imagine such a scenario? Compose a poem that explores this breakdown.
5. Works of notional ekphrasis are poems about imaginary works of art, that is, works of art that do not exist. These may be works invented for a real artist (e.g., a film noir thriller directed by Pablo Picasso), invented works by a fictional character (e.g., Harry Potter–designed tattoos), works by an imaginary artist (e.g., the corn-cob giants of Jeep Muenster), or impossible works of art (e.g., a sculpture sculpted from a black hole). Compose your own work of notional ekphrasis, employing concrete, sensual detail to fully bring the work to life.
6. Earlier in this section, you were introduced to three strategies for composing poems that work with both words and images. These strategies are: first, putting words into dialogue with physical visual images (e.g., by printing a poem on one page and an image on the facing page), second, integrating images onto the same page of the text (e.g., working with design strategies similar to that of a magazine or website), and, finally, totally integrating text and image (e.g., employing images at the level of the poetic line). Compose a poem on the topic of transgression by experimenting with one of these strategies.

Poems in Process

In our first poem in process, Katie Fewster-Yan explores what can seem like, for those who suffer in silence, a forbidden topic: eating disorders. Katie employs concrete and specific imagery to compose a painfully lush "room for the interim," the space between recovery and relapse, between living and dying. No matter how many times I read this poem, I am struck by the dynamic list of details that compose the girl's dreams, and by how the hand dryer in the first stanza, which powers the technology that saved the girl's life, returns in the last three lines as the groans of "[d]ead animals, the howl of inanimate carcasses."

Room for the Interim

The girl starved herself into a heart attack
and came back. Shocked into resurrection
by the same power forced into hospital hand
dryers, she catches a glint of the nurse's key ring
reflected in the third-story window. Beyond,
the sky remains visible through their image.

Sealed under short-term suicide watch, she
dreams of solitude, unkempt lawns, animals
in pastures, iron vices clamped down around
her lungs, of locks, plastic trays, styrofoam
plates and trees. Accompanied to the restroom,
she's uncertain whose side the walls are on.

If there were more mirrors in this place, she'd
recall what it was that she wanted to disown.
But the walls don't show her anything. All day,
the sound of air-power groans, artificial, down
the halls. Dead animals, the howl of inanimate
carcasses. She counts numbers. Tries to sleep.

Our next poem in process, one of my own, transgresses the boundaries of conventional poetry by borrowing its form from an image: the "Fold-In" that ends every issue of the humour magazine *MAD*. The *MAD* Fold-In is a joke that works like so: the set-up is an image with a corresponding description, and the punchline is the new image and description that results from folding the page to connect the points of an "A>" to a "<B." I ended my first book of poetry with a *MAD* Fold-In poem. I had tried and failed to write the poem for years. I succeeded after finding the right topic—a speculation on the "fold" as a way of understanding all the "big topics"—and realizing that the last line needs to be written first (so you do not end "is the the moon hope a [etc.]"). Be certain to fold your page so that the "A>"s and "<B"s kiss, revealing, in their touch, what a poem is.

A><B

A> <B
If all we are is
form, then folding in and folding out defines
the simplest fury of our clipped momentum,
and all life is deserted on a list of possible
hiding places for things inside of other things.
God is the unfolding of disbelief's failure
to outwit the demand for the infinity
of a larger voice enfolded in bunches of a more
fragile breathing. Death is felt as the folding of
nothing into the paths the present ploughs under,
enclosures surrendered to enclosures, like mind
as the first model for incarceration opening
up the possibility for profiles of tortured
mobility, or the belief that the moon
is some crazed fire ripped from the sky
on a moonless night and stuffed down
the throat of every enemy—until their
only irreverent gift to the world
is the least tangible example of silence for
the far-reaching force of the speaking
few. Love is the faintest feats of hate folding
tight around an impossible
adoration for distance. Hate
is love folding away from the hope
for some truncated distance, like a poem
as the folding in fingers which, in closing,
escape their fisty fixity and dissolve into the briefest
palm. A poem
A> <B

Composing with the Music of Language

Music—whether in terms of the musical arrangement of words in a poem or the factors that determine a Grammy-nominated song—is a subject on which people tend to have very strong opinions: you would be hard-pressed to sway a death-metal fan into grasping the pop-country genius of Taylor Swift. Such questions of **aesthetic** experience—what we like or dislike, our feelings about and sensory experiences of art in particular—are in the eye and ear, indeed in the full spectrum of sensory perception of the beholder. Through that same multi-lensed perception, we as poets aim to shape the aesthetic experience of our readers. For example, we use language to articulate the unexpectedly beautiful symmetry of an ugly grass tick's markings, or we can lead our readers to hear the stomach-turning swirl in a seemingly cute newborn kitten's first mewl.

Is there an entity or object found in nature that you find attractive or fascinating, even though it induces feelings of discomfort or repulsion in others? Call this entity or object to mind (or, better, go for a stroll and find it—though an image in a book or on a computer screen will also do) and undertake the following writing moment. This writing moment will encourage you to transform your reader's "beholding" through both your content (what you say) and your form (how you say it).

Writing Moment 1.5

- In the physical or recollected presence of your natural entity or object, gather the materials for a short poem that directly addresses this entity or object.
- Write down a list of observations that could compose a reflection on this entity's beauty. For example, you might consider the ways in which, despite its apparent status as "ugly," it conforms to classical ideals of proportion, harmony of parts, and splendour.
- While making the "ugly" "beautiful" in the content of your poem, you should also try to render it "beautifully" in your words by working with the sounds created by words. Take the opportunity to consider this question: what, for you, constitutes a beautiful sound?

Before continuing, I want to draw your attention to a practice you probably just undertook in your search for beautiful sounds: the act of reading aloud. This is a habit you want to nurture: read your poems out loud as you draft them, and, when possible, read the poems of other poets out loud. Poems—as we are about to explore in great detail—are auditory and sonic constructs, and reading aloud is the only way to fully access these aural attributes. This is the best way to inhabit the rhythms of your poems, to experience what flows and what sticks, slips, or falls flat.

Alliteration, Assonance, and Consonance

Having completed this writing moment, you have composed with the sounds of words, the most basic musical material with which we as poets compose. One way of working with this sonic material, of making language sing, is to attend to the repetition of consonant and vowel sounds. There are three tools at our disposal: **alliteration**, **assonance**, and **consonance**.

Alliteration is characterized by the repetition of the first consonant sounds of words, for example, "termite-tracked trees" or "birds in berry bunches." Assonance is characterized by the repetition of vowel sounds, for example, "the breeze is fleet and brief" or "a day of rain." Consonance is the repetition of internal or end consonant sounds in words, for example, "thick with crickets" or "muzzle the bee's buzz."

Poets have a number of reasons for working with alliteration, assonance, and consonance. For one, there is the joy of discovering and hearing these sonic associations in the act of composition. Readers, in turn, take part in the pleasure, or, depending on the specific sonic play, displeasure or anxiety or calm. The sounds stir the reader. Secondly, any one of these three tools can be used to create links between lines; alliterations with the "b" sound might be used in the first and last lines to create a sonic frame, or the "ow" vowel sound may be repeated to connect the "prowling owls" in line four to the "shouting down of cows" in line nine. Finally, these sonic qualities may be employed to mimic a quality of the subject under consideration or to heighten through repetition the expression of a strong feeling.

Beyond the musical qualities of language, you have practised working with **apostrophe**, one of the oldest conventions of nature poetry. Apostrophe is a **figure of speech** through which the poet addresses an absent person (dead or alive) or thing. In terms of nature poetry, poets have spoken to every object under (and including) the sun: the ocean, sunflowers, trees, spiders, dust, bears, the moon, and on and on.

One of the effects of apostrophe is that the address tacitly implies the inanimate or dead addressee's capacity to respond. You may choose to amplify this effect by employing forms of address that solicit a reply. For example, asking a question of the object suggests its capacity to reply. Giving a command suggests the entity's ability to act on this command. However, this amplification is by no means necessary. What is most important, as Stewart Cole aptly observed to me in an email, is that "[apostrophe] suggests a world of sentient forces beyond our comprehension—as though the world is charged with forms of vitality we only dimly intuit."

The final point to consider for your future work is that apostrophe is most powerful when employed as a single specific moment in a longer poem, creating a dynamic sense of shift (which accords with its etymology, from the Greek words for "turning away").

Rhyme Type, Rhyme Position, and Rhyme Pattern

For the next writing moment, which will give you hands-on practice with **rhyme** type, position, and pattern, let us reverse direction: instead of speaking *to* nature, we will speak *for* nature, employing the figure of speech **prosopopeia**. And instead of making the supposedly ugly object beautiful, we will work to make the seemingly beautiful object ugly, both in our reflections on nature and through our work with our new musical tool, rhyme.

The figure of speech prosopopeia, through which an inanimate object, non-human entity, or abstract idea is endowed with the ability to speak, should sound familiar to you. Prosopopeia is a type of personification, and is likely the first artistic tool with which you ever composed, whether this involved giving voice to stuffed animals, action figures, or the invisible bit of air that made up your imaginary friend.

When crafting prosopopeia, you need to pay careful attention to **perspective**. We will discuss the topic of perspective in greater detail in Chapter 2, so for now you can consider the basics. The prosopopeiac flower, cloud, or stone speaks from a specific position, in all that that implies, from a distinct vocabulary to a specific worldview. The imagined voice of a flower would be inherently different from that of a stone. For example, both would have very different view on the significance of rain: eroding for the stone and replenishing for the flower. Therefore, when composing a prosopopeiac nature poem, you want to consider both what is speaking and who is speaking, along with deciding on how and why.

In terms of the musical qualities of language, another way to compose with the sounds of words is through the quality most associated with poetry: rhyme. There are three aspects of rhyme to consider: type, position, and pattern.

Regarding type, perfect rhymes (also called full rhymes) occur when the last part (or parts) of a word make an identical sound, for example, rats-bats or bunting-hunting. Half-rhymes (also called slant rhymes) occur when either the vowel sounds are identical, as in mow-lower, or when the final consonants sound alike, as in smell-eel; in this sense, half-rhymes are examples of consonance and assonance. The least common type of rhyme is the eye rhyme (also called printer's rhymes); these are words that "rhyme" visually rather than in terms of any auditory quality, as in sow-sow (a female hog versus the spreading of seeds).

Regarding the position of rhymes, there are two types: end and internal. End rhymes (or terminal rhymes) are those that occur at the end of the line, while internal rhymes are those that occur between words within the same line or range of lines.

Finally, the patterning of rhyme refers to the organization of rhymes within a given poem. A **rhyme scheme** uses the letters of the alphabet to note which lines of a poem share a terminal rhyme. For example, the **ballad stanza** is a **quatrain** with the rhyme scheme *abcb*; in other words, the second and fourth lines rhyme, while the first and third do not.

It is also worth noting that the same motives guiding a poet's work with alliteration—to stir feeling, heighten meaning, and/or mirror the subject—also apply to a poet's work with rhyme. An added motive for those who compose with fixed rhyme schemes is the satisfaction derived from constructing within these conventions and the excitement of inventing new schemes.

For our next writing moment, let us return to nature in search of material to test out these conventions and tools, though this time we will attempt to make the beautiful ugly in both content and form.

Writing Moment 1.6

- Call to mind (or, once again, go for a stroll and find) an entity or object in nature that is commonly considered beautiful and about which you could compose a short prosopopeia.
- Write down a list of potential personality types or actual persons who could inform this entity or object's personhood and motivation.
- Write down a list of observations that could compose this entity or object's reflection on its ugliness. Consider the ways in which,

despite its apparent status as beautiful, it counters the classical ideals of proportion, harmony of parts, and splendour.

- While making the beautiful ugly in the content of your poem, you should also try to render it "ugly" in your words by working in one example each of three types of rhyme (perfect, half, and eye). Take the opportunity to answer this question: what, for you, constitutes an ugly sound?

Syllables, Rising Rhythms, and Falling Rhythms

Let us begin our turn to syllables and rhythms by continuing to explore aesthetic experiences, in this case the sublime. I think of the sublime as one of those things that, if this makes sense, I understood what it was before I knew what it was. I grew up on the pan-flat prairies, where, looking straight ahead, your visible world consists of 5 per cent grass and wheat terrain and 95 per cent sky (and, as the joke goes, you can see your dog run away for days). I came to appreciate and to be comforted by that vastness, the changing colours, shapes, and designs of that empty or starry or cloudy or glowing or storming endless sky. On my first trip to the West Coast, driving through the Rockies, I had my first in-the-flesh encounter with a mountain. Dad had stopped so we could take a bathroom break. I extracted my head from my book, hopped out of the car, and then, suddenly confronted with this sheer face of rock that towered all the way up to the soles of God's feet, I dizzied, almost fell, and nearly lost my mid-trip snack all over the highway. It was not until years later that I learned the name for what I encountered: the sublime.

The sublime is another aesthetic experience closely associated with nature poetry. There are many definitions of the sublime, and many explications and analyses of its workings. One of the first, and still most important, was Edmund Burke's *Philosophical Enquiry into the Origin of Our Ideas of the Sublime and Beautiful*, published in 1757.

The experience of the sublime, for Burke, occurs when one encounters a great vastness or vacuity, massive heights or yawning depths, the intensity of physical power, of severe colour, of relentless silence, the infinity of accumulation or the immeasurability of the little, that which is divided again and again and again. The result of this encounter, the sublime experience, is "astonishment, and astonishment is that state of the soul in which all its motions are suspended, with some degree of horror" (228). The senses and mind of the perceiver become so overwhelmed by the sublime object, so filled, that the self cannot think of any other object or tame the sublime with understanding.

It is worth adding that, building on Burke's work, philosophers have since taken two views on the sublime: the sublime as destructive and the sublime as generative. In both cases, the sublime is overwhelming and threatens to efface the self that beholds it. However, in the case of the destructive sublime, this effacement leads to inaction, to the shattering and fragmentation of the self. In the case of the generative sublime, effacement inspires the imagination to rise to the challenge and build.

When encountering the sublime in the next writing moment, this initial experience may not exemplify the level of astonishment Burke described. Unless you are lucky (or, perhaps more accurately, unlucky) you may have to use your imagination, play a little make-believe, and "manufacture" the sublime experience.

Writing Moment 1.7

- Call to mind a memory of (or, once again, go for a stroll and find) an experience of the sublime in nature.
- Re-write your experience twice, the first time using single-syllable words and the second time using only words with three or more syllables.

Undertaking this writing moment, you have worked with the music of rhythm, in the form of rhythm through word composition.

Rhythm through word composition involves attending to the **stressed and unstressed syllables** of words; it is the interaction between stressed and unstressed syllables that produces the music of the flowing line. There are two types of rhythms: rising rhythms and falling rhythms. Words, or combinations of words, that end in a stressed syllable constitute rising rhythms; these include, for example, "a **cat**," "en**flame**," and "and the **fall**." Words, or combinations of words, that begin with stressed syllables constitute falling rhythms; these include, for example, "**out**law," "**pig**eon," "**mar**vellous." (To give you a sense of the ubiquity of these rhythms, even in prose, take a second look at the rising rhythms in the line composed above: "the **mus**ic **of** the **flow**ing **line**.")

Now take a look at the pieces you just composed. What are the different effects produced by the two very different pieces and why? Which strategy better captures the sublimity of the experience, and why? Regarding stressed syllables and rhythm, consider how this writing moment encouraged you to compose both a more than likely heavily-stressed work (the monosyllabic piece) and a more than likely lightly-stressed work (the polysyllabic piece). Do you notice any patterns to the stresses in your piece? Which, for you, most effectively captured the sublime experience? Regarding tone and syllables, note how monosyllabic words (e.g., ask) with their predominantly Anglo-Saxon roots, often produce work that is considered down-to-earth. By contrast, Latinate polysyllabic words (e.g., enquire) will produce work that is abstract and cerebral and (however unfairly) considered by some to be pretentious.

Line Length

One trait that probably distinguished your piece on the sublime from your two nature-centred writing moments is a greater presence of your own body. This is not surprising. The sublime has long inspired poets to reflect on themselves as perceivers. A half-century after Burke completed his work on the sublime, nature poets (beginning with Romantic poets such as William Wordsworth and Percy Bysshe Shelley) enacted this shift, turning attention to the perceiver and to the perceiver's experience of the sublime.

In the contemporary context, this shift is greatly exemplified in ecological poetry or eco-poetry. The turn to the perceiver, in the case of these poets, manifests as a more compassionate and sensitive view on the so-called "object"; in other words, these poets recognize the dangers of the unchecked destruction of nature and in their poems nurture dialogue with, rather than the domination of, nature.

The experience of the sublime as potentially paralyzing astonishment often takes two forms in environmentally-centred or eco-poetry. The first is the natural sublime. This is the encounter with that which in its vastness, depth, intensity, power, and so on, transcends human domination. The second is the human-made sublime. This is the encounter with that which in its vastness, depth, intensity, power, and so on, threatens to destroy our inhabitable natural environs, fuelled by factors such as mindless urban expansion or enormous monolithic factories that result in unfettered pollution.

In our encounter with the human-made sublime, let us explore our final element of the music of language: line length. There are three forms to consider. The first form is the length of the line in **accentual and accentual-syllabic verse**. In the case of the former, the number of stresses in each line determines the length, while in the case of the latter both the number of stresses and the number of syllables in each line determines the length. The four-stress and the five-stress line are the most common. The second example is **syllabic verse**. With this second form, the length of the line is determined by a fixed number of syllables. This syllabic limit may arise from a traditional form, for example, the haiku with its 5, 7, and 5 syllable lines, or one invented by the poet. Finally, in the context of **free verse**, the decision of where a line break comes is determined by the poet: maybe after a few words or maybe near the far-right margin, perhaps by repeating the length of the first line or by varying the length line after line. Rather than speculate on why a free verse poet chooses one strategy over the other, here is the chance to try out two strategies for yourself.

Writing Moment 1.8

- Call to mind a memory of (or, once again, go for a stroll and find) an experience of the human-made sublime, an example of humanity threatening to destroy inhabitable natural environs.
- Write a poem using lines no longer than 4 syllables. Compose a piece that is 15 to 25 of these short lines in length.
- Revise this piece not by changing any of the words, but by simply adjusting the lines so they are between 15 and 20 syllables long.

Once again, re-read what you have written. What are the different effects produced by the two very different line lengths and why? Which strategy better captures the sublimity of the experience and why? Which strategy of **line breaks**, for you, rings most true to what you consider your voice?

This wraps up our first encounter with the musical qualities of language. Be sure to develop a poem or two from the materials you composed during your writing moments, and continue to practice with your musical tools—alliteration, assonance, consonance, rhyme, rhythm, and line length—with the aid of the following exercises.

In our final section of this chapter, we will engage the miracle of metaphoric vision as a means of encountering the unsaid.

Writing Exercises

1. Return to the material you created during your writing moments and compose one or two new poems. For example, complete your apostrophe by extending it, working it into a longer poem, or combining it with your prosopopoeia.
2. Go for a nature walk. Walk as far and for as long as you can. Then, for as long as you can, stay there. Compose a poem upon arriving. Compose a second poem (or second part to the first poem) when the need to leave overtakes you.
3. Alliteration was one of the foundational formal elements of early poetry (known as alliterative verse), and it remains a prime tool for many poets. Test your alliterative skills by composing a poem that praises the presence in daily nature of a certain single letter of your selecting. Use this letter's sounds as often as you can.
4. Compose a prosopopeia that is also an apostrophe, and use this poem as an opportunity to reflect on the so-called standards of beauty. For example, you could give voice to a birch tree (prosopopeia), and this birch tree could address a cigarette butt (apostrophe). The tree could meditate on beauty and then seek the cigarette butt's opinions.
5. Try your hand at a syllabic and accentual limit. Compose a nature poem in which each line is composed of eight syllables and rising rhythms.
6. What was the worst human-made environmental disaster? Compose a darkly **satirical** poem that actually *celebrates* this disaster. Pay close attention to the length of your words. One option is to begin by using more polysyllabic words and end by employing mostly monosyllabic words.

Poems in Process

Though on our writing trip we were surrounded by a wide variety of trees and brush, by flowing waters and twittering birds, Baxter Mills chose instead to write about something, um, man-made. To his credit, he succeeds at making the ugly—a glob of spit—beautiful, or, at least, he sounds it beautifully (though the speculation about "saving" the glob by licking it up turns my stomach). Sonically popping assonance and alliteration abound—and note, too, how he internalizes and repeats the rhymes (rather than ending each line with a rhyme) to at once amplify the musical powers of the poem and create a sense of rushing ahead.

Apostrophe to a Spot of Spit, Narrowly Avoided on My Way Down the Stairs

O Spit on step, listen: why do you glisten?
Are you a vision of the wisdom of all things
that bring singing attention to the next step?
Is your impermanence an innocent signal
of beauty's prerequisites: impending silence,
the violence of a gutless black hole guzzling
galaxical swirls? If I saved you, swiftly licking
this step, taking you, Spit—frothy, moist,
oysterial—into my stomach, what vibrancies
would I expel, besides the burgundy of bile
and this pretty pastiche of jumbo shrimp,
limp kale, and pasta once white as a unicorn
newborn?

Agatha Cheng sublimely explores the destruction of nature in "Progress." She generates this sublime quality from the connection she makes between hunger—this inevitable, sustaining, universal bodily experience—and the dismantling of the planet under the guise of "progress." She further heightens this sublime feeling (to the "highest heights," to quote her) through the repetition of the word hunger, and the relentless refiguring of hunger's disfiguring force.

Progress

Hunger sucks this gaping hole inside the earth.
Hunger is a hard master. It drives steel-tipped
prongs into soil's fleshy guts then works raw
the forged conches of our hands.

> Hunger draws us up the many steps, teetering
> through choked spires, reaching, finally,
> the highest heights, the Babel of hard-won glory,
> the ease of mangling fury, this naked chant:
>
> hunger is a fire-hewn sorrow, forget the numb
> gnawing, and keep on digging, and keep on
> digging, and keep on digging and digging, and dig.

Making Metaphors

Why do you write poems? What is it that inspires an individual piece?

For many poets, and I would put myself in this category, the need to write poems arises from an obsession with (or, really, an addiction to) the process of writing poems. For me, this addiction originates in both an experience of lack and of liberation.

The lack is what drove me to my notebook in the first place; there was this feeling of something missing within myself, and the experience that none of the usual modes of communication (from a personal journal to a private conversation with family to a public chat with friends) was equipped to help me encounter this feeling. In the poetry I read, and the poetry I began to write, I found the means of undertaking this encounter.

The "limits" of poetry—its conventions, tools, and traditions—were in fact liberating. For the first time, I felt free to explore these impossible-to-communicate feelings, record strange perceptions, and follow the threads of unexpected connections. I felt free to sing. I felt liberated to make something right or good or true, to (as Coleridge phrased it) put "the best words in their best order" (293) for my own sanity and solace, and, perhaps, for the solace and satisfaction of a friend or family member who might read a piece I finished.

How does poetry allow for this experience of liberation? As I suggested, this capacity arises from poetry's "limits"—its conventions, tools, and traditions—the most central of which relate to its use of figurative language. "The devices of figurative language," as Chris Baldick notes, "are the tools writers use to shape language and to uniquely render thoughts and perceptions" (83). We have already practised with one type of figure, figures of sound ("expressions that focus on patterns of sound" (83) such as alliteration, assonance, and consonance), and we will now turn to metaphor, the central figure of thought ("expressions that depart from 'normal' or accepted literal meaning" [83]). (In future chapters, it is worth noting, we will discuss other figures of thought as well as the final type of figure, figures of order (expressions that "depart from 'normal' order" [83].)

The goal of this section, then, is really the unstated goal of every section of this book: to nurture your writing addiction. Here, I hope this will be accomplished as we turn to our third foundational tool, the core figure of poetry: metaphor. We will also take a slightly more self-conscious turn by inhabiting the different motives that drive different poets. My hope on this front is that investigating these motives will help you grasp more fully what motivates you.

To begin with our first example, the transformative capacity of figures of thought makes them suitable for encountering and giving form to the unsaid. For example, a figure such as metaphor is indispensable for poets who seek to accurately represent the world not in terms of its basic material presence, but in terms of its strange, wondrous, irrational, ecstatic, and even violent manifestations. In this sense, the unsaid is the "not yet said" because the world has not been spoken into being in this way. It is made new.

The following writing moment gives you the chance to test out three processes through which this renewal occurs.

Writing Moment 1.9

- Process 1: The Different Use. How might a gardener use a stethoscope? What tool, for a gardener, might the stethoscope become?
- Process 2: Misperception. Choose an entity or object within your sight, and watch it out of the corner of your eye, so that it is just barely visible. What other object or entity, when glimpsed, does this thing become?
- Process 3: Revelation of the Hidden. Think of someone close to you who has a hidden quality. What animal or object would this person have to transform into in order for this hidden quality to be evident?

Metaphor's Two Parts: Tenor and Vehicle

In undertaking this writing moment, you have inhabited one of the motivations that guides many artists: the hope to faithfully and accurately represent the world by revealing the many possible worlds that remain hidden within it.

You also had the opportunity to test out the tool best equipped for undertaking this work. Most simply, a metaphor draws a connection between two things, puts an equals sign between them, without using "like" or "as" (whereas a **simile**, metaphor's familial companion, is a comparison that uses "like" or "as"). Put another way, a metaphor reveals an invisible thread connecting, for example, leafless treetops to the shot nerves they resemble, or the spurned lover's broken heart to the shattered shards of a bottle or the husks of back-bound, long-ago starved crickets. Metaphor transforms not only our vision of the world, but also our experience of it.

A metaphor is composed of two parts: a tenor and a vehicle. The tenor is the literal term—in our examples, the treetops and the broken heart—while the vehicle is the figuring term, the term that reshapes the literal term—in our examples, the nerves, bottle, and crickets. As these examples suggest, John Crowe Ransom was correct to observe that the transformative power of the metaphor allows any individual to work miracles (60). Though these transformations are of a perceptual order, rather than a physical one, they are, when well executed, no less able to inspire awe and wonder.

Metaphor and Associative Thinking

Other poets seek a more internal fidelity, fidelity with their emotions, perhaps, or the motion of their minds. This approach is best exemplified by two different poetic perspectives or poetic voices: the poet as confessor and the poet as visionary.

For confessional poets, the unsaid refers to the subjects about which they speak. These subjects, in many family and social circles, are taboo: mental or physical illness, drug or alcohol addiction, sexual or psychological abuse, silenced personal or familial history. Form-wise, confessional poets, at all times, keep their eyes keenly fixed on the "I," and, in doing so, communicate the intensity of emotion, whether through blunt statement or silence, through the description of action or the shaping of highly expressive figures.

Visionary poets, like confessional poets, address personal experience. However, visionary poets turn even further inward, delving into the depths of the unconscious, surveying the fringes of perception, and activating and reconfiguring the many switches and circuits and dials they discover in the convergences of language and imagination. Their goals are many, and vary from poet to poet: to liberate language from the rigidity of corporatized directives, to give expression to the untapped depths of the mind, to deliver prophetic speculations on the future or highly symbolic alterations of received history. Their forms are also many, ranging from the heavily figurative and dreamlike burst to the stripped, raw howl, from the highly allusive to the extremely illusive, from the innovative mash-up of styles and voices to the crude stream of mono-vocal expression.

These two kinds of poets, though very different, are linked by their shared interest in employing metaphor as a means of exploring the expressive power of associative thinking, particularly as it pertains to speaking the unspeakable. For the confessional poet, for example, this can take the form of an unspeakably traumatic experience or mind-silencing anguish, while for the visionary poet this can take the form of a similar encounter with the traumatic or, by contrast, an encounter with the prescribed way of speaking or thinking, and, in turn, what this prescription cannot say, or refuses to say. Metaphor provides relief and liberation insofar as the inexpressible trauma, the tenor, is given expressible, communicable form by the vehicle of the metaphoric association. The following writing moment will give you the opportunity to attempt both approaches to metaphor.

Writing Moment 1.10

- For the confessional approach, recall a personal experience that caused you great pain, an experience that you have not shared (and, it is worth saying, that you will not be asked to overtly share in this writing moment), an experience that is considered taboo to discuss. What is the action or instant that embodies the initiation of this pain? Referring to this action or instant as "It", write down any object, interaction, perception, happening, and so on that can serve as a vehicle for figuring this "it." Let your senses and mind move as freely as you possibly can as you fill in this blank, repeatedly: "It is _______."

- For the visionary approach, look around and write down the first thing you see. This first word or phrase will serve as your initial tenor. What is a metaphor for this? In other words, write "The [thing perceived] is _______." Whichever word you place in this blank becomes your new tenor. Find a vehicle for this tenor. Repeat this process, composing metaphors for metaphors for metaphors for as long as you can. Return to your initial tenor once or twice more and start again, discovering the different paths your imagination uncovers.

Extending Metaphors

Other poets deeply consider their audience when composing their poems. Activist poets, for example, create with the goal of educating their readers and listeners. They seek to rally an audience pushed to the fringe and challenge the dominant, mainstream consumers. Their work seeks to expose that which is missing from the dominant conversation. It speaks what too often goes unsaid.

The extended metaphor, or conceit, is a central tool for any poet, but it can be particularly suited to performing the more didactic poet's work. An extended metaphor is a metaphor that, as the name suggests, extends beyond the initial, line-length incarnation and continues to explore the connections between the tenor and the vehicle of the metaphor. For example, in George Herbert's "The Windows," humankind (tenor) is a stained-glass window in a church (vehicle). In the three stanzas of his poem, Herbert extends this metaphor as a means of considering the complexity of humankind's relationship to God. There are innumerable ways to extend a metaphor, and different motivations that inform this extension, which we will discuss in Chapter 4. For now, though, it is worth noting why the conceit is such a useful tool for an activist poet. The concrete vehicle gives shape to an otherwise abstractly understood relationship, making this idea more pleasurable for the reader to conceive and easier for the reader to grasp.

The following writing moment asks you to inhabit the activist impulse, and conceive of conceits for a specific audience.

Writing Moment 1.11

- Imagine you are an activist poet, and a group of entrepreneurs have asked you to compose a poem to perform at a gathering to celebrate a successful year. "Money" is the tenor for the poem and "seeds" are the vehicle.
- Rather than seeds, what would your vehicle be for the tenor "money"? How could you extend and explore this connection?

Metaphors between Mediums

During the twentieth century, a number of artists in all fields brought greater attention to bear on the conventions and material of the work itself. They sought to experiment with form. Painters such as Picasso and Pollack, for example, were more concerned with locating the essential components of their medium, or in discovering a more authentic means of expression. Experimental composers such as Schoenberg and Glass abandoned melodic scales in favour of atonality or repetitive sound, and novelists such as Proust, Joyce, and Woolf sought new "realisms"—through myth, memory, or the unconscious—that saw beyond the dominant psychological realism.

Many poets, too, broke radically from accepted convention, and poets working today continue to undertake these experimental efforts by turning their attention to form. One fertile method for doing so, a method that links very different undertakings, is to work metaphorically, to imagine that the poet's material—that is, language—is something else. **Sound poets**, for example, proceed in their work by imagining that sounds themselves are the material for composition. Many **visual poets** see a connection between the written word and different kinds of visual art, creating totemic masks, nudes, and nonsensical logos out of the letters of the alphabet.

For the following writing moment, focus your attention in a new way on the materials with which you compose.

Writing Moment 1.12

- Make a list of other mediums and forms that you enjoy creating with or consuming. Be both general (music) and specific (Jack Kirby–era *The Avengers* comics).
- Fill in the following blank with each of the items from your list: "Language is _______."
- How, with this metaphoric connection established, does your chosen vehicle transform the tenor "language"? How does it transform the sonic material of language? The visual material? The syntactic (or sentence-making) material? The conventions of grammar and expression?

This completes our overview of metaphor's many forms. Continue to work your way toward mastery of these various types by composing poems from your writing moments and by undertaking the following exercises.

Writing Exercises

1. Return to the material you created during your writing moments and compose one or two new poems. For example, expand into a complete poem one (or all) of the transformations you created in the first writing moment. You could also complete your confessional or your visionary piece.
2. A *manifesto* is a public declaration of an individual or collective's opinions, motives, and goals. Throughout the twentieth century, radical artists and political radicals alike employed the manifesto as a means of firmly establishing their public presence and gathering together fellow travellers. Compose a manifesto poem in which you state the motives and goals of your writing. Remember that *how* you make your statements (how, for example, you employ figurative language) should reflect the goals and motives you proclaim.
3. We have looked extensively at the connections and similarities that metaphors locate or forge. However, the exploration of differences and dissonances is just as important to poets. One of the key figures for

thinking about difference is **irony**. Compose an ironic poem by "mismatching" abstractions and their concrete manifestations. For example, for the abstraction "True Love," one mismatched concrete example might be "never looking at your lover's face." Write a poem in which you sincerely present ironic concrete examples as embodiments of an abstraction—for example, Wealth, Compassion, or Pain.

4. What is a cause that you believe in deeply but that you feel remains invisible? Compose a three-stanza or three-part poem in which you inhabit three positions, respectively: the confessional, the visionary, and the activist.
5. Choose a figure for, or manifestation of, the invisible (a ghost, a god, something microscopic). Ask someone (a friend or a stranger, whoever is closest) for a noun. Compose an extended metaphor in which you explore how this figure of the invisible "is" this noun. Show us how this noun makes the invisible material.
6. What if the letters of the alphabet were actually insects? Choose three letters and provide the following information for these insects: Name, General Description, Size, Life History, and Did You Know?

Poems in Process

The opening metaphor in Ardyn Geddes's "A Newer (Cuter) Tongue" is at once so surprising and so spot on: Hello Kitty—the pink-bowed, iconic kitten—is language. I say this metaphor is spot on not because it is self-evident, but because of how smartly Ardyn extends this conceit to insightfully transform the way we think of language, expression, and ourselves. In a wonderful irony, she comments on the power of popular, consumer culture to efface original, individual expression in a poem that is a highly original, individual expression. It is also worth noting that Ardyn's piece is a **sonnet**, a form we will try our hands at in Chapter 3.

A Newer (Cuter) Tongue

Hello Kitty is now what language is.
Through those doe eyes of hers, do we read much?
Like Hello Kitty, bow-ed, showing no frizz,
Language now bears a bow and ribbon crutch.
Is Hello Kitty's tongue a whiskered fake,

Delicate sounds pawed clear of real meaning,
Worse than slang, less than nonsense aches?
Are words downgraded from aged to young to weaning?
Yes, words, like Kitty, are now expressionless,
Lacking a mouth through which to be released.
Hello Kitty's the lone global address;
In silences fast as sound she spreads and breeds.
In backyards, boxed, we bury the words we spite.
"Hello Kitty!"—youth's first phrase, last rite.

One of the most compelling features of Laura Kanabe's "Paint the Scene" is the variety of ways she figures the self. There is the very private, painful experience of a woman cleaning up after a domestic dispute shaped through a series of public metaphors: the concert, war, and the work of art. There is also the violent diminishing of the self, imagining the self as garbage, imagining suicide as just another mess. Laura's handling of perspective and pronouns also warrants comment. She impressively renders the muted intensity of the woman's pain, which is heightened by Laura's precise use of language. Laura maximizes the presence, and violence, of the "rejecting" he, by minimizing his presence. Finally, Laura also manages to draw us, the readers, into the scene, figuring us as the unspoken "you" she addresses at the beginning and end of the poem.

Paint the Scene

Begin at the end,
the clean-up, her solo:
shrieks that echo inside,
forbidden to escape.

The sour scent of red wine,
which he rejected
but the carpet drinks up,
turns her stomach
as she clears evidence,
struggling to withhold
the vomit that creeps up
the back of her throat.

Back bent,
she picks crystal
flecks from a once grey
carpet and fills the broken
glass that has no leg
left to stand on.

Pain pounds, perpetuating
the unvoiced screams,
but she dares not
kneel in the battlefield,
not till the fallen
are laid to rest,
wrapped prudently
in advertisements
for an unachievable life.

She considers joining
the packaged garbage
on its final voyage.
It would be easier
to understand
the scene if it were painted
with red liquid
as warm as her skin,
an arterial spray
upon white walls—
but then who
would clean up
the mess?

Conclusion: Ending at the Beginnings

We began with the question: when did you compose your first poem? This question was meant to encourage you to reflect on the way in which, to return to the epigraph by Robert Penn Warren, poems grow out of our lives. It was meant to prepare you to dig deeply into these three foundational tools—image, music, and metaphor—and into the complex tangle of threads that compose the knot where you, your world, and your words converge.

Now, having dug into these many occasions, imagine a curious friend asks you the more general question, "Where do poems begin?" Where would you begin? Would you begin with the experiences of the forbidden, sublimity, or the unsaid that strike the body and move us to speak? Or would you begin with the topics of personal experience, nature, or artistic perception that have inspired poets for centuries and continue to urge us to compose? Or would you begin with the tools with which we create, the images, music, and metaphors?

You would not be out of line telling your friend, in summary, that there are all of these different lenses of experience and encounter and language, but you choose, again and again, to look through this one. Nor would you be off the mark if you said that there are so many paths of experience and encounter and language down which you have barely travelled, but, a few steps at a time, you are making your way down each one. Either way, the key insight to share with your friend is that what links each lens, what unites each path, each occasion, is that it is not an answer, but a question. It shuts the eyes and opens them wide, at once.

In this sense, what John Crowe Ransom says about the miracle of metaphor applies, really, to all of the moments and movements and manoeuvres out of which poems are born: they initiate acts of attention. For whereas so many of the communities, orders, and systems of which we are members seek conversation-concluding answers, the metaphor "leaves us looking, marvelling, and revelling" (60). The occasions of poetry leave us looking, marvelling, and revelling in this way, too, and, if we have done our work well, our poems will leave our readers doing the same.

We will thus remain on the topic of attention in Chapter 2: Voice and Tradition. We will try out the elements with which we construct our voices, and we will explore the voices of traditions and poets who will initiate in us acts of attention, rousing us to look and marvel and revel in ways that we enjoy, or do not enjoy but should, or in ways that we did not know were possible but now that we do we cannot un-know, and cannot stop.

Recommended Resources

- *Poetry Anthology*: A poetry anthology is an excellent and efficient way to get introduced to a great number of top-notch poets. Poetry anthologies come in all shapes and sizes. To ensure you are getting work of the highest quality, pick up an anthology published by a university press (for example, Oxford University Press) or an academic publisher (for example, Norton). I recommend you start with an anthology that spans the centuries (beginning with the likes of Chaucer and Anonymous and wrapping up with poets who are still active today). My go-to anthologies when I was starting out were *The Broadview Anthology of Poetry* (though I left my first edition in Daejon, South Korea—intentionally, to help spread the poetic word) and *15 Canadian Poets x 2* (now *70 Canadian Poets*). Most recently, I have been enjoying *Language for a New Century: Contemporary Poetry from the Middle East, Asia, and Beyond* and *Scanning the Century: The Penguin Book of the Twentieth Century in Poetry*, which is not organized by poet, but instead by historical event, theme, and mood.

- *Poetry History*: To add another dimension to your reading and writing, I also recommend you explore a little literary history. I strongly recommend starting with James Fenton's *Introduction to English Poetry*. He casts his net wide—spanning the centuries and counting show tunes and prisoner work songs in his definition of poetry—and yet his easy-to-read volume weighs in at a slender 152 pages.

- *Dictionary*: I am guessing this one needs no explanation. Ideally, you want to use a dictionary (print or online) like *The Oxford English Dictionary*, which provides historical usage information as well as etymological information (tracing a word's roots is always a fertile undertaking).

- *Literary Dictionary*: A literary dictionary, which, as the name suggests, provides detailed definitions of literary terms (such as "malapropism," "bucolic poetry," "peripeteia," etc.), will not only allow you to look up words like "malapropism," "bucolic poetry," and "peripeteia," but it will also serve as an excellent resource for discovering new poetic tools. I am partial to both Chris Baldick's *Oxford Concise Dictionary of Literary Terms* and M.H. Abrams's *A Glossary of Literary Terms*. There are also poetry-specific dictionaries. When you are fully committed to the poetry cause, you will definitely want to grab (with two hands and, perhaps, the help of a strong friend) *The New Princeton Encyclopedia of Poetry and Poetics*, which, in its fine-printed 1,664 pages, contains everything.

- *Books by local poets*: It is never too soon to start learning about how poems are being composed in your community and region. If you are looking for direction, visit a library or bookstore for advice.

CHAPTER 2

Voice and Tradition

Introduction: On Necessity and Voice

"Sometimes I say to a poem,
'Not now,
Can't you see I am bathing!'
But the poem usually doesn't care."
—Hafiz

The moment I read these lines by Hafiz, I set his book aside to scribble them in my notebook. I was struck, of course, by the familiarity of the "not now" (though in my case, you should replace bathing with grading—"meeting grade submission deadlines is next to godliness," as we say in the teaching biz). I am sure I was also a bit pleased to learn that someone as wise and prolific as Hafiz also felt the pull of daily duties.

More than any of that, though, I loved how suggestively Hafiz addressed the intermingling of necessity and voice. The personified poem's refusal, the fact that it "doesn't care," succinctly sums up the sense of necessity that accompanies the experience of inspiration, the unquenchable urge to explore this experience with pen and page. Connected to this urge is what Hafiz suggests about the poetic voice. We, as poets, have two voices. There is the voice that says, "not now, I've gotta bathe" (or grade, or, fine, I'll admit it, watch a Jays game), and there is the voice of the poem, the voice that speaks to us until we turn from the bath and speak in unison with it.

In the following chapter, we will explore this meeting of necessity and voice. I want us to delve into voice in two related forms: the voice of tradition and the voice of the speaker. By the voice of tradition, I mean the **metrical verse** tradition and the free verse tradition, two foundational approaches to determining what constitutes the conventions and qualities of a poem. By the voice of the speaker, I mean the nuts and bolts of a specific voice in a specific poem, all the different elements you can compose with when constructing your speaking "I" or "you" or "we."

As we dig into the traditions and techniques of voice, I hope we can also strive to nurture this sense of necessity. It was the overwhelming experiences—the forbidden, the aesthetic, and the unsaid—that allowed us to accomplish this in the previous chapter. In what follows, we will encounter a pair of motivations and a pair of topics that have spurred, spur, and will continue to spur artists of every ilk. These motivations are the desire to make the strange familiar and the desire to make the familiar strange. The topics are the lost—as in the irretrievable—and myth.

We will begin by turning again to the music of language. This time we will explore how these tools are utilized in one specific example of metrical verse, Emily Dickinson's "There's a certain Slant of light."

The Musical Impulse and Metrical Verse

The musical impulse has manifested in the written and spoken word across historical periods and cultural boundaries. These works are linked by the attempts to make the written and spoken word sing. In this section and in Chapter 3, we will explore specific historical and current traditions of metrical verse. However, to begin, I thought it would be better for us to first explore our personal understandings of the way words can sing, and to reflect upon our local traditions.

I, for example, grew up on a farm in southern Saskatchewan, near a town called Moose Jaw in the rural municipality of Baildon. Though I know it sounds like things do not get much more "country" than that, I had MTV pop music beaming into my brain (as well as USA Network zombie flicks and Nickelodeon reruns of *Mr. Ed*) from an early age via one of those old-school, van-sized satellite dishes.

My influences were diverse, ranging from the local cowboy poets who wrote about their lives and the land to the book of Robert Service poems my grandpa kept beside his bed ("There are strange things done in the midnight sun / By the men who moil for gold; / The Arctic trails have their secret tales / That would make your blood run cold" [1–4]) to *Rap Traxx 2*, which featured the likes of Rob Base, Salt-N-Pepa, and Will Smith (back when he was still a Fresh Prince).

The results were diverse, too. In grade eight, I wrote a sort of mock macabre narrative poem (in the vein of Service and Edgar Allan Poe) that told the true story (there's the farmer poet influence) of the evening my dad spent with his cousin and his cousin's friend, the Cat Man. The poem, "Michael, the Cat Man, and Me" (I was more than a bit presumptuous, I see, having used my own father as the speaker), began like so:

> My cousin was he whom I called on that eve,
> a man of good mind, though I still can't perceive,
> how he found interest in such a strange friend,
> how he could stay with that man 'til the end.

Around that same time, I wrote a rap in praise of (for some reason) the Kansas City Royals. The brain being the brain I still remember the line: "they've got a fastball pitcher and they call him the Flash." Nothing else of that poem remains, though I wish I still had a copy. I would love to see what my adolescent self rhymed with the last names Seitzer and Gubicza.

I do not hold up these sources or these excerpts as models—far (actually, far, far, far) from it. Instead, I want to use these personal examples as a way of extending to you an invitation to explore your own past poems and local environs. How, in other words, have the poets, singers, and lyricists you know and admire shaped how you make language sing?

Writing Moment 2.1

- Of your strongest poetry influences, which ones most stir your musical impulse?
- How does the poetry you have written reflect this influence?
- How have these poets influenced how you craft with consonance, assonance, and rhyme?
- How have they influenced how you pattern these sounds and the stressed syllables of words?

With these reflections in mind, we can now turn from our particular personal and local influences to a particular example of the metrical verse tradition. The following sections will give you the chance to do a few things: to try your hand at metrical verse, to respond to the work of another poet, and to animate one of the foundational artistic motivations, the desire to make the strange familiar.

Emily Dickinson and the Strange

Every now and then, each of us has an encounter with the truly strange: an unexplained glow ascends through the treetops without any recognizable source, a flash of déjà vu becomes a full-on fit of clairvoyance when you know for certain yet another detail seconds before it happens, or in the background of a voice-mail message—that is nothing but static and clicks—you can just make out a voice whispering your name.

Even stranger than these strange occurrences, and more pressing to explore in a poem, are those strong feelings that seem to arise out of nowhere, knotting the gut or tingling the skin or weakening the knees without any apparent internal or external stimulus. These are the mundane moments—walking to get groceries, brushing your teeth, watching the clouds pass, reaching for a dropped coin—that suddenly become extraordinary for engendering a barely nameable feeling of connection or isolation, of joyous fullness or depressive emptiness.

These encounters are strange insofar as they are estranging, buoying you beyond daily cares or alienating you from your reality, your community, or yourself. Furthermore, these encounters are stranger than those named in the previous paragraph because they can occur with greater regularity and with greater familiarity and intimacy, and yet remain just as unnameable in their manifestation and cause.

Writing Moment 2.2

- What feeling most often strikes you without explanation? What is the feeling that overwhelms you? Is it a joy that moves you to spread it in the world, or a joy that is fleeting and leaves you empty? Is it rage, helplessness, mania, longing, anxiety, exhaustion, sadness, or disgust? Is it a mix of these or something else? Does it have a name or names?
- When and where does this feeling most often manifest? Is there a specific time of day or a season? Does it come to you in a type of venue or is it caused, again and again, by the same stimulus? Consider, perhaps, the most recent experience of the feeling or the strongest you ever felt.
- One way to enter into conversation with another poet is to borrow from that poet. The most basic way to do this is to borrow the terms of the poet's subject. With your strange feeling embodied, consider and note responses to the following, which are taken from the poem we are just about to approach, Emily Dickinson's "There's a certain Slant of light" (118–9): the **stimuli**, the time/location, and a description of the effect of this feeling.

The mid-nineteenth-century American poet Emily Dickinson sublimely explores the experience of the strange in her poem "There's a certain Slant of light." Dickinson was a prolific yet reclusive poet, publishing only seven of her nearly two thousand poems during her lifetime. She remains highly influential today, easily recognized for her hymn-like rhythmical verse and valued for her mind-bending ability to explore topics ranging from God to death to pain (often all three at once) in mundane objects and deceptively simple terms.

In this poem, she begins with the mundane origin, the "certain Slant of light, / Winter Afternoons," and then she goes on to explore the powerful feeling this light inspires, the way it "oppresses" and provokes despair.

There's a certain Slant of light

There's a certain Slant of light,
Winter Afternoons —
That oppresses, like the Heft
Of Cathedral Tunes.

Heavenly Hurt, it gives us —
We can find no scar,
But internal difference
Where the Meanings, are —

None may teach it — Any —
'Tis the Seal Despair —
An imperial affliction
Sent us of the air.

When it comes, the Landscape listens,
Shadows — hold their breath —
When it goes, 'tis like the Distance
On the look of Death —

In the very first stanza, Dickinson describes the basic coordinates of her experience of the strange. There are two aspects to her mundane moment. First is the stimulus, the "certain slant of light," and second is the locale, "winter afternoons." Note how Dickinson's careful work with word choice foregrounds the strangeness, the **ambiguity,** of her experience: "certain slant" suggests both the specificity of this light and her inability to name or describe it exactly. Dickinson also offers her first assessment of the effects of this light; it "oppresses."

Let us now look at how Dickinson makes the strange familiar—and then make familiar our own experience of the strange.

Dickinson and the Strange Made Familiar

To make the strange familiar does not mean to make the strange ordinary, soothing, or powerless. Dickinson's poem evidences this, as might, more than likely, your own experience composing the beginnings of your companion piece. The goal, in this case, is to give the faint feeling a familiar form, to make the illegible legible without diminishing any of the force of the extraordinary.

Dickinson's poem is a rich work of art, one we could explore together for the remainder of this chapter. So, for the sake of focus, let us attend to her imagery. The first two questions to ask are: what type of imagery did Dickinson choose and why? Possible answers are that she chose bodily (subjective) imagery and Christian (symbolic) imagery, and she chose this imagery because the light, the feeling it inspired, disturbed her on a bodily and a spiritual level.

The third question to ask is: how did she use this imagery and figurative language to make the strange familiar? The answer is a number of ways. There is the simile "like the Heft Of Cathedral Tunes," which combines the bodily (the heft) and the religious (the cathedral tunes). The light, metaphorically, is "an imperial affliction," suggesting both God-like majesty and bodily sickness. Finally, she personifies the absence of the light (in other words, the dark that follows) through "Death." Using both a simile and the "Distance," she renders this personification of the (absent) light in a perfectly and powerfully **askew** way; for despite the many layers to this figuring, the message is clear: the look of death is like the (physical and spiritual) darkness that we look into, and that looks into us, when this light goes.

To turn from Dickinson to our own poems, how do we decide what types of imagery to use when constructing with figures of thought, such as metaphor, simile, and personification? There are, I think, two basic practices, one that concerns reading and one related to writing.

The first (reading) practice is to study your favourite poets the way we just studied Dickinson. What types of imagery do they choose? Why? How do they shape this imagery with figurative language? And to what end? (For example, to make the strange familiar.)

The second (writing) practice is, quite simply, to go with your gut and let your imagination wildly wander. One option in this regard is to work associatively. Imagine, for example, ascending the stairs of a subway station and just as you resurface in the city an ineffable feeling of hope, of renewal, lifts you suddenly. Working with the associative method, you would choose metaphorically connected imagery that we commonly link to renewal, for example, the birth of a child, the rising sun, or the invention of a new means of space travel. Another method is to work by contrast. Imagine the same subway-station scenario, only this time the hope is replaced by despair. The contrast method might lead you to choose the act of flight or the harvesting of a ripe field, which are more often connected to hope. The possible options and the methods for choosing them are as plentiful as the inspiring happenings that call them into action. The key, as always, is to set forth with an adventurous spirit but to choose with care.

The next writing moment will give you the opportunity to brainstorm some possible types of imagery and test one of them out using Dickinson as your model.

Writing Moment 2.3

- Return to your strange feeling and consider which aspects of your life this experience affects, troubles, or amplifies. Make a list of possible types or fields of imagery. Answer the following questions for further stimulation. Placed in your shoes, which types of imagery would Dickinson choose? What do you come up if you work by the associative or the contrast method?
- Once you have finished your list, select the type of imagery that you think is most apt, fertile, and original. Employ this field of imagery as the means of making your feeling familiar. We will again borrow from Dickinson, this time by testing out two of her techniques: the simile and the "but."
- The simile, remember, is a comparison using like or as. Compose a simile that compares the force of your feeling to a figure from your field of imagery. Use the following line as your model: "oppresses, like the Heft / Of Cathedral Tunes."
- Poems often gain momentum from contrast. A simple way to achieve this is through a "not X but Y" structure. In the second stanza, Dickinson utilizes this structure to show the effect of this feeling on her: there is no scar, but there is the new experience of difference. Using this example as your model, describe the manifestation of your feeling as "not X but Y."

Dickinson and Metrical Verse

The other practice Dickinson employs to make her strange feeling familiar—as well as powerfully presented—is to sing. She composes with three of the key musical qualities of language that we discussed in Chapter 1: rhyme, line length, and rhythm. The fixed form Dickinson works with is hymn-like and almost exemplifies the ballad stanza; in other words, the conventions of these forms determine how she works with rhyme, line length, and rhythm.

In terms of this first tool, she rhymes the first and third lines, and the second and fourth lines. Thus, her rhyme scheme is: *abab*. The first and third lines, and the second and fourth lines, are also paired according to line length and rhythm. They are, respectively, eight and five syllables in length. Rhythm-wise, lines one and three possess four stressed syllables each, while lines two and four possess three stressed syllables each. The rhythm in lines one and three is a falling rhythm, a heavy stress followed by a light stress. Lines two and four begin with a falling rhythm, but then end with a rise. Here is what the stanza looks like with the stressed syllables bolded.

> **When** it **comes**, the **Land**scape **list**ens,
> **Sha**dows—**hold** their **breath**—
> **When** it **goes**, 'tis **like** the **Dis**tance
> **On** the **look** of **Death**—

For this final writing moment, you can continue to explore your strange feeling, your type or field of imagery, and Dickinson's work—this time within the metrical tradition.

Writing Moment 2.4

- Fill in the following blanks. Each blank corresponds to one syllable and bolded blanks require a stressed syllable. The goal is to pursue your musical impulse so be sure to stick to Dickinson's rhyme scheme, line length, and the stress pattern established by her rhythm.
- When it comes, the ____ ___ ____ ___, / ____ ___ hold their ____; / When it goes, it's like the ____ ___ / On the ____ ___ ____.

This concludes our first creative journey with a fellow poet. I encourage you to develop poems from the materials you composed during your writing moments, or to continue to test out these new insights with the aid of the exercises listed below.

Having explored the metrical verse tradition, we now need to give ourselves over to the free verse tradition, a jaunt that takes us to the steaming streets of NYC (as well as to the frozen Russian tundra).

Writing Exercises

1. Return to the material you created during your writing moments and compose one or two new poems. For example, complete your Dickinson-centred piece or return to the initial writing moment and head in a completely different direction.
2. To extend David Foster Wallace's description of fiction writers to include all of us scribblers, "[writers] as a species tend to be oglers" (21). We are always looking and listening, with all of our sensory and intellectual and imaginative faculties, and we are always preserving what we witness with words. For this exercise, you will go one step further and watch your watching. Pay close attention to your body—to your senses and systems and organs, to sensations and feelings and impressions. Isolate different receptors in yourself (for example, a specific section of your brain, an itch on your side, and your liver) and, personifying them, explore how they metaphorically watch and record the world.
3. We undertook a writing moment based on a strong feeling that manifests unexpectedly during a mundane experience. The opposite occurrence can be just as surprising, even startling. Compose a poem that explores a moment in which you experienced a total lack of feeling during what was supposed to be momentous occasion (for example, when receiving an award or recognition of some kind, or at a birthday, graduation, wedding, funeral, or some other significant occasion). Again, try working in the metrical verse tradition of Dickinson.
4. The ability to make the strange familiar with ingenuity and rigour requires both our imaginative and rhetorical powers. The following exercise will help you practice both. Choose two objects, entities, or activities at random (perhaps ask a friend for one or select one at random from where you are sitting). Compose a poem in which you prove how each creates or gives birth to the other. For an added focus, work in the tradition of Dickinson.
5. Emily Dickinson employed a variation on the hymn, a metrical form popular during her time. What are popular metrical or rhythmic forms in your cultural moment? Consider, for example, a pop song, an advertising jingle, or a TV theme song. What conventions—in terms of line length, rhythm, and rhyme—does this particular example follow? Determine these rules for one or two examples and then write your own based on these same rules.

6. As you read, take note of the poems you most admire. For poems written in the metrical tradition, determine which musical conventions the poet employs and compose your own poem using the same restraints. Feel free to borrow that poet's first line to help establish the rhythm, and build from there.

Poems in Process

I would like to take the opportunity to share a little Saskatchewan cowboy poetry. My great-uncle Edmund Tysdal composed the following Dickinson-esque poem in 1960. The rhythm gets a bit ramshackle in places, but the ballad stanza pattern is there: four stressed syllables in the first and third lines, three stressed syllables in the second and fourth lines, and the *abcb* rhyme scheme. This poem also demonstrates how we can craft with varying sentence lengths; in other words, the rhythm of sentences. Note how my great-uncle gains very different effects in the three stanzas by composing with, respectively, one long sentence, four short sentences, and two two-line sentences.

The Ballad of a Rifle

The rifle founds an epic where
the fist just founds a dream
about a hand that fires fingers
in a deadly steady stream.

A baby is an ancient thing.
A stone is something young.
Hunger's in the apple's skin.
Nutrition's in the tongue.

Bullets make two promises:
to kill and uphold peace.
One promise they just make to break,
and one they make to keep.

The ***duende*** just crackles in the four elegant yet ferocious couplets that compose Diane Tucker's "Barbed Wire." The poem hinges on a richly rendered metaphor: the heart (the lover's love) as barbed wire, and Diane cunningly illustrates the speaker's transformation by framing this barbed heart with two very similar couplets that describe two very different acts of breathing. In terms of the metrical verse tradition, notice how she employs a four-stress line throughout and yet varies rising and falling rhythms to great effect. Note, too, how, as the violence increases, the rhyme devolves (from perfect rhyme to almost-eye rhyme—the avoidance of the word "pyre" is highly suggestive here—to no rhyme). What do you make of the return of the perfect rhyme in the closing couplet?

Barbed Wire

I start with a long and slow desire:
breathe out love, breathe in fire,

but now your heart is barbed wire
upon this empty funeral bier,

a binding wire, trussing noose,
gouging and goring as it grips.

I end with a long, slow breath:
breathe out love, breathe in death.

The Freedom Impulse and Free Verse

Like the musical impulse, the freedom impulse is a shaping force of the written and spoken poetic word across time periods and cultural boundaries. In the metrical verse tradition, the freedom impulse manifests in the renovation of received forms and the invention of new forms. In twentieth-century English-language poetry, the freedom impulse revolutionized *how* we write poems with the rise of free verse poetry.

In Chapter 3, we will look closely at a range of these innovations in both the metrical verse and free verse traditions. For now, we only need to recognize that innovative poets often embody the dual-aspects of the freedom impulse: negative freedom (freedom from) and positive freedom (freedom to). On the one hand, these poets desire freedom *from* inherited forms of speaking and freedom *from* prohibitions on what can be written about. On the other hand, they also nurture the freedom *to* invent new forms and the freedom *to* explore any subject under the sun.

Beyond shaping these grand historical shifts, the freedom impulse also manifests for each of us on the personal level. Like many, when I first discovered free verse poetry I had the "you mean it doesn't have to rhyme" moment, and *how* I wrote changed: I abandoned fixed rhythm in favour of a more fluid rhythm, I traded in end-rhymes for subtler internal rhymes, and rather than aligning all of my poems to the left margin I experimented with line length, line breaks, spacing, indentation, and so on. Here is a sample fragment from those early days:

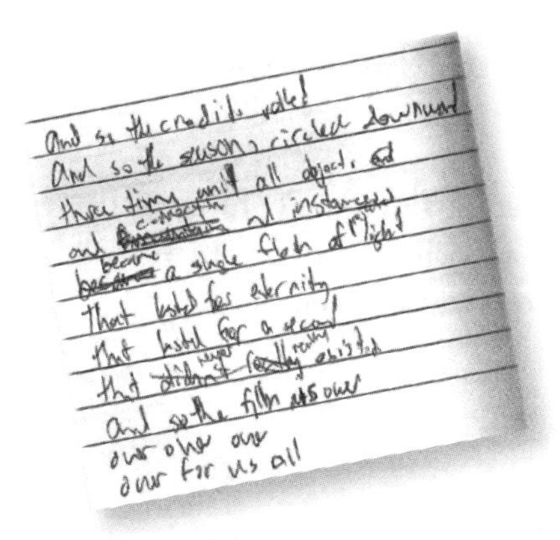

And so the credits rolled
And so the seasons circled downward
thru time until all objects
and connections and instances
became a single flash of projector light
that lasted for eternity
that lasted for a second
that never really existed
and so the film is over
over over over
over for us all

A few years later, I shifted again. I wanted to investigate the boundaries of the poem and started to write poem hybrids: little wannabe mythical creatures that were part-poem, part-non-poem. Here is an excerpt from a poem that was also part-zombie film and part-department store catalogue (hence the letters A through H connecting the text to the different parts of the zombie form/fashion), titled, "Zombies: A Catalogue of Their Return":

A. The zombies arrive neither to represent the flow of capital nor to join cyborgs and man-eating sharks on the postage

> stamps recently released to commemorate only the bearable terrors projected across the last one hundred years.
>
> B. The zombies return. Rising up, experts suspect, against moribund comparisons to minds stalled blandly before electronics and coldly burning screens (with looks that barely aspire to the condition of the living dead). Local shop-owners anticipate the promotion of a new clothing line. Senior citizens are thankful for a respite, however pungent, from game shows and Reality TV.

Once again, please read these poems less as textbook (forgive the pun) examples and more as samples from which you can springboard into the ocean of your own environs. The questions asked in relation to the musical impulse can also be asked here.

Writing Moment 2.5

- Of your main poetry (or, even, non-poetry) influences, which ones most stir your freedom impulse?
- How have these influences inspired you to seek freedom from a rigid view of poetry?
- Have they filled you with a sense of the freedom you needed to speak about things that felt taboo?

With your reflections in mind, let us again turn from the personal and local influences to a particular traditional example. Through Frank O'Hara's "[The Light Presses Down]," you will have the opportunity to respond to the work of another poet—though a free verse one this time around—and animate another foundational artistic motivation, the desire to make the familiar strange.

Frank O'Hara and the Familiar

While Emily Dickinson is an exemplar of both the metrical verse tradition and the ability to figure strange feelings in familiar forms, another American, the mid-twentieth-century poet Frank O'Hara, is an ideal companion to join as we turn to the free verse tradition and the desire to make the familiar strange. For O'Hara, as his friend and fellow poet John Ashbery reminds us, the poem is "the chronicle of the creative act that produces it" (viii). This belief moved him to "constantly [experiment] in his poetry in different ways without particularly caring whether the result looked like a finished poem," and it accounts for the often breezy feel of his work, and its surprising turns of thought and phrase.

Both of these qualities are exemplified in our sample of O'Hara's work, "[The Light Presses Down]" (475–6).

[The Light Presses Down]

The light presses down
in an empty head the trees
and bushes flop like
a little girl imitating
The Dying Swan the stone
is hot the church is a
Russian oven and we
are traveling still

you come by to type
your poems and write a
new poem instead on my
old typewriter while I sit
and read a novel about
a lunatic's analysis of
a poem by Robert Frost
it is all suffocating

I am still traveling
with Belinda Lee where
does she take me Africa
where it is hot enough
even to make the elephant
angry and the grass is
all withered and TV color

why do I always read
Russian exile novels in
summer I guess because
they're full of snow
and it is good to cry a
little to match your sweat
and sweat a little
to match your tears

Perhaps, upon first reading, "[The Light Presses Down]" appears to be an example of O'Hara at his most extreme, providing, as Ashbery put it, "the inspired ramblings of a mind open to the point of distraction" (ix). A host of familiar features—heat, books, friends, and writing—swirl together in an unpunctuated blur. However, these are not details chosen at random and presented willy-nilly. There is a pattern, a developmental arc designed to allow O'Hara to make the familiar strange.

Before taking a closer look at this pattern, however, let us first undertake the following writing moment and document our own experience of the familiar.

Writing Moment 2.6

- Take a moment to observe your current surroundings. If you wish, stand up and explore, or remain right where you are.
- Make two columns, "Sensory Experience" and "Activities or Objects," and while you are observing write down all the examples that strike you.
- For "Sensory Experiences," draw on your own senses and feel free to speculate on the sensory experience of those around you. Meanwhile, for "Activities or Objects," keep an eye out for activities both big (for example, a politician giving a speech on TV) and small (for example, a child picking a scab).

O'Hara and the Familiar Made Strange

What I love most about poets who seek to make the familiar strange is the way they draw us to attention with striking transformations:

suddenly a plain old spoon is a space arm reaching into the unexplored atmosphere of an overcooked casserole, or the garage door's rusted hole is the abyssal opening of a frozen volcano. These poems remind us that nothing is neutral, nothing "just is."

O'Hara accomplishes this transformation through two techniques: amplification and the metaphoric vehicle. He amplifies sensory intensity, suffocating us in a molten environment in which "the church is a / Russian oven" as "the light [of the day] presses down." In concert with this amplification, he explores the "light" of the imagination, its more literary productions in particular. He begins with the imagining mind's rendering of the heat of the day ("in an empty head the trees / and bushes flop like / a little girl imitating / The Dying Swan"), passes from a friend composing a poem to watching a Belinda Lee movie (based on a book), before concluding with "Russian exile novels."

Both the amplification and the vehicle are employed to create a uniting horizon. The heat touches all things in the present, inflects O'Hara's perception, and, even, impels him to read the "Russians." The activity of literature holds O'Hara's attention in the present, while also allowing him to make connections across time.

Most importantly, both of these techniques are deployed as a means of reaching that powerful final image: O'Hara is at once self-enclosed in his emotional pain (and physical discomfort) and connected across time and distance to those who share his pain, those with whom, through literature, he sympathizes. This connection—between O'Hara and the exiled novelists—in turn reflects onto us, as readers of O'Hara, who enter into the room of the moment he builds. We share in this isolation and this union.

Writing Moment 2.7

- Return to your list of "Sensory Experiences" and choose two or three dominant qualities. Amplify each one on its own, à la O'Hara. How can you make this experience all-encompassing? To what other experiences, activities, and insights does it lead you?
- Return to your list of "Activities or Objects" and choose two or three potential vehicles with which to travel, again à la O'Hara.

For example, if you are in a restaurant, your vehicle might be food, eating, or cooking. If you are on the street, your vehicle might be modes of transportation, rooftops, or mobile phones. Like O'Hara, who moves from his own imagining mind to the Russian novelists, develop in a linear fashion from the most intimate to the most external.

O'Hara and Free Verse

There are two key differences to note between Dickinson and O'Hara. The first difference relates to their respective encounters with the familiar and the strange. Dickinson makes the strange familiar: she gives form to an almost ineffable estranging feeling through familiar sensory and symbolic imagery. O'Hara, by contrast, makes the familiar strange, refiguring the familiar city through amplification and a metaphoric vehicle. The second difference is formal. Dickinson, composing metrical verse, the dominant convention of her time, follows a strict accentual and syllabic form. O'Hara, composing free verse, the dominant convention of his time, is fixed in the now, letting the poem, to return to Ashbery, serve as "the chronicle of the creative act that produces it" (viii).

Nevertheless, this formal difference between these poets is not black and white. Most obviously, O'Hara distinguishes himself from Dickinson with the formal traits that make his poem feel breezy, almost disposable: the free short lines, the peculiar line breaks, the lack of punctuation, and the uneven stanza lengths. Yet, despite these loose standards, O'Hara shares Dickinson's faith in the power of the music of poetry. Though he seeks liberation from inherited metrical forms, he attends carefully to the rhythms and sounds of words. Take for example the line, "a lunatic's analysis of / a poem by Robert Frost." The stress pattern creates a very musical line ("a **lu**nat**ic's** a**nal**ysis of / a **poem** by **Ro**bert **Frost**"), a music that is heightened early on by matched stress patterns and the exciting vowel- and consonant-play in the pairing of "lunatic's" and "analysis."

For the following writing moment, do not feel obliged to attend over-consciously to rhythm. O'Hara's ability to compose both with such spontaneity and musical ingenuity is the result of years of practice. However, do keep his example in mind as you continue to compose.

Even if you seek an anti-rhythmic poetry, this will be a choice you make and, in turn, an effect you will need to carefully nurture.

Writing Moment 2.8

- Drawing on your earlier materials, or simply returning to the now, compose a poem that is "the inspired ramblings of a mind open to the point of distraction."

For many artists—not just poets, but painters, novelists, film-makers, and cartoonists—the chief end of their work is transformation. Two interrelated approaches to acts of artistic transformation are to change the strange into the familiar and the familiar into the strange. At the core of both processes is convention, the expected, or the so-called "normal": both in terms of form and perceived reality. Poets who practice this transformation seek, in the most basic way, to **defamiliar-ize** our experience of language and our day-to-day lives. Often, their activity is phrased more overtly in terms of audience via the old saw, "Comfort the uncomfortable and bring discomfort to the comfortable."

We have practiced these two approaches as we travelled with our poet companions. We tried our hands at the strange made familiar in the context of the metrical verse tradition and Emily Dickinson's "There's a certain Slant of light." The free verse tradition and Frank O'Hara's "[The Light Presses Down]" served as our vehicle for making the familiar strange. Perhaps most striking of all is the fact that despite the temporal, formal, and temperamental differences between these two poets, they both composed poetry that is powerful and commend-able for the same reasons; their work, to quote Steven Heighton's def-inition of poetry, "[possesses] poetry's surprise and bizarre aptness and rhythmic/acoustical unity" (17). Aim for this same aptness, surprise, and music as you develop poems from the materials you composed during your writing moments and as you test out these new insights with the aid of the exercises listed below.

We will now turn from tradition to two sets of tools: the elements of voice and perspective and the features of voice and structure.

Writing Exercises

1. Return to the material you created during your writing moments and compose one or two new poems. For example, compose a series of O'Hara-style pieces in the same locale (the way a visual artist might sketch and re-sketch the same nude) or return to the initial writing moment and head in a completely different direction.

2. Returning to the "writer as ogler": compose another poem in which you "watch watching." However, this time turn your gaze outwards and watch how others watch. Choosing a specific locale (or locales), attend carefully to what others watch and how they watch and, even, what they do (or what you think they do) with what they take in. Add a twist to your piece by watching for what others miss or do not pay attention to.

3. We undertook a writing moment based on a familiar object or experience that is transformed in an unexpected and surprising way. The opposite strategy can be just as effective. Compose a poem in which you explore a marvellous and miraculous occurrence or object through mundane and everyday images and figures. For an added focus, work in the free verse tradition of O'Hara.

4. The ability to make the familiar strange with ingenuity and rigour requires both our imaginative and rhetorical powers. The following exercise will help you practice both. Choose two objects, entities, or activities at random (perhaps ask a friend for one or select one at random from where you are sitting). Compose a poem in which you prove how each creates or gives birth to the other. For an added focus, work in the tradition of O'Hara.

5. Frank O'Hara mastered the breezy, conversational poem. His poems seem to capture the musing of the curious, chatting friend in action. However, as many of us know from personal experience, conversational expression is not necessarily breezy and musing. Instead, we stammer, repeat ourselves, resort to platitudes, and fill silences with statements we do not believe. Write a parody of an O'Hara poem in which you reflect upon art and life "in the moment," but you do so in a voice (word choice, figures, developmental logic, comfort level, etc.) that is closer to a real, awkward conversation.

6. As you read, take note of the poems you most admire. For free verse poems, ask yourself: which features make the poem a poem (and not, say, prose with line breaks) and which tools and techniques do I most admire? Compose a poem based on your answers to these questions.

Poems in Process

"A Meal at McDonald's" is Fiza Arshad's excellent take on Frank O'Hara's breezy form and a poem that exemplifies the desire to make the familiar strange. Fiza works with short, punchy lines to lead us as readers to proceed with great speed, while her careful compiling of concrete detail and specific images keeps us firmly fixed in the swirling of the chaos-broken peace. Two of my favourite estranging moments are the speaker as "holey scarecrow" and the hand dryer as a "lonely railroad."

A Meal at McDonald's

Sitting at McDonald's
invites chaos into peace
by welcoming a barrage
of intruders to lean in
on the calm
of this holey scarecrow
guiding its fields

I hear music in
the pitter-patter of
tiny feet bringing
joy to my heart
but the hand dryer
is a lonely railroad

yet the old lady
sits in the corner
mindful of her food
and of all her meals
while the young prime minister
holds an emergency meeting
on the television set
ecstatic about his country's
financial state

In "Companion," Sopika Sathyaseelan reminds us that along with the poets, thinkers, and forms that serve as our artistic companions, we are always joined in our work by another companion, a form-transcending feeling or experience or idea that drives us to write, and rewrite, and write it again. Sopika's line breaks in the first stanza create a gut-punching reversal when the hope stimulated by "infinite / number of ways" is undercut by "pain," while her "over, and" construction, repeated, almost simulates the experience of starting and stopping and starting this endless process. That closing "again," set out on its own, both describes the repeated process and takes the form of an imperative, speaking the demand that our art makes on us. Sopika's poem—as evidenced by the fact that I have only shared about 5 per cent of the remarks I wish to make about "Companion" (don't even get me started on the wonderful "verbing" of the noun "wright")—also demonstrates the richness of a carefully crafted minimalist work.

Companion

There are an infinite
number of ways
to feel pain.

Pick one.

It becomes the
poem
we wright
over, and
over, and
over,

again.

Voice and Perspective

It is through the lost that we will encounter elements of voice and perspective. The act of bearing witness to someone we have lost is an essential reason for writing a poem, and this approach will allow us to continue engaging with the tools of poetry through the occasions of poetry. Furthermore, perspective is always a perspective on something. Our approach to the elements of voice thus requires this "something" in order for us to more practically get a handle on these elements.

Let us begin, then, with a moment of reflection. Who did you most recently lose? Who did you lose long ago? Who is it that you cannot let go? Who is it that you have grown apart from, or who is it that has moved away, or passed on, that makes you say, "I want you with me, right now?"

Write down this person's name, and reflect first on your memories and then on your experience now, in the present moment. If it helps, jot a few of your reflections under your chosen person's name. As you did when reflecting on the forbidden in Chapter 1, consider how this person endures in terms of your personal experience, but also consider how this person endures in relation to the communities you shared with this person, whether familial, social, cultural, national, virtual, or otherwise.

Pronouns

Pronouns are one of the simplest, and yet most expansive and flexible elements of voice. We have three central options: "I" (first-person perspective), "you" (second-person perspective), and "he"/"she"/"it" (third-person perspective). There are also the plural forms of first- and third-person: "we" and "they," respectively.

Since these pronouns often name the active agents in your poem, you also want to consider **tense** as a writing tool. Close attention to shifts between the past, present, and future, or situation in one temporal stream, can add existentially authentic or intellectually striking temporal richness to your poem.

Another approach is to avoid personal pronouns altogether, to speak only of the chesterfield, the cigarette, the skyline through the window, or the things of the world, rather than through the perspective of particular selves. This approach is often effective for producing distance and estrangement, or for undertaking more philosophical reflections.

During the following writing moment, remember the process involved in composing subjective, sensual imagery. Encountering the lost, you need to put yourself in the presence of the absence of the one you have lost. Immerse yourself in this blend of memory and feeling and sensation.

Writing Moment 2.9

- Compose three short reflections about this relationship between yourself, your lost one, and your community.

- For your first reflection, delve into a specific strong memory of an experience you share with your lost one. Speaking from your perspective as "I," tell your lost one both what you remember most about that moment and how your present experience differs from that past experience.
- For your second reflection, return mentally to the site of the specific strong memory. Explore the events of this memory without using any personal identifiers or personal pronouns. Instead, let the story of the memory unfold through the concrete details presented and the movement of the objects. For example, rather than writing, "he smoked a cigarette," write, "the cigarette seethed between chapped lips."
- For your final reflection, imagine your community speaking from the perspective of "we." What would the "we" say, reading your two previous reflections?

The goal of this writing moment is, quite simply, to get you practicing with the full range of perspectives available to you, and, through the practice, to get you thinking about the different effects and potentials of this range. Notice how the different perspectives reveal different elements and aspects of the same experience. Notice the breadth of vision gained as these different voices resonate together. Be sure, too, to reflect on your experience of different pronouns: With which of the perspectives did you find it easiest to compose? Which was the most challenging? Why? What, for you, are the strengths and weaknesses of the different perspectives?

The Speaker and the Persona

At the heart of every speaker in a poem is a sort of feedback loop. The speaker's perspective—personality, motivation, senses, etc.—influence how we work with the elements of voice (determining everything from word choice to pronouns to tone). These elements of voice in turn shape perspective, making it palpable and material, something real to which readers react, whether with comfort, curiosity, or revulsion. To get a sense of this, I want you to do something that might initially seem strange in the context of an exploration of your poetic voice: inhabit the mind of an alter ego.

Each of us is filled with more selves than can be substantially expressed in our daily lives, or, really, explored in full depth in the short span of our lives. These selves take many forms: the hidden, the repressed, the ideal, the archetypal, the imaginary, the culturally inherited types, and so on. Take a second to reflect and give one of these selves greater, more specific form, make her or him an alter ego with a name and a voice, with aptitudes and allegiances, with hopes and needs and fears and longings. Once you feel comfortable in this alter ego's skin (or, better, when this alter ego feels comfortable in yours) undertake the following writing moment.

Writing Moment 2.10

- Imagine that you (the real you) have told your alter ego about the lost one you reflected upon in the previous writing moment. Imagine you have shared the emotions these memories stir up, as well as the core of your personal struggle.
- How would your alter ego respond to this story? What form would your alter ego's response take? What would your alter ego think of your emotion and struggle? What advice would she or he give you?
- After reflecting upon these questions, write your alter ego's reply.

Having undertaken this alter ego writing moment, you have made a pair of gains.

First, by writing in "someone else's" voice, you have brought into relief the many different choices we make as writers. Just consider how your alter ego's reply contrasts with your regular way of writing. Did your alter ego speak in a form that you might not have normally employed? How did writing from the perspective of your alter ego influence your word choice? What sorts of details attracted your eye, in contrast to the details you might have selected when writing from your own perspective? Did your alter ego's sentence structure differ from your own? In other words, to move to the more general question again, how did perspective shape the different components that combine to create your voice? And if your word choice, sentence structure, attention to detail, and form of reply did not change, then did you not do something wrong?

The second benefit of this writing moment is that you tested out a variation on a creative tool popular among poets: the persona. A persona, most simply defined, is "an assumed character or role." Thus, in poetic practice, the word strongly retains the classical Latin etymological roots of the *persōna* as mask. Once again, the lens of the persona influences everything from word choice to choice of detail to the length of your lines to the shifting of your attention. Put another way, your choice of words, details, sentences, and so on are performed to create an authentic persona, a believable personality.

The persona can take a number of forms. It may be an unnamed individual who represents a specific identity (e.g., the Irish fighter pilot in W.B. Yeats's "An Irish Airman Foresees His Death"), a specific historical figure (e.g., Richard Howard's *Untitled Subjects*, which includes the voices of the painter Philip James de Loutherbourg and the composer Richard Strauss), or, even, a specific character borrowed from a famous fictional work (e.g., Lynn Crosbie's work with Fredo from Francis Ford Coppola's *The Godfather* films in her poem sequence, "Fredo Pentangeli"). Compose a poem with one of these types of persona. It will be a great way to practice thinking carefully about the different choices we make as poets, while also allowing you to take part in a rich poetic tradition.

Tone

The tone of a poem is the feeling or mood expressed through the poem. The feeling or mood may permeate the piece as a whole, or may shift from stanza to stanza, creating what Helen Vendler fittingly labels the poem's "emotional curve" (123). A list of all the potential tones would fill pages and pages, with the possibilities ranging from abusive, affectionate, and apologetic to vexed, whimsical, and zealous.

The benefits of attention to tone vary poem to poem. If you are composing as or about a specific persona, careful attention to tone will create a more authentic, lively, and realistic self. If your speaker is less specific and embodied, a speaker whose presence is barely felt in the poem, tone is still key to creating an energized and dynamic speaker (or, even, an effectively flat and emotionless speaker). To turn to Vendler's phrase again, you may also choose to craft an emotional curve as your poem's developmental structure—the same emotion could amplify in force from the first line to the last (from touchy to enraged, for example) or a uniform tone could shift drastically in the final stanza (from hope to despair, for example).

Any feature of the poem—from the words to the images to the sounds to the metaphoric vehicles—can be crafted to express your desired emotion or generate just the right mood. Whichever range of choice you are working with, an important feature of tone to keep in mind is that it is often established retroactively. For example, the opening line, "The man who left me," hints at a bitter tone, through the word "left," yet for the most part is relatively toneless. If we add two more lines, "The man who left me / never listened to the music / I suggested," that initial line takes on a truly bitter, even angry tone. By contrast, we could replace one word and end up with a completely different tone: "The man who left me / always listened to the music / I suggested." The "always" inflects that first line with a tone of nostalgia and longing.

Another important feature to remember is that how something is said can be just as expressive as what you say. For example, changing the length of sentences, and how they are punctuated, will also change the tone. Here is a very exaggerated but I hope also effective example:

> Our family cabin on the cliff overlooked the lake where the man in the bright orange swimsuit drowned when we were kids who thought he was playing at drowning as he flailed, the way we played at falling to sharks and squids in shallow water, his trunks the bright bottom of the fireflies who always managed to slip back into the dark before we could catch them.

> Our family cabin on the cliff overlooked the lake. That's where the man in the bright orange swimsuit drowned. We were kids. We thought he was playing at drowning as he flailed. The way we played. We fell to sharks and squids in shallow water. His trunks were the bright bottom of the fireflies. They always managed to slip back into the dark before we could catch them.

Both speakers recall the same traumatic event—a man's drowning—in the same words. Yet the tone drastically changes through the addition of punctuation and the resulting change in sentence length. The first speaker's urgent mania is transformed into the mature melancholy of the second speaker. The first speaker remains traumatized. The second speaker is still affected, but this speaker is more emotionally distant from this past event.

The following writing moment will give you the opportunity to at once reflect on your work with tone and to practice crafting tone.

Writing Moment 2.11

- Choose one of the pieces you wrote for writing moments 2.9 or 2.10.
- Read your selection carefully so that you can both name the tone or tones and grasp the features that create the tone or tones.
- Add another line to the opening or ending of your selection as a means of shifting the tone and changing the piece's emotional curve.
- Rework your selection's punctuation and sentence length, while changing the words as little as possible, as a means of transforming the tone.

Line Breaks

Our final element of voice transcends the topic of perspective. It is the characteristic that distinguishes your speaker as a speaker in (or of or by) a poem from a speaker who is a character in a novel or a play. This element, or, more accurately, this tool, is the line break. Before digging into the what, why, and how of line breaks, let us begin with a writing moment that will ask you to re-break some lines I have mended.

Writing Moment 2.12

- The following sentence opens Stanley Kunitz's very powerful meditation on loss, "The Portrait." I have removed the line breaks: "My mother never forgave my father for killing himself, especially at such an awkward time and in such a public park, that spring when I was waiting to be born."
- Add line breaks to Kunitz's opening (and no cheating by glancing down the page) with the goal of creating a sense that the speaker is off balance.
- Add line breaks to Kunitz's opening (and, again, no cheating) with the goal of stimulating a sense of suspense and surprise in your reader.

For the sake of comparison, take a look at Kunitz's original. Of the two motivations I gave you, my reading is that Kunitz was aiming to stir suspense and surprise, rather than establish an off-balance speaker. Here are Kunitz's line breaks:

> My mother never forgave my father
> for killing himself,
> especially at such an awkward time
> and in such a public park,
> that spring
> when I was waiting to be born.

How does your work compare with his? Did you make the same choices to the same end? What are the different effects of your different choices? As you reflect on this variety of choices and effects, it is worth keeping in mind that when we break lines there are only two options: end-stopped lines and enjambed lines. However, from these options, a wide range of possibilities arises.

End-stopped lines break at the end of a phrase, sentence, or clause, most often with a punctuation point (such as a period, semi-colon, or comma). In Emily Dickinson's "There's a certain Slant of light," for example, 12 of the 16 lines are end-stopped (significantly, only the third line of each stanza is enjambed). Another point to note here is the variety of Dickinson's end-stopped lines. Whether composing metrical or free verse, you want to avoid ending every line with terminal punctuation, such as a period or question mark. Endless end-stopped lines create a monotonous poem and suggest a lack of attention to craft.

Enjambment, by contrast, involves running the sentence over to the next line, breaking it, in other words, mid-phrase, clause, or sentence. Frank O'Hara's "[The Light Presses Down]" is an excellent example of a heavily-enjambed poem. O'Hara's barrage of enjambments forces us forward, pulls us quickly to the next line, then the next, then the next.

As you compose, consider how you can use end-stopped and enjambed lines to guide your reader's pace. Think also about how you can use the line break to stimulate everything from suspense to desire to expectation to double meanings. Even an enjambed line creates a microsecond of a pause as the line forms a discrete unit of meaning.

Take, for example, the line, "I never wanted her to leave me," and break it as follows as a means of creating an unexpected reversal, "I never wanted her / to leave me."

Finally, in terms of enjambment more specifically, pay attention to the types of words with which you end an enjambed line. What is the effect of a line broken on a noun as opposed to a verb, adjective, preposition, or article? Most poets tend to prefer the solidity of a noun or verb at the end of an enjambed line, saving articles and conjunctions for particular occasions.

This concludes our exploration of the elements of voice and perspective. I encourage you to develop poems from the materials you composed during your writing moments, and to test out your new insights into the elements of voice and perspective. Get comfortable inhabiting the position of different speakers as we transition to strategies for ordering and organizing what these speakers say.

Writing Exercises

1. Return to the material you created during your writing moments and compose one or two new poems. For example, combine the multiple perspectives of the first writing moment; try working the voices together in one draft and arrange them in separate stanzas in another.
2. Write a "lost poem" (i.e., an only just discovered poem) in the voice of someone you have lost. Be certain to consider how this individual's way of knowing and being in the world is reflected in both *what* you say and *how* you say it.
3. One way to order your poem is to move centrifugally, to begin with a centre point and to move outward, orbit by orbit, to the different horizons that encircle this centre point. Pronouns provide a useful means for distinguishing and composing with these distinct layers. Recall a time when you were lost, literally or metaphorically, and compose a poem that moves centrifugally from "I" (your experience of being lost) to "you" (address the one (a person, perhaps, or an ideal) from whom you felt most "lost" to) to "they" (the group that searches for you) to, finally, "we" (speak on behalf of yourself and all similarly lost individuals or things).
4. Compose a poem that develops centripetally, moving from the broadest, encircling outside to the centre point. What is something that humanity, or a large community of people, has lost? Is it an object, an identity, an

ideal, or something else? Begin your poem with "we" (speaking on behalf of yourself and the rest of this community) and move inward to "they" (the ones in the past who possessed what is now lost) to "you" (someone in the future who could retrieve what is lost) to "I" (your personal relationship to and/or opinion of the lost) to "it" (the lost object, identity, ideal, etc.).

5. Compose a poem using one of the popular types of persona: the unnamed individual who represents a specific identity, the specific historical figure, or the specific character borrowed from a famous fictional work.
6. Compose a poem with an emotional arc, perhaps an arc that amplifies an emotion or an arc that shifts between contrasting emotions. Consider how you can employ line breaks as a means of effectively expressing this emotional arc.

Poems in Process

What makes Marc Adrian DeLeon's "Baby," our next poem in process, such an effective elegy is that it sensitively bears witness to two losses. The first loss is his grandmother's loss of Adrian, her grandson, when "the steel vulture" carried him from the Philippines to Canada. The second loss is Adrian's loss of his grandmother, the foundation of his love of learning, who has passed away. Notice that even though this is a work of mourning, Adrian indulges his musical impulse, singing as he celebrates the grandmother he loved. This is most evident in the many S-sounds throughout, most strikingly rendered in "your wispy / Spirit whispered."

Baby
for "Baby" Alcantara (1940–2012)

The vaguest of images hobbles into
My skull: me poring over tomes
At that unripe age, and your excited
Trembling as subtle as your slow,
Successful endeavour to fill
My gray matter with statistics
And skills. Only when the steel vulture

Scooped me up and soared away
Did your distance drone on longer:

Longer than my personal undulating
Ebbinghaus curve, longer than
Albert's parsec-measured gravitational
Lens. At this riper age, your tie to me
Breaks, and I wail as you lay bare-boned

And withered: Baby, only when your wispy
Spirit whispered away did the scaffolding
You set for me become the home you always
Wanted me to see and be.

In "The Truth Is," Mawaver Phillips expertly crafts a persona, one, I am sure, bound to make you roll your eyes (though do not feel guilty if you laugh). Mawaver creates a specific identity (a male chauvinist) and cleverly exposes the difference between the persona's public and private selves. Perspective, in her poem, is effectively employed to shape voice. This is most noticeable in her choice of words (knowing folks like this, I just had to recommend the slang term "peeler") and the imaginary presence of the girlfriend, who spurs the rapid-fire shifts in the persona's rant.

The Truth Is,

yes, that dress does make you look
fat. You talk and talk and yet all
that comes out is blah, blah, blah
(wish someone'd invent a human mute
button). Why can't you take
your girlfriends shopping with you?
I'm tired of holding your purse
(and this thing you tell me's a man
purse) while you try on dresses
two sizes too small. The last time
you asked me if there were peelers
at Jimmy's bachelor party, I gave you
the facts: they were highly trained
exotic dancers. No, I didn't stop smoking;
that's what I do in the garage as I
"clean" it out on Saturdays. The truth is
I would never tell you any of this
because lying is a whole lot easier.

Voice and Developmental Structure

Having inhabited the perspective of the speaker, we can turn to the structures that underpin the arc, order, or development of what the speaker says. The elements of voice and perspective, as you just experienced, are quite personal, and thus easy to just dive into and test out. Developmental structures, by contrast, can be a bit more abstract. The trick to engaging them in a practical way is to write about a topic that possesses the features of these developmental structures. I have chosen myth. Myths have provided a fertile field for poets for centuries. The topic is also broad enough that we should all be able to hit on an imagination-stirring example.

Your myth may take the form of a mythic story, such as the 12 labours of Hercules, or a mythic figure, such as Orpheus, the poet-musician whose songs could stir rocks and calm Hades, the ruler of the dead (and about whom so many poets have written that you might not be made a card-carrying bard until you have composed your Orpheus poem). Your mythic stories and mythic figures, of course, do not have to be borrowed from Greek myth. You may also draw from other ancient civilizations, historical events, local legend, or popular culture. You may also choose figures and events from fairy tales, fables, legends, and other forms of popular literature.

The key point regarding order is that in many instances you will find ordering structures in the myth itself, and in other poems written about this myth or mythic figure. The following writing moment will help you locate some of these structures by inviting you to sketch out an outline for two potential poems.

Writing Moment 2.13

- Choose a mythic figure.
- Compose an outline for a poem in which you introduce your reader to the importance of your chosen mythic figure.
- As you compose, reflect upon what you believe an outline is, considering the purpose it serves and the form it takes.

Outlining Structure

There is no right or wrong way to compose an outline, whether a numbered list or a quasi-flow chart, whether a description of the parts to come or blank-filled lines of verse. There is also no incorrect purpose; the outline may serve as a means of getting the gears turning or as the detailed schema that is developed in concert with the poem.

One of the benefits of outlining is that it allows you to, in a sense, see through the scenery of the poem to the road that will bear the reader through. An outline enables the distillation of three interrelated elements: the poem's parts, their order, and the development and interaction of these ordered parts. Outlining is also an indispensable skill for those of us (the majority) who cannot write poetry full-time. Many poems have struck me on the subway, mid-commute, poems that a week filled with lecturing, grading, and meetings would keep me from composing. The outline is a great way of quickly capturing everything you can in quasi-poem form. It gives you seeds to water in the soil of your spare time.

Now that we have considered the elements of the outline—the poem's parts, their order, and the development/interaction of these ordered parts—the next step is to explore some of the methods for conceiving of how a poem develops and how its parts interact. First up: the narrative.

Narrative Structures

When setting out to compose a narrative poem, the most obvious organizational strategy is to follow a traditional **plot structure**: beginning with, perhaps, a one-line or one-stanza exposition (the "normal" state of affairs), introducing the initiating incident, and then following the rising action to the climax (or anti-climax) and dénouement.

For example, the outline for a narrative poem about Orpheus may plot the poem as follows: Orpheus and Eurydice in love (exposition), Eurydice is killed by vipers (initiating incident), Orpheus descends to the underworld and, through his song, is able to save Eurydice (rising action), Orpheus is warned by Hades not to look back at Eurydice as they ascend to the earth's surface (rising action), Orpheus looks back and Eurydice is sucked back into the underworld (climax), and, finally, Hades refuses to give Orpheus another chance (dénouement). (Alternately, if you are the grim type, you could end with Orpheus being ripped to shreds by maenads.)

Beyond this basic plotting, there are a number of other elements to consider, all of which concern the order and developmental arc of the poem. Keep perspective in mind at all times—inhabit it fully. My very linear outline for a possible Orpheus poem would be suitable for a detached objective narrator. However, I would need to make changes if I wrote my poem from the first-person perspective of a character, such as Hades, who had witnessed the events. I would need to account for many factors: Hades' investment in the events, his specific listener, and his motivation for telling the story. My outline would have to be further revised if I decided to write my poem from the perspective of multiple characters.

Time is another factor to consider when conceiving of your narrative poem. The story may take place in one mode (past, present, or future), or the story may be told in the present, as the narrator reflects on the past and looks to the future. For example, as Eurydice ascends with Orpheus before her, she reflects on the events that led to her death and she imagines the variety of ideal futures that await them. The story could also be told in reverse or in a single frozen moment—the pause before, during, or after disaster.

For the following writing moment, return to your mythic figure and compose an outline for a narrative poem.

Writing Moment 2.14

- Choose one of the following perspectives: detached narrator, first-person narrator (with a specific listener), or multiple perspectives.
- Choose one of the following temporal options: linear, reverse, or present telling that looks back on the past and ahead to the future.
- Return to the outline you composed for Writing Moment 2.13, and, based on these selections, rework it into the outline for a narrative poem.

Meditative Structures

Meditative structures are those dedicated to introspection and argument, inner reflection and public debate. If, in the outline for the narrative structure, we plot events, then, in the outline for the meditative structure, we plot the movement of perception and the development of thought. At their purest, as Helen Vendler notes, meditative poems consist of "successive 'takes' on the subject being considered" (114).

In terms of content, meditative poems can be written on any topic, contemplating one's relationship to a secret crush or one's relationship to the divine, celebrating the joys of a rediscovered childhood toy or the virtues of a globally renowned leader.

If the goal is to generate dynamic and animated thought, then the key is to approach the aspects of your topic that produce this type of inquiry. One option is to explore what is unknown or unknowable in the topic, the mystery of its hold (for example, the population of the underworld meditating collectively on the power of Orpheus' song) or the inconsistency of its nature (Eurydice, for example, meditating on Orpheus' love, post-failed rescue).

Another option is to approach the **thematic** tension in the topic, the complex interaction of a pair of connected but distinct terms: self and other, self and community, past and present, nature and culture, innocence and experience, loss and preservation, the transcendent and the mundane, art and reality, the unconscious and the conscious, and so on. The list of possible pairings is nearly limitless, and their presence in our lives ubiquitous. Any one of them, for example, could be fruitfully animated by the Orpheus myth, whether through the nature–culture divide overcome by Orpheus' singing or the strange self–community experience Eurydice is thrust into in Hades.

The activity of the process of meditation itself is another factor to consider. One way to conceive of this is the felt presence of the poet or persona, ranging from the most detached to the most implicated. The meditative "takes" of the former may materialize through the accumulation of un-reflected upon attention and perception, while the latter can take the form of outright argument and investigation, attempting to answer or prove, and drawing on the tools of the debater: thesis, reason, example, and so on. In between these two poles, lay the more common approaches, perhaps a hybrid approach or the figurative articulation, one that contrasts metaphoric figures to reflect on the similarity and difference between two terms or approaches to the unknowable through an ever-changing range of metaphoric figures.

A final feature to consider is the climax. The word "meditate" is more commonly associated with the practice of religious self-emptying than reflection or contemplation, while the word "climax" brings to mind an explosion-stuffed, robot-army-infused chase scene at the end of a Hollywood summer blockbuster. Yet, as we all know—having considered, mulled, deliberated, speculated, reasoned—thought has its climax, its moment of revelation, whether because a solution has been reached, a new vision achieved, or the thinker is confronted with the thought she did not want to face.

For the following writing moment, return to your mythic figure of choice and compose an outline for a meditative poem.

Writing Moment 2.15

- Return to the story surrounding your mythical figure and choose one thematic tension that it crystallizes. Use the list above or come up with your own tension.
- Choose one of the following processes of meditation: perceptual, figurative, or investigative/argumentative.
- Return to the outline you composed for Writing Moment 2.13, and, based on these selections, rework it into the outline for a meditative poem.

Shapes and Other Forms of Order

Within the poles of narrative and meditative structures, there are a variety of mechanisms for determining the order of a poem's parts and the development/interaction of these ordered parts.

Shapes, as we have seen, can also serve as a very simple yet effective device for determining a poem's structure. In the previous section's writing exercises, I invited you to compose poems that, respectively, developed centripetally or centrifugally. The line, both straight and arcing, is the shape we most often use to think about narrative structure. The circle, square, triangle, squiggle, gyre, and so on, can all be used as a means of conceiving of the movement of attention through space and time, from interior to exterior, or of envisioning the developmental activity of a narrative or meditative structure.

Other forms of order are easy and often unique ways to give your poem structure. To name only a few examples, poets have drawn on the chronicle, catalogue, anatomy, inventory, and list. My own Orpheus poem, "Beautif: Orpheus after Eurydice," is an example insofar as I took the questionnaire from an adult dating site, and filled it out from the perspective of Orpheus.

For the following writing moment, return to your mythic figure of choice and compose an outline in which you test out one of these new alternatives.

Writing Moment 2.16

- Return to your mythical figure and choose one shape or form of order. Use the examples above or come up with your own.
- Return to the outline you composed for Writing Moment 2.13, and, based on your figure, shape, or form, rework your outline.

For ease of introduction, I have presented these different structures in isolation. However, as your experience as a reader and writer of poetry tells you, these structures interact. Poems are often a blend of narrative and meditative elements: interior reflection might counterpoint the events of an unfolding story, or the meditation might cut short a developing tale, or the events of a story might metaphorically stand in for the processes of thought. One strategy is to remember that the word "verse" originates in the word "turn"; employ these developmental structures to at once give your poems shape and to create dynamic, engaging, and surprising *turns* in story, thought, or perception.

Writing Exercises

1. Return to the outlines you created during your writing moments and compose one or two new poems. You could also try out one of the many techniques suggested throughout, such as a meditative structure composed from multiple perspectives or a narrative structure that branches off into a variety of possibilities.
2. Write your Orpheus (or Eurydice) poem.
3. Outline and then compose a poem that contains a combination of narrative and meditative structures. For example, the story and reflection could both get their own, separate stanzas, or the story and reflection could take place in parallel, alternating back and forth, line by line.
4. A whole range of ordering forms preserve the exploits of our contemporary legends and mythic heroes (with "legends" and "mythic heroes" placed in quotation marks, if you prefer). The adventures of the baseball superstar are preserved in the box score. The pop music icon finds a home in sales charts. An instruction manual accompanies every "must-have," "revolutionary" technology. Choose a contemporary mythic figure and compose a poem that derives its structure from the form that often preserves this mythic figure.
5. When I first started sharing my poems as an undergraduate student, one of my professors, the poet Andy Stubbs, showed me a number of great tricks for shaking up the structure of a stale, predictable poem. Three of the techniques that I still employ today are: one, rewrite the poem in reverse order; two, randomly rearrange lines or stanzas into a new order; and three, cut every word, line, or section that strikes you as flat. You do not necessarily end with a finished poem (though this can happen). Instead, you are given a new view on the material, one that will often show you a new route for your revision. Give one of Andy's tricks a try.

Poems in Process

Safa Minhas' "Frog Prince" is a self-conscious, rather cheeky struggle to tell a famous fairy tale. Safa's narrative poem, however, is less about the story of the frog prince and more about storytelling itself, insofar as the persona gets entangled in conventions and the story gets lost in bracketed asides. Safa effectively renders this experience through her work with repetition and simple language. The darker turn she makes at the end, furthermore, gives the story a dynamic arc, an arc effectively punctuated by her thought-provoking twist on "happily ever after."

Frog Prince

There once was a time, once
upon a time, where once
upon a time a rock existed
(a stone?), which perhaps
was man-made (or woman-made)
and there was a frog (a frog
prince!) and a peasant
woman who was pretty
pretty (by human standards
anyway). So the frog lived
on the rock (not that the rock
was comfortable (but it was
his rock, see)), and the woman
lived in her hut (not that it was
charming (but it was her hut,
see)). Oh! The woman fell
in love with the frog (some
sort of fetish, I guess),
and the frog fell in love with
the woman (another sort of fetish,
I've heard). The frog kissed
the woman and the woman
kissed the frog. They both
transformed. There were also
some villagers with pitchforks
and flaming torches. The end
(lived happily ever after).

In "A Real Fairy Tale," Novelette Munroe also engages the fairy tale tradition. She uses the fairy tale as a way of exploring the process of personal mythmaking that we all undertake, reflecting on the relationship between fantasy and memory, between what is longed for and what is. Novelette quite movingly blends the narrative and meditative, both telling stories and more self-consciously addressing the act of storytelling. She also works with sensuous images and concrete details, adding an element of the "real" to her real fairy tale and connecting us deeply with the world of her poem.

A Real Fairy Tale

Ever had a memory of a memory of a memory of a memory?
As a child I believed in talking teenage turtles
who ninja-ed under the New York city streets
and half-scaled humans who breathed
through gills and sang under the sea.
My grandmother told me once that as a child
she saw a mermaid on the beach. And that
confirmed it all for me. She said
she was told stories about how mermaids were lonely
but did not want to be disturbed by us land geeks.
When a memory becomes a fantasy
the fantasy becomes the memory. I have
a memory of a memory of a memory of a memory
that my soul fell in love once for it reached out
and touched the nose of another. But that's
when I sneezed. It's hard to depend
on a memory to know what's true
when the longing for what used to be there
is more tangible than the birth of its cheer.
It reminds you that the fairy tale is all
that was there. My grandmother's right:
mermaids do live under the sea.

Conclusion: On Multiplicity and Voice

In our extended exploration of voice, we have come a long way since we, with Hafiz, were called from the bath by the poem. I am guessing you have already revised my initial statement, again via Hafiz, that we have two voices: the voice of daily responsibility and chatter, and the voice that meets the poem's call, that joins this voice, sings and lifts and turns with it.

If you have not tweaked my statement already, how would you revise it? Here are a few possibilities: we have multiple voices, manifold voices, infinite particular voices. The metrical verse and free verse traditions provide conventions and techniques that inform and multiply our voices. Within these traditions, so many particular voices, such as Dickinson and O'Hara, have renewed the conventions, providing unique models we can further rework and renew. The elements of perspective and developmental structure further expand the range of our possible voices, providing us with the tools and techniques we need to compose unique and authentic speakers who speak in dynamic, engaging ways.

The voices in which we choose to—or, more accurately, are driven to—speak, the lives we pursue and the time we spend travelling with specific traditions, will differ from poet to poet. For one of you, the form you choose might be a Dickinsonian hymn, and you will spend a lifetime writing them, and exploration will mean varying the form's topical, rhetorical, and musical conventions, just so. For another, the life of the choral poet might suit you best, and you will explore this feature of this persona and this swerve from this community and never inhabit the same voice twice. What is essential, as with any aspect of poetic practice, is that you work with rigour, dedication, intensity, care, and an insatiable craving for adventure.

We will remain with the metrical and free verse traditions as we turn to Chapter 3: Poetic Forms. Our next passage together will lead us to try our hands at fixed forms poets invented centuries ago, forms concocted in more recent years, and even forms that have nothing to do with poetry but can inspire us to rethink entirely the what and why and how of our work with words.

Recommended Resources

- *Books about Metre*: There are a number of excellent books dedicated to the study of metre. There are the more academic books, which exhaustively catalogue every element, rule, and variation. My favourite in this category is *Poetic Designs: An Introduction to Meters, Verse Forms, and Figures of Speech* by Stephen Adams. This book has served me well as a writer and a reader. There are also more practical guides. A recent addition to this club is definitely worth your time. In *The Ode Less Travelled: Unlocking the Poet Within*, Stephen Fry teaches the composition of metrical verse in a manner that is equally insightful, hilarious, and very readable.

- *Full-Length Collections*: At the end of Chapter 1, I recommended that you buy an anthology (or two) and read widely. At the same time, you also want to be reading with depth. When you discover poets whose handful of anthologized poems stir your appetite for more, get your hands on their books, or, if available, their collected or selected works. Not only will you discover more incredible work, but you will also see how many different poets that one poet is over the span of her or his career.

- *Writers on Writing*: There is also much to be gained from reading writers on writing. In these types of works, you will gain insights into everything from craft to tradition to the publishing world to the practical aspects of living the writer's life. Two absolute must-reads are Annie Dillard's *The Writing Life* and Rainer Maria Rilke's *Letters to a Young Poet*. Interviews are also a valuable venue for probing a writer's thoughts on writing. *Where the Words Come From: Canadian Poets in Conversation*, edited by Tim Bowling, is a unique example because the book is composed of emerging poets interviewing their veteran peers. *Prismatic Publics: Innovative Canadian Women's Poetry and Poetics*, edited by Kate Eichhorn and Heather Milne, is a must-read recent work; it provides both interviews and poems by some of Canada's best living poets.

- *A Writing Routine*: Of all the companions we have encountered in this chapter, perhaps the most important companion has remained unmentioned: yourself. I mean the self who puts off writing poems for the sake of watching cat videos on the Internet or waiting for the phone to ring or fixing that one screw on the door knob that might eventually come loose. The best way to get this companion on board (or keep her or him under control) is with a writing routine. Pretty much every writer I have met or read has listed the routine as the most indispensable element of her or his practice and life. The obvious payoff is that you get work done. For the uninitiated, the less known benefit is that the writing process, once you are hooked, invigorates and animates. No matter how distracted or exhausted you are, 15 minutes into a writing session you will be recharged and two hours of scribbling will pass, just like that. The process sustains.

CHAPTER 3

Poetic Forms

Introduction: Service and the Force of Form

> "My best writing seems to have to
> be forced from me by some other
> force but that force has to be one
> whose power I agree to serve."
>
> —Ariana Reine

While writing this chapter, I received the above Ariana Reine quotation from a student along with the comment, "It made me think of you." As someone whose working life has been dedicated to service (from bartender, waiter, and barista to, today, teacher), I took this as a compliment and saw, in a way that I had not before, the connection between poetry and service-centred vocations.

They are linked by the interpersonal connections they form (often between strangers), the sharing of a skill (whether through the creation of the best Bloody Caesar you will ever taste—I guarantee it—or the composition of a well-crafted metaphor), and the act of giving someone what they are after. There is also a connection between the respective unhappy "customers": for example, the vicious and obtuse reviewer and the woman who spit at me, "You're a waste of skin," when I let the honey on the condiment stand at Starbucks run dry. However, this latter connection is one we can leave for another day (and textbook, perhaps, *How and When to Bite One's Tongue*).

More particularly, I love the link Reine makes between service and a poem-inspiring force. She sums up an experience we all share as poets: the experience of the force of form and the decision to serve this form, whether through reproduction or reinvention. Poetic forms—whether **fixed forms** or forms of voice—are most simply characterized as sets of rules and conventions that we follow when composing a poem. They are forces insofar as they set generative borders around the creative process, and we serve these forms insofar as we choose to observe their rules and conventions.

In what way, though, are the restraints, rules, and conventions of these forms productive and generative? In what way do they function as poem-inspiring forces? Think of the act of writing a poem as reaching into a river. Reaching into these rapidly passing waters with our hands, a net, a metal detector, or a fishing rod will end with the retrieval of very different things, whether just a few drops of water or treasure or a gasping bass. Similarly, reaching into the rapidly passing experience of our lived lives with different poetic forms and conventions and practices will result in the creation of very different poems. The restraints of a form, then, do not inhibit; instead, they allow for a specific kind of reaching and retrieval, they enable us to take hold of certain experiences and to shape them in a specific—whether striking, beautiful, or estranging—way. As T.S. Eliot aptly observes, "freedom is only freedom when it appears against the background of artificial limitation" (187).

In the following sections, our three forms—metrical forms, twentieth-century forms, and other mediums—will be paired with three more poetic motivations—to sustain fidelity, to rebel, and to found a new language.

We will begin with the basics of metrical form before turning to one of the oldest examples, the sonnet. Even though this form dates back to thirteenth-century Italy, it remains popular today because it is so challenging, enlivening, and, to borrow an excellent turn of phrase from Edward Hirsch, "one of the enabling forms of human inwardness" (39).

Metrical Forms

What does it mean to be faithful?

What different forms, for example, does your faithfulness take? To whom are you most faithful—your family, a friend, or a lover? How do you express this fidelity in your day-to-day life?

Perhaps you are most loyal to a cause; there is a good in the world to which you remain faithful, to preserve it, or there is an injustice whose wrongness you devotedly work to right.

Maybe a deeply held belief is what holds your devotion, whether a belief you have inherited from a long tradition or one you have discovered through your own lived experience.

With these questions in mind, undertake the following writing moment.

Writing Moment 3.1

- Choose the person, cause, or belief to which you wish to express your faithfulness.
- Select an entity or object that does not usually serve as a symbol for fidelity (in other words, do not choose a dog or a ring).
- Write down a few of the ways in which the state or activity of this entity or object serves to represent, or, even, practice, fidelity.

Fidelity as Subject and Practice

The concept of fidelity, as I hope this writing moment hints, is a bountiful topic in poetry. Whether the object of devotion is God, a cause, or a lover, poetry will always serve as a dynamic and expressive medium for us to celebrate, prove, rationalize, or question this devotion.

Beyond subject matter, fidelity plays another important role in our respective practices. As we change as poets throughout our writing lives, we support different traditions and practices, consciously or unreflectively. This is always a two-tiered exercise. We inevitably express fidelity both to a specific aesthetic program and to a community's way of speaking, whether this community is religious, political, economic, or any number of other categories.

In the context of one aesthetic example, poetic forms, the central type of fidelity we work with is fidelity to the rules and conventions. With metrical forms, these rules govern the length of the line, the rhythm of the line, and the rhyme. As you might imagine, for poets who compose with these metrical forms the ability to artfully and originally craft with these elements is highly valued. Metrical forms come in two varieties: types of lines and fixed forms.

Let us begin with one of the oldest and simplest types of line, one that still remains essential today for poets of almost every ilk: blank verse.

Blank Verse

Blank verse has been a central type of poetic line throughout the development of English-language poetry. Blank verse's defining features are almost non-existent: unrhymed iambic pentameter. Unrhymed, of course, suggests the lack of rhyme. Iambic refers to the type of rhythm. An iamb is an unstressed syllable followed by a stressed syllable. The words "a**lone**" and "ex**cel**" are both examples of **iambs. Pentameter** refers to the number of stresses the line contains, and, thus, the line's length. A pentameter line contains five stressed syllables. (For a list of the six central rhythms and other types of lines, see the glossary entry for "metrical verse.") These three simple limits that characterize blank verse have provided poets with a fruitful poetic line. Blank verse served as the metrical foundation of Shakespeare's plays and Milton's epic poem, *Paradise Lost*, and it remained a central line for many twentieth-century poets.

There are a number of reasons for the popularity of blank verse. Formally speaking, the lack of rhyme removes a potentially hindering constraint, while the steady metre, and use of internal sonic elements, retains the musical features of verse. Regarding this steady metre, the iamb is the most natural rhythm in spoken English, and thus provides poets with the most freedom. The pentameter line, similarly, is ideal because it can be read comfortably in one breath.

Here is a self-reflexive couplet I composed to serve as an example:

These **i**ambs **lined** in **fine** pen**ta**met**er**
will **help** you **build** this **form** so **blank** yet **verse**.

Here is another example of blank verse from one of the line's twentieth-century masters, Wallace Stevens. These are the first two lines from his masterpiece, "The Idea of Order at Key West."

She **sang** be**yond** the **gen**ius **of** the **sea**.
The **wa**ter **nev**er **formed** to **mind** or **voice**.

The trick to writing quality blank verse, and any other metrical line, is to develop your ear. The best way to develop your ear is to practice. The following writing moment will help get you started by providing a mix of advice and exercises.

Writing Moment 3.2

- The first step is to read, read, and read some more. Fix the pattern firmly in your head. For the present exercises, reread my sample and Stevens' sample. You can exaggerate stressed (bolded) syllables and mute unstressed (not bolded syllables).
- One way to practice, as you know from previous writing moments, is the fill-in-the-blank (pun intended). Remove words from a line with a fixed rhythm and replace the words with your own choices. The goal is to maintain the rhythm. Note, in the following example of "blanked" blank verse, that each blank is a syllable, and the bold blanks are stressed.

  She **_____** be**yond** the **___** __ **of** the **_____**.
  The **wa**ter **nev**er **_____** to **mind** or **_____**.

- Another, more challenging practice, is to revise a line that does not fit the form. The following couplet is meant to be the closing two lines of a sonnet. This means the rhyme scheme is right, but the rhythm (iambic) and line length (pentameter) are both off. Revise the following couplet into a pair of iambic pentameter lines. You are allowed to cut and change words; however, try to change as few words as possible, and you must retain the couplet's original meaning.

> If one day soon I finally forget the way to go
> Remind me that ashes are really just the body's snow.

- For further practice, visit the website "For Better For Verse" at prosody.lib.virginia.edu. This interactive website is incredible and indispensable (and highly addictive). It allows you to practice **scansion** (the act of marking the metre of a poem) by scanning the line with the click of the mouse (or tap of the screen) and then with another click or tap it reveals if you scanned the line correctly. The site also includes other excellent tools, lists of resources, and rules of thumb.

The Sonnet

One of the most enduring and dynamic fixed forms is the sonnet. The sonnet, whose name derives from the Italian *sonetto*, meaning "a little sound" or "a little song," was invented in southern Italy around 1235. Since taking up the form in the early-sixteenth century, English language poets have employed the sonnet to express love, celebrate nature, meditate on God, attack death, reflect on time, promote politics, and document history. The sonnet is, to turn again to Edward Hirsch, "both the most traditional and the most experimental of forms" (36).

In terms of its fixed features, the sonnet is a 14-line poem written in iambic pentameter. So, put another way, you compose 14 blank verse lines, only now you add the requirement of a rhyme scheme.

Two of the most popular sonnet forms are the Petrarchan and the Shakespearean. The Petrarchan consists of an eight-line stanza (an octave) with a rhyme scheme of *abbaabba* connected to a six-line stanza (a sestet) with a rhyme scheme of *cdecde* or *cdcdcd*. The Shakespearean consists of three linked quatrains rhymed *abab*, *cdcd*, *efef*, and a closing couplet rhymed *gg*.

Sonnets are also characterized by the *volta* or turn, which usually begins with the ninth line. The *volta* is defined by a substantial change, whether the presentation of a counter-argument, a shift in a conceit, the turn to a resolution, or the further amplification of a strong emotion.

Writing Moment 3.3

- Return to the elements you composed in Writing Moment 3.1: the person, cause, or belief to which you wish to express your faithfulness, and the (surprising) entity or object that best figures your fidelity. (If you had trouble conceiving of an entity or object, feel free to employ one of the following examples: a rat, the wind, or Silly Putty.)
- Compose two lines of blank verse. In the first line, state that you are as faithful as your chosen entity or object. In the second line, state how this entity or object serves as a surprising emblem for fidelity.
- Once you have read and written a substantial amount of blank verse, the line becomes second nature (and sometimes all-consuming, like a song you cannot shake). Until then, here are two approaches you can take to help ease yourself into the practice. First, you can write your two lines in free verse and then revise the line, replacing words and adjusting syntax. Alternately, you can build the line, iamb by iamb, not advancing until you have the correct rhythm in place.

The Mini-Sonnet

The sonnet, though a fertile and dynamic form, is a massive challenge. One method I developed for myself when starting out, to help ease myself into the sonnet, was the mini-sonnet.

The mini-sonnet is composed of five iambic pentameter lines, rhymed *abcba*. The mini-sonnet is a shrunken version of the Shakespearean sonnet, insofar as it retains the Shakespearean's developmental structure. The first two lines of the mini-sonnet replace the first eight lines of the Shakespearean sonnet. Lines 3 and 4 replicate the *volta* or turn undertaken in lines 9 through 12 in the Shakespearean sonnet. Finally, the fifth and last line replaces the summative or synthesizing couplet.

Try your hand at the mini-sonnet in the following writing moment.

Writing Moment 3.4

- For the first two lines of your mini-sonnet, use the two lines of blank verse you previously composed.
- To undertake a turn in lines three and four, expose the infidelity of other, more conventional figures of fidelity that contrast with your choice. For example, if you discuss the rat in your first two lines, you can now discuss (and expose as unsatisfactory) a dog.
- For your final line, compose an **epigram** that sums up the authenticity of your faithfulness as represented in your initial choice of figure.
- Be sure to compose in iambic pentameter lines and to rhyme *abcba*.

This marks the end of our approach to metrical verse forms. I encourage you to turn these writing moments into poems, and I also hope you will continue to engage some other popular metrical forms and other types of fixed forms by attempting to compose a few of the examples described in the ensuing writing exercises. In our next section, we will explore the full range of free verse (and, really, anti-verse) forms refined and invented in the twentieth century.

Writing Exercises

1. Having completed a mini-sonnet, try your hand at a full-length Shakespearean sonnet. The Shakespearean sonnet consists of three quatrains rhymed *abab*, *cdcd*, *efef*, and a closing couplet *gg*. Remember that the *volta* or turn, which begins with the ninth line, is characterized by a substantial change, whether the presentation of a counter-argument, a shift in a conceit, the turn to a resolution, or the further amplification of a strong emotion. Go against the grain and take as your subject a person, cause, or belief to which you do not wish to remain faithful.
2. On the topic of fidelity, liturgics are a fitting poetic **subgenre** to turn to. Liturgics include the prayer (the devotee invokes the higher power), sermon (a devotee's public address), carol (a celebratory song), canticle

(a work for public worship based on religious writing), and even the curse (a devotee invokes the higher power, wishing punishment on a rival). Compose a blank verse version of one of these liturgics.

3. The sestina, a French form invented in the twelfth century by the **troubadour** Arnaut Daniel, is a very challenging form that many of my students have nonetheless had a lot of fun with. Do not let the limits scare you off. First, the form's 39 lines are divided into six sestets (6-line stanzas) and a closing tercet (3-line stanza) known as an **envoi**. Second, the six words that end the first 6 lines are repeated at the end of each line in the ensuing stanzas according to the following order: i) ABCDEF, ii) FAEBDC, iii) CFDABE, iv) ECBFAD, v) DEACFB, vi) BDFECA, vii) (envoi) ECA (with BDF appearing, respectively, in the middle of lines 37, 38, and 39). If you are looking for some consolation, there is no limit on line length (though you will want to keep your line length consistent.) For an example of a sestina, see Christine Tan's Spike Lee–inspired piece in the Poems in Process below.

4. The pantoum is an accentual-syllabic form that originated in Malaysia. The form is composed of quatrains (as many as you wish) and the metre of your choosing. The unique feature of the pantoum is that the second and fourth lines of each stanza become the first and third lines of the next stanza. (The repeated line is known as a repeton.) The poem ends with a quatrain in which lines one and three of the first stanza become lines two and four of the final stanza. The rhyme scheme is **interlocking**: *abab*, *bcbc*, *cdcd*, etc.

5. The tanka, like the haiku (5-7-5), is a Japanese syllabic form. The tanka is composed of five unrhymed lines, which consist of, respectively, 5-7-5-7-7 syllables. The tanka is often divided into a tercet and a couplet with the couplet marked by a turn (in thought, perception, and so on).

6. Imagine that the topic of fidelity required a fixed metrical form and you were asked to write it. Determine the rules for line length, rhythm pattern, and rhyme. Which conventions would make for a truly fidelity-expressing form? Be sure to give your form a name.

Poems in Process

Though many of this poem's fine qualities tempt me, I do not want to break down its inner-workings for you. Instead, I would like you to use Marc Adrian De Leon's "These windows: bright and crystal-clear" to test what you have just learned. What type of fixed form is this poem an example of? What are its features? How has Adrian played with the conventions? Has he stuck strictly to the rhythm or has he taken poetic licence and varied it?

These windows: bright and crystal-clear

These windows: bright and crystal-clear, the sea-
Struck tainted sky does peek like silver blush.
Of wandering eyes do storytellers dream;
And slender thighs do make the singers hush.
Newly-cleaved rhododendrons, scarlet beasts,
Eclipse these trickling, pathetic rays; for days
Your seraphim-sculpted form I eagerly feast
With iris-ignited hunger. These talons belay
You like buccaneers who hoist the sails and sail
For days, for weeks, for months, and years—not me!
My privilege: the condor's shadow. Frail
Are these feathers—insatiably craving, weary and hungry.
  Your corpse around which I spiral tempts me so;
  My beastly blessing: indulging in flesh of snow.

Christine Tan's "Brooklyn Heat" is a sestina about Spike Lee's *Do the Right Thing*. Much of the power of this piece results from the meeting of old and new: the meeting of the old form (the sestina) with the new, unexpected content (the film), and the meeting of this form's conventions with the popping, spoken word rhythms Christine works in throughout, exemplified right off the bat by the opening pair of short, stress-stuffed sentences. Note also how Christine works effectively with enjambment throughout the poem, and how she productively manages the limit of her six line-ending words by bringing out their respective multiple meanings.

Brooklyn Heat

after Spike Lee's *Do the Right Thing*

Lips on beer cans. Heads in the ice-box.
Minds off the heat. As children are left
to their own devices, parents stay cool
or try to. Using every last bit of power
to keep one's skin from catching on fire.
To get that body temperature just right.

New Air Jordans. A scuff on the right
shoe. Bugged out Bugging Out can't wait to box
clever into Clifton, who has really ignited his fire
by bumping into him, even if it was from the left.
Bug just craves the chance to exercise some power
when he sees he's justified. He's cool, he's cool,

he tells Mookie, but he quickly loses his cool
when he sees there's no brothers on the wall right
beside him. Symbolic of his people stripped of power?
In his favourite pizza parlour? Sal is ready to box
Bugging Out in the ear. Prepared to take that left
jab or a cross from the rear. He's ready to fire

Mookie if Bugging Out don't shut up. Hang fire
'til everyone's too hoppin' hot, too angry to cool
down, 'til there's absolutely no space left
for any more hate. Bugging Out walks right
out of the pizzeria. Radio Raheem's stereo box
blasts on full volume Public Enemy's "Fight the Power"

while Bugging Out starts his futile search for power
in numbers. A boycott against Sal's Famous. (A future fire
ruining much more than pizza box after pizza box.)
Bugging Out asks Radio Raheem to join his boycott. He's cool,
he's down with it. Smiley also tags along. And off the three go to right
a wrong of no black man's picture on the right or the left

of photographed Italian-Americans. Public Enemy's volume left
on high. Bat to the boom box, then it loses its new 22-battery power
while voices of the angry and passionate still sound loudly left and right.
Is this about the noise or the pictures? Start a fight. Start a fire.
Sal's Famous up in flames. Arson mocking Brooklyn heat. Night's cool
absent. NYPD arrives and suffocates. Raheem's body-sized box

waits. If we never do right by each other, what's left?
The boom box no longer plays "Fight the Power."
The brave finally put out the fire, and still no one is cool.

With "*StarCraft*: The End of the Hive," Sheen Pardinas utilizes a fixed form that is characterized by a syllabic limit. This form, the haiku, one of the most popular fixed forms, is composed of three lines and a syllable count of 5-7-5. Like Christine, Sheen puts a new twist on the old form. First, in writing about a videogame, he encounters another medium as his subject matter, a practice we will discuss later in this chapter. Secondly, Sheen also composes one of the twentieth-century forms we will look at in this chapter: the **found poem**. Sheen, you see, did not write these lines. Instead, each line is dialogue of a character in the video game. Sheen, I should add, has also made a recording using the game's voices. As someone who loves found poetry, and who spent six great months in South Korea (where *StarCraft* is a national religion), I could not resist including this poem.

***StarCraft*: The End of the Hive**

Goliath online
Nuclear launch detected
Ready to roll out

Our minds are as one
Twilight falls upon us all
My life for Aiur

Must place that on creep
Our base is under attack
Spawn more Overlords

Twentieth-Century Forms

The type of poetry this book has more than likely steered you to write is **lyric poetry**. The term lyric, with its roots in ancient Greece, originally referred to a song sung to the accompaniment of a lyre (a hand-held, harp-like instrument), but "[it] is now used for any fairly short poem in the voice of a single speaker" (Ferguson 2027–8).

I have a number of reasons for steering you to write lyric poems. Lyric poetry is the poetry with which I am most familiar. It remains a dominant strain. Composing lyric poems—by turning you to personal experience and encouraging you to remain brief—is an efficient way to introduce you to the tools and techniques of poetry. Once you have a handle on these tools, you can abandon the lyric and utilize these tools to write your great epic or dramatic poems, or turn with greater confidence to the lyric's more performance-based siblings, spoken word and slam.

I bring your attention to the lyric poem as we turn to the twentieth century because this period saw both the ascendancy of the lyric and the lyric's dismantling. A number of times in this book I have used a phrase like, "there is an exception to this rule," or I have observed, "such and such is only one perspective." In the context of twentieth-century poetry, this is an understatement. Not only are there exceptions to rules, but also—more than any other period—there are vigorous counter-practices, schools of writing that rebel against their predecessors, or contemporaries who aim to expose the flaws and failures of their fellow writers.

In the following section, then, we will encounter this range of twentieth-century lyric (and anti-lyric) forms through one of the period's major artistic motivations: the desire to rebel. Let us begin with both a bit of review and a rebellion. In the following writing moment, you will first immerse yourself in your surroundings and, as I have encouraged you since "Working with the Image" in Chapter 1, you will practice composing with particularity and specificity. Having done so, you will have the chance to rebel against this approach, to consider other potential practices and outcomes.

Writing Moment 3.5

- The following lines have a number of issues, most central of which is a lack of specific detail and sensuous imagery. Rewrite the following stanza, changing as many words as you see fit and restructuring the sentences (though maintaining the three-line limit). Your goal is to communicate this strong feeling or mood without naming the mood or feeling.

  I looked out my window and saw
  this thing, and it gave me, like,
  this really strong feeling.

- Return to your revised passage, and revise it again. Beyond translating it back into its original form (that is too easy), consider how you can rebel against the dominance of particularity and sensuousness.

Form and Free Verse Poetry

This writing moment, in the context of form, has led you to make a pair of aesthetic choices beyond the "choice" to value (or not value) the concrete and specific over the general, vague, and indistinct. Can you guess what these choices are? These choices can happen so unconsciously that, prior to picking up this book, you might not have even known you were making them.

First, this writing moment forced you to write a lyric poem. Second, it encouraged you to compose in free verse rather than metrical verse. I draw your attention to these choices as a reminder that we should not take them for granted. The lyric "I," as we will see, can take many different shapes, and, furthermore, is not a poem's sole source. Similarly, free verse poetry, despite its apparent "naturalness," has revolutionary and rebellious historical roots.

Let us begin with the rise of free verse poetry, since it is out of the free verse revolution that transformations in the lyric "I" arise. In the English-speaking tradition, free verse poetry is quite young by comparison to metrical verse. It was a decade into the twentieth century that poets such as Ezra Pound, Amy Lowell, and H.D.—known as **Imagists** and flying the banner, "Make it new"—created this major shift in English poetry.

Freedom for them meant freedom from inherited tradition and convention; thus, free verse poetry can be characterized both by what it overthrows—fixed rhyme schemes and fixed rhythmic patterns—and by what it founds—a quest for a new practice, for, as Lowell puts it, "new rhythms—as the expression of new moods" (vi).

Imagists were characterized by both a negative and a positive move: the abandonment of overdone emotion, overdone abstraction, and overdone metrical conventions, on the one hand; and, on the other, the taking up of free verse as their poetic form and the immediate "instant of time" as their poetic experience. According to Lowell, she and other Imagists fought for free verse "as a principle of liberty. We believe that the individuality of a poet may often be better expressed in free verse than in conventional forms" (vi).

The inherent (and inevitable) irony is that these poets, in challenging established conventions and traditions, found new traditions and conventions. They thus exemplify this essential poetic motivation: to rebel—they break radically with received popular practice and instead champion an alternative, less accepted strategy for creation. Let us continue to trace the features of these different rebellions by testing them out for ourselves. We will first turn to the idea of subjectivity as a means of exploring how other poets took up the free verse rallying cry and reshaped it, before reflecting upon how we can do the same in our work.

Form and Subjectivity: Three Approaches to the Lyric "I"

As with the English metrical tradition, the free verse tradition has a complex history and has taken a wide variety of forms in the hands of practicing poets. One means of charting its diversity is to trace the changing shape of this quest for a new form based on the turn to a unique subjective experience or position. It is from these turns to different experiences that different incarnations of the lyric "I" arise.

One approach is, quite simply, to compose in a manner that mirrors common speech. This may involve speaking as much in your everyday voice as you can, in a manner that is straightforward and unadorned. In the first quarter of the twentieth century, Marianne Moore, in the American context, playfully characterizes this as writing in "plain American which cats and dogs can read" (15). A more particular approach is to employ a vernacular language, "to learn the speech of the place" (7), as Wallace Stevens put it. This involves utilizing the jargon, unique rhythms, and specific grammar of a people or region.

Another approach is to generate your form by turning to your particular body and the particular moment of composition. Charles Olson first consistently outlined this approach in his 1950 essay "Projective Verse," laying the foundations for the **Black Mountain School** of poetry. Olson argued "[a] poem is energy transferred from where the poet got it (he will have some several causations), by way of the poem itself, all the way over to, the reader" (16). In order for this transfer of energy to occur, the poet needed to adopt a new poetic form and new poetic experience: the rhythm and length of "the line comes (I swear it) from the breath, from the breathing of the man who writes" (19), and the content of the in-the-moment-experience determines everything from the layout on the page to the structure of the sentences.

To give you a sense of what I mean, here are two very different examples by two poets inspired by this same turn to breath and the body. The first is the opening of Robert Creeley's "The Language":

Locate I
love you some-
where in

teeth and
eyes, bite
it but

take care not
to hurt, you
want so

much so
little.

And here, by contrast, is an excerpt from Daphne Marlatt's "Imagine: a town":

Imagine a town running

(smoothly?
a town running before a fire
canneries burning

(do you see the shadow of charred stilts
on cool water? do you see enigmatic chance standing
just under the beam?

A third approach to free verse results from poets breaking off from received traditions to more deeply explore the different poetics of **non-hegemonic identities**. These poets seek poetic forms and poetic experiences outside the traditions founded by predominately white, male, and heterosexual writers. In the context of the Black Mountain tradition, for example, Marlatt sought new forms for exploring the lesbian feminist experience. Fred Wah, most notably in *Diamond Grill*, created a hybrid text as a means of investigating the ways in which stories are told about the Chinese immigrant experience (Wah's grandfather), the mixed race experience (Wah and his father), and the land (both the prairie and the nation) itself.

These are only three of the approaches to free verse lyric poetry that arose in the twentieth century, manifesting out of these meetings of poet and body, identity, community, and region. As you read and compose new poems, be certain to also explore other foundational schools, such as the **Harlem Renaissance**, **Beat poetry**, **Confessional poetry**, **Language poetry**, and on and on.

Writing Moment 3.6

- First reflect on these three approaches to identity in free verse: everyday/vernacular, embodied (Black Mountain School), and embodied (non-hegemonic identities). Would you align yourself with any of these practices? Which are you most keen to explore?
- Return to the three lines you composed for Writing Moment 3.5.
- Rewrite these lines in a vernacular with which you are familiar. Consider, for example, a manner of speaking you share with a specific community: your family or friends (past or present), your workplace, your favourite pastime, or your favourite online site or forum.
- Rewrite these lines through a more embodied poetics. Compose in line lengths that suit your breath, and feel free to toy with layout and spacing.

Form and Materials: Sound Poetry and Visual Poetry

There were poets composing at the same time as the Imagist poets who were even more radical. These poets sought to break so fully with tradition that they ceased to be concerned not only with metrical forms and conventions, but seemingly essential elements such as meaning and grammar. Instead, these poets turned to two respective material qualities of language—sound and graphic form—and founded two new types of poetry: **sound poetry** and visual or graphic poetry.

Sound poetry, since it is essentially a spoken form, is difficult to truly grasp in print form. For this reason, I ask that you read the following sample, "Karawane" (UbuWeb), composed in 1916 by **Dadaist** Hugo Ball, out loud (preferably with great passion, if not at the top of your lungs).

jolifanto bambla o falli bambla
großiga m'pfa habla horem
egiga goramen
higo bloiko russula huju
hollaka hollala
anlogo bung
blago bung blago bung
bosso fataka
ü üü ü
schampa wulla wussa olobo
hej tatta gorem
eschige zunbada
wulubu ssubudu uluwu ssubudu
-umf
kusa gauma
ba-umf

More than simply attempting to get you thrown out of wherever you are (or, if you were really brave in your reading, arrested for disturbing the peace), Ball was, in the words of his contemporary, **Futurist** Velimir Khlebnikov, exploring how "the element of sound lives a self-oriented life" (in McCaffery 7).

What this means, as Steve McCaffery effectively outlines, is that sound poets undertook a three-fold process of liberation: liberating a word's sound from its graphic form, from what it refers to in the world, and even from its history; liberating the poem from common modes of reading for theme or edification; and liberating the mind and body from traditional decorums of creation and communication (7).

As for the actual process of composing a sound poem, your imagination is your only limit. Sound poets employ a whole range of strategies, including, but not limited to: uttering nonsense, creating an imaginary language, repeating words to allow a sort of unconscious voice to take over as the word drifts into other words and sounds, arranging letters of a sentence into new nonsensical words, or mangling the speeds, pitches, and tones with which one speaks. With the advent of new recording technologies, as McCaffery notes, many sound poets began using tape recorders to record and manipulate their poems pre-performance and to provide a recorded voice to duet with the live voice (10).

At the same time that sound poets were first seeking to explore, and to liberate, the sounds of words, other poets were taking as their compositional material the graphic or visual aspects of words. Though the end result was always a transformation and defamiliarization of language, the motivations and practices were very different.

For example, another one of Ball's contemporaries, the Futurist F.T. Marinetti, sought to transcend the limits of syntax and meaning, and, in turn, fully express his (often violent) creative emotion, by manipulating the size and shape of letters, as well as their placement on the page. By contrast, Guillaume Apollinaire took a more measured, mimetic, and meditative approach with his calligrams. Calligrams are works that make an iconic shape, for example, a woman in a hat or the Eiffel Tower, out of words, which in turn compose a poem.

Here is a visual poem composed for a class assignment by Katie Fewster-Yan. I include it here because it exemplifies both Marinetti's play with typography and the pictorial quality of Apollinaire's calligrams. And since it is a portrait of yours truly (my initials are DST), I thought it would be nice to let you put a face to the voice behind these lines.

DST

As we have experienced in our own work with the graphic image in Chapter 1, poetry that employs a graphic element, that unites the image and the word, remains a fertile region of creation. Poets today also continue this encounter with typography that characterizes so much early visual poetry. Helen Hajnoczky composes wonderful graphic poem/advertisement hybrids, creating consumer objects out of typography and "setting" them within the frame of a newspaper advertisement. Glen Robson creates stunning typographical masks, limiting himself to the lower- and upper-case manifestation of a single letter for each piece.

For the following writing moment, you will want to don your experimental hat (and gloves and glasses and tongue) as we turn to the materiality of language as our material for composition.

Writing Moment 3.7

- Employing one of the sound poem strategies mentioned above (or conceiving of your own process and practice), return to the material you wrote for Writing Moment 3.5 and compose a 15-second sound poem.
- Once again, return to the material you wrote for Writing Moment 3.5. Reflecting on this passage, jot down a few iconic images this poem could form if written out as a calligram. Give the calligram a try.

Form and the Anti-I: Cut-Up, Found, Aleatory, and Conceptual Poetry

Fidelity to the "I"—to the self's times, body, and identity—as the source of form characterized our first two examples of twentieth-century poetic forms. With this turn to the materials of language as the materials of composition, we encounter poets who—despite the potentially expressive quality of their work—make two surprising moves: first, they rebel against the lyric "I," the self as the controller of creation; and, second, they rebel against the conventional poem as the ideal object of creation. The "I" and the traditional poem, for these poets, fail as the loci of creation for a number of reasons: they are too egotistical, too overused, too limiting, and too tied to a certain set of established tendencies.

Three popular techniques for poets of this tradition are the **cut-up** poem, the found poem, and the **aleatory** (chance) poem. To compose a cut-up poem, choose a set piece of printed text—for example, a newspaper article, photocopied poem, or a tax form—and cut out each individual word. You then rearrange the words to create new poems. I had a lot of fun in my first year of university doing this with Shakespeare's sonnets (I had planned to do all 154, but only made it through the last three), and in my first book I made a cut-up poem that combined an excerpt from Guy Debord's *Society of the Spectacle* with George W. Bush's post-9/11 speech, combining two extremely different voices into one, unified voice. Found poems are composed of text discovered written on anything from posters to scraps of paper to the book covers of commuters to tattoos, often searched for within a limited time and/or space. Aleatory poems involve placing a limit—often, conceptual, spatial, or temporal—on composition. For example, a poet friend of mine stood on the same street corner at the same time for an hour for a week straight; the poems he composed could only contain the words, sounds, and phrases he overheard from passersby.

Beyond these three more basic methods, poets achieve this "escape from the I" by working under conceptual constraints, hence the term **conceptual poets**. Beginning in the 1960s, the French group OULIPO, whose full name is roughly translated as "workshop of potential literature," invented some of the most innovative sets of poetic constraints. Their many members share the motivation to sidestep the "I" and the conventional poem, as well as sharing another, more reader-centred goal: to make the reader an active agent in the moment of composition.

To return to the topic of the sonnet, for example, Raymond Queneau's *Cent mille milliards de poèmes* (1961) is a book of 10 sonnets that call the reader into tactile and creative action. The innovation is that every page is split into 14 strips, one for each line, so that the reader can flip line by line, rewriting the sonnets, and producing a new work at every turn, bringing, in a sense, a new meaning to the term *volta*. If this book interests you, you might want to pick up your copy sooner rather than later since it contains 100,000,000,000,000 different possible poems.

Christian Bök is notable for both sustaining traditional conceptual practices and for innovating new ones. In *Eunoia* (2001), he forwarded the tradition of the lipogram (a text that intentionally avoids using a particular letter or set of letters) by composing a series of univocalic poems (poems, in other words, that are limited to the use of one vowel each). I use the word "forwarded" because Bök went further than any poet before him, composing a narrative poem for each vowel, exhausting a vast majority of possible words for each vowel, and operating under many other self-imposed restrictions (for example, each chapter alludes to the art of writing and contains a culinary banquet). The result is a truly one-of-a-kind mind- and mouth-bending postmodern epic.

Bök has also invented new constraints that took him beyond the bounds of poetry itself. Poets often explore the intersections between poetry and other artistic mediums, for example, music or painting, or, in even more extreme cases, other forms of knowledge, such as biology or math. Here, Bök is truly the avant-garde of the avant-garde. His current work, *The Xenotext Experiment*, is the attempt to compose the first bio-poem, a virus whose DNA will compose genetic poetry as the virus reproduces.

Since, I am guessing, you lack the tools for manipulating viruses and DNA, we will instead turn to OULIPO for our next writing moment. Return to the material you wrote for Writing Moment 3.5 and try your hand at one of the most popular OULIPO formulae, N+7.

Writing Moment 3.8

- For this writing moment, you will need the material you wrote for Writing Moment 3.5 (though, of course, any poem written by you or another poet will do) and a dictionary.
- The task is simple: look up in the dictionary the first noun in your poem, locate the noun that appears in the dictionary seven nouns after yours, and then replace the noun in your poem with the new noun. Repeat this process with every noun in your poem.
- If you are feeling adventurous, you can do the same with your verbs.

This whirlwind tour of twentieth-century poetic forms, in combination with our trip through the component parts and forms of metrical verse, have shown you, I hope, that poetry nurtures fidelity and rebellion on two fronts. First, at the level of content, poetry allows us to articulate our faithfulness to, or dissent against, a person or people or cause or belief. Second, at the level of form, poetry is a medium in which we practice this fidelity and rebellion. This occurs through the types of poems we write: firmly fixed, metrical forms, or free verse forms, or a blend of the two, or, even, their near total abandonment in the choice of sound *as such* as the core compositional element. Whatever your preference, I recommend as always that you remain curious and daring as you turn your writing moments into poems and try out the following exercises.

In our next section, we will remain within the horizon of both fidelity and rebellion as we adopt as our motivation the desire to found a new language. However, as a means of doing so, we will shift from poetic forms to non-poetic forms: the comic book and social media.

Writing Exercises

1. Two of the doctrines of Imagism are, according to Ezra Pound, "direct treatment of the 'thing', whether subjective or objective" (3) and "to use absolutely no word that does not contribute to the presentation" (3), while Amy Lowell invites Imagists to "use the language of common speech" (vi) and "create new rhythms" (vi). Taking the rebel as your "thing" (whether a specific rebel or the rebel in general), compose an Imagist poem in which you follow these four principles. Alternately, compose a poem about the rebel in which you rebel against all four of these principles.
2. Many Black Mountain School poets followed Charles Olson's demand that they practice what he called "composition by field." This practice involves diminishing the ego as the centre of attention and refusing to bring pre-determined forms to bear on nature and reality. Instead, for Olson, poets need to seek a unity between self and the site of composition, let perceptions lead always to more perceptions, allow form to gain its shape from the content, and create works that explore the process of creation, works that value the process over the final product. Choose one or more of these traits and try your hand at "composition by field."
3. Imagine that you are a world-famous sound poet and you have been asked by the Coca-Cola Company to compose a 30-second sound poem advertisement based on one of their former slogans. Employing one of the sound poem strategies mentioned above (or conceiving of your own process and practice), choose one of the following slogans and compose a 30-second sound poem: "The Ideal Brain Tonic" (1891), "The Cold, Crisp Taste of Coke" (1958), or "America's Real Choice" (1985).

4. In two of the examples given above, we noted how letters and other typographical symbols can be utilized to create advertisements and masks. One could also create mythological creatures, a coat-of-arms, or spaceships. Try your hand at the practice by creating two examples based on my suggestions or a concept of your own.
5. Following in Christian Bök's footsteps, compose your own lipogram (text that excludes a particular letter or letters of the alphabet). Compose a treatise on remaining faithful to the letters that you choose to exclude.
6. Imagine that the topic of rebellion required a conceptual form in the vein of OULIPO and Bök. Determine the constraints. These might involve anything from limits on word choice and structure to defined types of action/thought to constraints on the time/location of composition to the requirement of appropriation. There are no limits to the limits you can choose. Remember to give your form a name.

Poems in Process

Joseph Luik's "The Fence" is an elegant little Imagist poem that contains many of the qualities Pound and Lowell valued: precision of language, dedication to the image, and a voice that captures the music of everyday speech. I am also impressed that in such a short poem Joseph is able to crystallize the two poles of the subjective (as Pound would put it) "treatment of the thing": the imaginative transformation in the first two lines and the rational interpretation in the closing two lines.

The Fence

The rickshaw parts of a broken line
Clacked together in spinal columns
A message to all passers-by
I'm easy enough to cross

One day before class, Calla Paleczny and I were talking shop in the hall. We were discussing the act of composition, and Calla was saying things about the body and breath and their relationship to layout and the line. I mentioned Charles Olson off-hand, assuming I was adding to Calla's explication of her Black Mountain School–inspired practice, and she gave me a blank stare. She had heard of neither Olson nor the school. I mention this anecdote not as a way of saying, "see, someone else thought it first," but, instead, to show how organic our connection can be to the traditions that will speak to us. We find these schools not to rigidly obey them, but to enter into conversation. In "A Little Concrete House," Calla makes some very powerful opening remarks.

A Little Concrete House

I was once trapped
in a little concrete house
on days raindrops calmed
the road's red dust and sang
their last notes on the tin roof
as I crouched—doors open and inviting
elbow deep in buckets
of rainwater and swaths of fabric
dyed the colours
of imagination

I was once held captive
in a little concrete house for a year
and a lifetime
I sat on that hill and listened
to the village and the bar's blaring
speakers and demons from the church
and crickets and shotguns
filtering through the iron clad windows
of the little concrete house

I once tried to escape
a little concrete house
but I could not
for I feared staying
and leaving
lest I became that headless man
on the highway
the fugitive butchered
with eyes gouged out
and pieces of him singed for
a potion its maker
eating truly believed
was magic

I once held myself
in a little concrete house
opened myself up
to the dark
and came out charred

Dahlia's Dead is a sequence of poems I wrote for a friend who was killed by a drunk driver. It consists of a collection of calligrams/concrete poems drawn on cocktail napkins and a few hand-drawn, incomplete comic book pages. The following poem, "The Label," takes its design from a Budweiser bottle.

Mediums and a New Language

In the summer of 2000, I was living in South Korea, teaching English and struggling through a writing rut. I had composed another flat, lifeless, subpar love poem, which opened as follows:

you sleep motionless alive but dead or the reverse
the shadow cast
by afternoon light sneaking through closed curtains
do not touch you
the breeze does not disturb anything meaningful
on your body

As I reread the poem, anxious to fix it, to compose something that felt honest and vital, I let this hypercritical voice I could feel babbling in the background take control of the pen and scribble its **lyrical** critiques in the margins. Rereading these criticisms, and feeling somewhat detached from the original poem, I took pity on the poem's "author" and I allowed this author to come to his own defence. I ended up working these two voices into the poem, which I titled "~~An Experiment in Form*~~" and formatted like so:

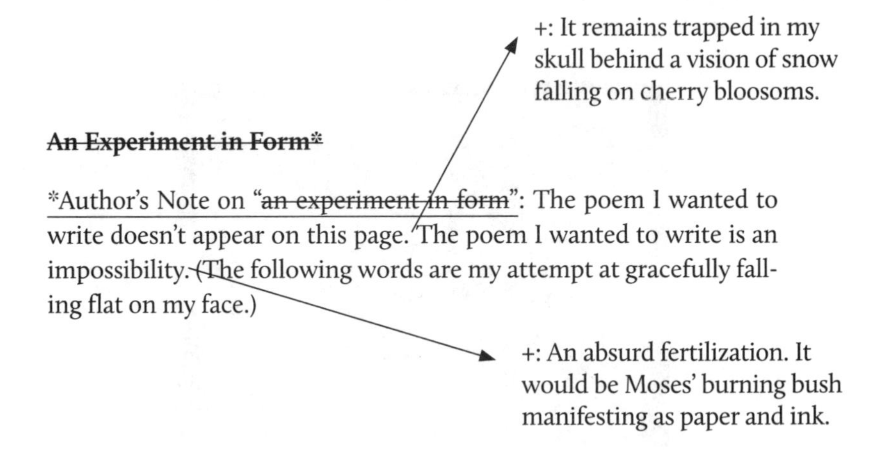

+: It remains trapped in my skull behind a vision of snow falling on cherry bloosoms.

~~An Experiment in Form*~~

*Author's Note on "~~an experiment in form~~": The poem I wanted to write doesn't appear on this page. The poem I wanted to write is an impossibility. (The following words are my attempt at gracefully falling flat on my face.)

+: An absurd fertilization. It would be Moses' burning bush manifesting as paper and ink.

Reader's Question: Why the apology before the deed? Why the white flag before the declaration of war? Is this what they meant when they said, "modern western insecurity is the ultimate tool of self-defence?"

This is only the opening section of a much longer poem, but I think this should give you an idea as to what I was after. The sincerity of the voices added energy and authenticity to their figures and to their respective attacks and defences. The variety of the voices—original poem, reader, and author—made for a much more dynamic read, and opened up for me a whole new range of compositional possibilities.

This is one example of how a poet discovers a new language. As this example suggests, when poets seek a new language, they do not necessarily go off in search of new words or simply borrow words from a foreign tongue. In "~~An Experiment in Form*~~" we have the language of literary criticism integrated into the language of the poem, and we also have a more visual form employed to help better depict the clutter and conflict of this encounter.

Regarding the search for new languages, two different types of **mediums** have long been the companions of poetry: other artistic mediums and mediums of communication. The rich tradition of ekphrastic poems about paintings is an example of the former, while, more recently, an example of the latter is the capacity of different social media to link poets to other poets and new audiences. One way to explore these forms, then, from the perspective of the poet, is to approach specific artistic and communicational mediums as a means of generating new poems and as a means of reworking the form of the poem as such. There are four different areas in which these resonances can be investigated: content, theme, form, and dissemination.

In the following section, we will explore comic books, as an example of an artistic medium, and **Internet comment threads**, as an example of a medium of communication, in relation to three of the areas of resonance: content, theme, and form. In Chapter 5, we will return to the topic of dissemination.

The particular encounters we stage between poetry and comics, and poetry and comment threads, respectively, are, of course, designed to inspire you and to provide you with some new tools to test out. You should, however, also undertake this same approach to the artistic mediums you are most passionate about (whether sculptures, movies, or video games) and to the communicational technologies you are most involved in or most anxious about (whether Facebook, Twitter, YouTube, or those not invented at the time of this writing).

For now, though, you will want to grab a superhero comic (in print or online) and load up a favourite comment thread, as we take our first steps with our companion mediums into the regions of content and theme.

Comics, Comments, Content, and Theme

With your comic in hand and your comment thread loaded, give them both a careful perusal: read, glance, flip, stare, and scroll. Become intimate with the life and language of the pages and posts. Once you have done so, undertake the following writing moment.

Writing Moment 3.9

- Write a three to four sentence free verse poem about your comic book (any aspect that you see fit).
- Write a couplet about your comment thread (any aspect you see fit). For the sake of practice, compose in blank verse or, simply, 10-syllable lines.

This is the most common approach to other mediums, taking the medium as the content or subject of your poem. To say this approach is the most common, though, is not to diminish it. In fact, this practice is both complex and essential.

For one, composing with a specific medial content invigorates your form. Can you find the ways in which this happened in this writing moment? If not, can you think of ways in which you could revise your work to encourage this influence? Three elements to consider are word choice, imagery, and voice.

In relation to your comic book, you could take on the diction of the heroes or villains, or you could employ the distinctive sound effects (for example, *BWKSSSSSS* for a Bat Plane–fired missile) or the shared symbolia (the icons comics use to represent different states, such as a light bulb for an idea or bubbles for drunkenness). Attending to words could also prompt some play with puns; for example, you could riff on the link between Spider-Man's web and the Latin root of the word "text" (*textus*), which means web. The lush colours and energetic shapes might influence your imagery, or, on this same front, you may employ the at once visceral and iconic forms and actions of the heroes and villains who fight it out in the frames. Finally, regarding voice, comic books are easily teamed with personae. You could speak in the voice of a specific hero or villain, or explore her or his thoughts in a poetic register.

The same methodological invigoration occurs when poetry is paired with the comment thread. You could inflect your diction with popular Internet slang or chatspeak (OMG, WTF, LOL) or you could meditate upon the deeper meanings and implications of stock, meme-ified (the modern-linguistic version of mummification) phrases: lurk moar (the command to read more before posting), copypasta (any text that gets copied and pasted repeatedly), and tl;dr (too long; didn't read).

The social sphere that underpins the comment thread would especially make for a fertile subject. You could delve into the "Rules of the Internet." For example, I have always felt there are deep life lessons expressed in Rule 38 "CAPSLOCK IS CRUISE CONTROL FOR COOL" and the equally important Rule 39 "EVEN WITH CRUISE CONTROL YOU STILL NEED TO STEER." You could also explore the Internet's transformation of Wordsworth's "spontaneous overflow of powerful emotions," whether by drawing on a sample of the Internet's lifeblood, *schadenfreude* (taking pleasure in the misfortune of others), or by exploring what it means that in a comment thread all anger, even the most justified, registers only as "butthurt."

The persona could also foster some original work in this context, too. The Internet troll, the white knight, the spambot, and all of the other comment thread regulars are ripe for celebrating, interrogating, and lampooning; they are voices through which to reveal unique views on what is beautiful or good or true.

As this remark on the true and good suggests, composing a poem about an artistic medium or a medium of communication can allow you to think about the timeless themes—the ideas we have long struggled with or in which we have found solace—in a new way. Superhero comics, for example, lend themselves to meditations on topics such as justice, power, and the nature of evil. As a poet, though, working always with the aims of looking awry, you might not want to proceed so directly. Perhaps you could write a poem about Superman in which you reflect on weakness, or a poem about Batman in which forgiveness is the theme. Superhero catchphrases could also serve as fertile material. Take Spider-Man's lesson (via Voltaire), "with great power comes great responsibility," and explore its opposite: "with great weakness comes great irresponsibility." Poems about comment threads could act as vehicles for meditations on communication, community, and freedom, or on silence, isolation, and oppression.

The Gutter and the Leap between Lines

Comic books can also help you develop your practice, expanding your range of compositional strategies, whether you are writing about a comic book or not. For example, the comic book can serve as a model for how you transition from one line to the next. This exercise is beneficial on three fronts, insofar as it helps you nurture three of the interconnected traits that often characterize a quality poem: concision, originality, and the **leap**. In order to understand how this exercise works, though, we must first step away from poetry for a moment and turn to the gutter.

The gutter is comic book terminology for the gap between panels. It most often takes the form of white space between two black borders. The gutter divides panels, but it just as forcefully connects moments, providing the pause needed to create a distinct transition between panels rather than a senseless blur. Put another way, the gutter joins action in one panel to the action in the next, forming a sort of comic book sentence.

Take a look at one page from your comic book, ideally a page that has a few gutters. How does the action transition from one panel to the next? How little or how much do we move in space and time? How does the new panel shift our attention? What is the new focus in terms of subject, proximity, and angle? These are the sorts of questions you can ask about the comic book page to, in a sense, spur it to shape your own practice. Once you have asked and answered enough of them, you can turn to your poem with new questions. How can these shifts between panels manifest in the shifts in my poem? How can these panel transitions influence the transitions in my poem between images, sentences, or stanzas?

Writing Moment 3.10

- Return to the three- or four-sentence free verse lines you composed for Writing Moment 3.9.
- Write another sentence. The transition from your original text to the new line should mirror or mimic the transition between your comic book page's first and second panels.
- Add another sentence. This time mirror or mimic the transition between your comic book page's second and third panels.

The central benefits of this exercise are threefold. Greater concision often results as the comic encourages you to remove lines that fill the "gutters" of your poem, cramming the effective blanks with unneeded information, superfluous words, and conventional digressions. Furthermore, we all fall into ruts when it comes to ordering our poems. This exercise helps shake you out of your habitual developmental logics. Not only are your usual organizational patterns challenged, but also you are inspired to refine new patterns. These new structures, coupled with concision, will combine to fill your poems with leaps, those jumps between lines that surprise and challenge your reader.

The Reply and the Swerve

The same generative exercise can be undertaken in relation to the comment thread. Here, though, the reply—the back and forth responses that make up the thread—replaces the gutter as the active element.

The questions we ask of the reply and the comment thread differ slightly from the questions asked of the gutter and the comic book page. For example, you want to consider the voice of the reply. What is the poster's motivation and persona? Composing lines in combination with different posters can give your poem a thrilling choral effect. Attend also to the language of the replies: sentence structure, word choice, speech acts. You could even quote replies. For example, borrow a question from the thread and then answer it in your poem. Ignoring all the replies that come in between, ask: what is the logic that connects an original comment to its most distant reply? Can you compose two lines of poetry bound by this same logic? Add to the comment thread and see what type of new replies, and, in turn, new potential material, is generated by your contribution. (We will explore the possibilities of collective creation in Chapter 5.)

Writing Moment 3.11

- Return to the comment thread couplet you composed for Writing Moment 3.9.
- Adopt the persona of one of your comment thread's contributors and compose a couplet that "responds to" your initial couplet.
- Borrow a comment from your comment thread and rewrite it in couplet form.

Concision might not result from this exercise. However, the reply, like the gutter, breaks us out of habits of order and organization and nurtures the leap. In this instance, the leap comes from the unusual swerve, the surprising jump in thought, shift in attention, or striking image.

Comics, Comments, and Layout

What if we went one step further in the meeting between our poetic form and these non-poetic forms? What if, to perhaps stretch the metaphor too far, we, as poets, hopped onto these mediums' respective backs and created poems that were comic books and comment threads?

This is one of the most exhilarating, challenging, and border-bending ways we can write with a new language. In a way, this practice involves composing with a **new pen** and responding to a new speaker. The new language is the combining of image and text. The new speakers are all of those who favour such **hybrid works**: comics, websites, graphic literature, and so on. Our new pens are the technological devices, such as laptops and phones, and the accompanying programs, such as Photoshop and InDesign, which allow us to bring these innovative poems to life.

This practice is undertaken in the same manner as our two earlier encounters with comics and comments. Only now, instead of attending to one element, we attend to all possible elements, in particular the physical, visible appearance of the medium. In other words, you transform the material appearance of the poem by adopting the layout conventions of your chosen medium. Compose a poem about a comic that is itself a comic. Create a comment thread poem that is a comment thread.

The means of proceeding are many. The high- and low-tech are both options: utilize the authenticity gained with a laptop and its programs or go with old-fashioned pen and paper. While designing the layout, you could also take the opportunity to draw your readers in further by making them active participants. Ink your poem into word balloons but leave the panels blank for your reader to fill, figuratively or literally. Leave blank comment boxes for the same purpose. You may also go "right to the source" in both cases. Digitally or manually remove the words from an actual comic book page and add your own. Post your poem on the comment thread of your blog, one comment box for each line, so your friends and readers can add to the poem with their replies.

With these possibilities in mind, undertake the following writing moment.

Writing Moment 3.12

- What are two or three different ways that you could transform your poem about a comic book into a poem that is also a comic book?
- What are two or three different ways that you could transform your poem about comment threads into a poem that is also a comment thread?

This concludes our final encounter with poetic forms. This pairing of type and motivation, in taking us so far from conventional practice, demonstrates the benefits of leaping away from conformity with convention and swerving from the uniformity of tradition. In fact, this pair of companions offers a new slant on the word "uniformity," suggesting the need to, every now and then, break with uni-formity (work with a single form) and test out some hybrid, mongrel, and Frankensteinian forms.

As always, I encourage you to develop poems from the materials you composed during your writing moments, or to continue to expand the horizons of your practice through the ensuing exercises.

Writing Exercises

1. Return to the material you created during your writing moments and compose one or two new poems. For example, compose a poem in the language of comics or comment threads, or compose a poem employing a comic book character or an Internet commenter as your persona.
2. Translate a famous poem into a comic book. This may involve making an actual comic or writing a lyric description of the poem-cum-comic.
3. Compose a comment thread for a famous poem. You could people the comment thread with other famous poets, with critics, with a series of less distinct poetic voices, with the usual band of Internet commenters, or with some combination of all of them.

4. Advertising is the mix of mediums (at once artistic and communicational) by which we are most inundated and which has become the predominant "lyric" form (concise, figurative, concerned with desire) in the lives of most people. In what ways are poetry and advertising similar? In what ways are they different? Create a poem that is an advertisement for the ultimate poem. If possible, format the poem like a specific type of ad (magazine, newspaper, public, online), so that upon first glance it appears to be an ad.
5. Choose an artistic medium you are passionate about (for example, painting, film, or videogames) and reflect on the content, thematic, and formal resonances between poetry and this medium. Consider the questions we asked and activities we undertook in relation to the comic book. Which elements of language, for example, could you borrow from this medium? How could an element of this medium stimulate you to reconceive your approach to a poetic tool? How might a poem mimic the layout of this medium?
6. Choose a medium of communication you are most involved in or most anxious about (whether Facebook, Twitter, YouTube, or those not invented at the time of this writing) and reflect on the content, thematic, and formal resonances between poetry and this medium. Consider the questions we asked and activities we undertook in relation to the comment thread. Which elements of language, for example, could you borrow from this medium? How could an element of this medium stimulate you to reconceive your approach to a poetic tool? How might a poem mimic the layout of this medium?
7. In the future, poets' acts of expression and exploration, their renderings of the beautiful and the sublime, will be undertaken in practices of creation and will require processes of consumption that we, right now, would deny have anything to do with the creation and consumption of poetry. Poetry in the future will take the form of pills, pulse-bearing wires, neuro-implants, grafts, virtual realities, and genetic manipulations. Every poet will be half-poet, half something else: half-plastic surgeon, half-programmer, half-pharmacist. In anticipation of this revolution, compose an elegy or an obituary in which you memorialize the lifework of one of these future poets.

Poems in Process

Julia Pedota, in "*Eight Elvises*, 1963 (The First Four of One Hundred Million Tweets)," employs the most minimal of minimal new forms

(Twitter) in her attempt to contain multiple excesses: the massive pop culture icon (Elvis), the icon of pop-cultural proliferation (Warhol), and the excessive amount of cash this particular painting generated (a cool $100 million). Julia's efforts point to Twitter's paradoxical nature: short in form (140 characters or less) but, like Warhol's prints and his iconic stars, endless in their reproduction and proliferation.

Eight Elvises, 1963 (The First Four of One Hundred Million Tweets)

The eye moves along the delicate lines
in black and white to disguise a change,
he's a mere blur now.

That rock 'n' roll cowboy,
made his way in Memphis
America the beautiful
with a steel guitar in his soul.

Eight overlapped,
meaning relinquished to shape the world
of reproduction.

High is now low,
a career based
on the selling of stars.
The impression of the dead
forever imprinted on his canvas.

Jakub Wasikiewicz's "10 Weird Confessions of a Belieber" is your usual run-of-the-mill poem/Craigslist Personal's hybrid that redoes Rilke through the voice of a verbosely eloquent and uniquely-dictioned cybersex fetishist who cries out "purely as a bird" in his own self-interested self-defence. Jakub, it seems to me, has just founded a new lyric subgenre: the poetic upgrade (in which one downgrades the work of a canonical poet through a contemporary technological form). I am sorry to note that I had to crop Jakub's poem, so you are missing out on some really nice touches. (You will have to wait for the upgrade.)

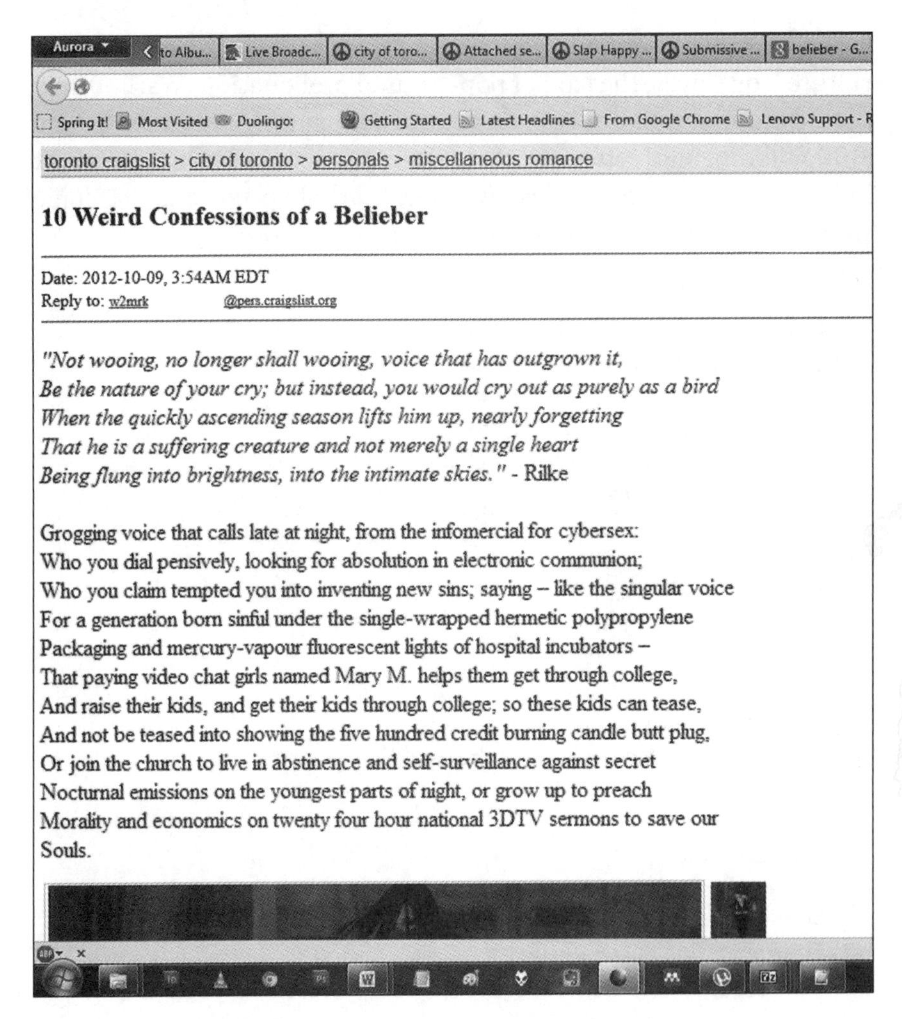

toronto craigslist > city of toronto > personals > miscellaneous romance

10 Weird Confessions of a Belieber

Date: 2012-10-09, 3:54AM EDT
Reply to: w2mrk @pers.craigslist.org

"Not wooing, no longer shall wooing, voice that has outgrown it,
Be the nature of your cry; but instead, you would cry out as purely as a bird
When the quickly ascending season lifts him up, nearly forgetting
That he is a suffering creature and not merely a single heart
Being flung into brightness, into the intimate skies." - Rilke

Grogging voice that calls late at night, from the infomercial for cybersex:
Who you dial pensively, looking for absolution in electronic communion;
Who you claim tempted you into inventing new sins; saying – like the singular voice
For a generation born sinful under the single-wrapped hermetic polypropylene
Packaging and mercury-vapour fluorescent lights of hospital incubators –
That paying video chat girls named Mary M. helps them get through college,
And raise their kids, and get their kids through college; so these kids can tease,
And not be teased into showing the five hundred credit burning candle butt plug,
Or join the church to live in abstinence and self-surveillance against secret
Nocturnal emissions on the youngest parts of night, or grow up to preach
Morality and economics on twenty four hour national 3DTV sermons to save our
Souls.

FIGURE 3.1 "10 Weird Confessions of a Belieber"

Then we have another excerpt from *Dahlia's Dead*, the sequence of poems I wrote for my friend who was killed by a drunk driver. This poem, titled, "After the Crash (The Continuing Adventures of Daniel)," is one of the incomplete comic book pages. Dahlia and I had always planned to create a comic book together, but never did. She was the artist. I left the panels blank in her honour.

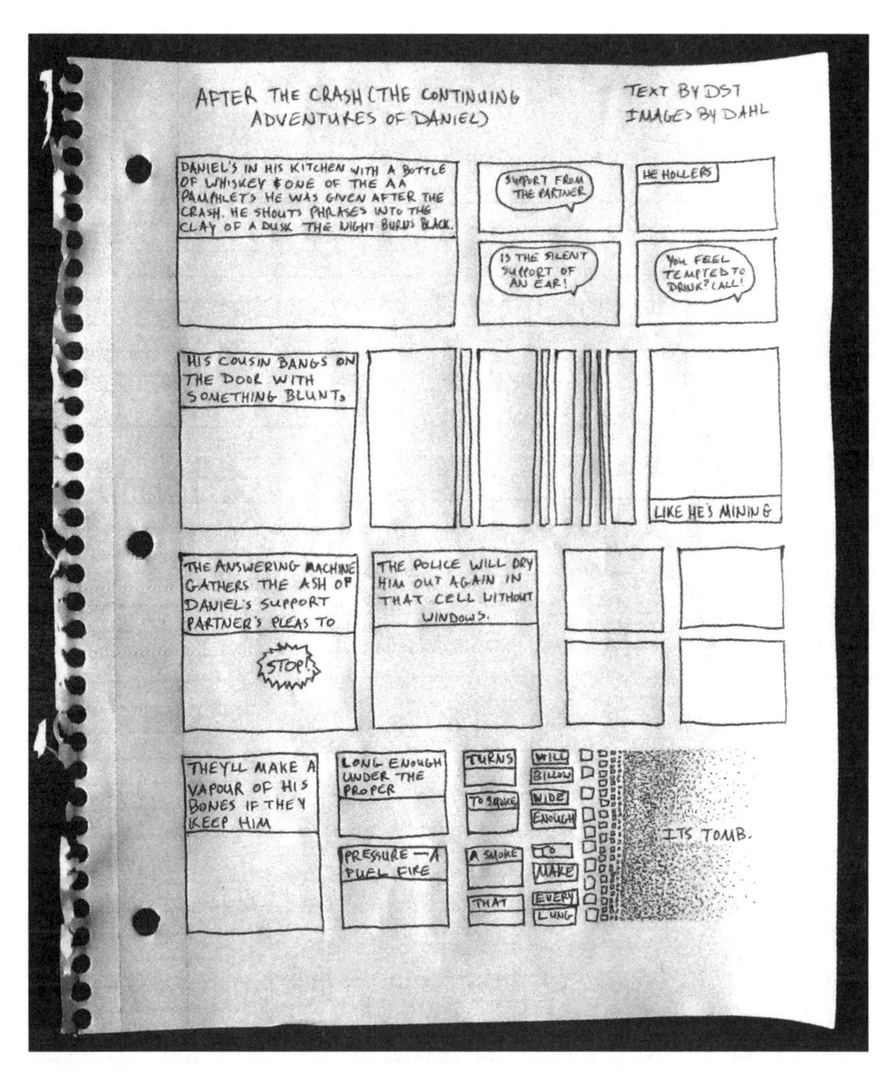

FIGURE 3.2 "After the Crash (The Continuing Adventures of Daniel)"

Conclusion: Inspiration and the Force of Form

How do you beat writer's block?

Writers of every sort get asked many of the same, foundational questions, class visit after class visit, reading after reading. "Who are your biggest influences?" "How do I get published?" Of these common questions, the one about writer's block is probably the most important.

If we cannot beat writer's block, then what exactly are our influences influencing us to do? What work will we have to publish?

A walk, nap, or a shower can usually overcome short-term writer's block; get the blood flowing with some burpees if you are the active type. Other popular remedies include a smoke, coffee, or, fine, something healthy like a piece of fruit. There are, though, those more extended (and dreadful) periods of the page remaining blank, when a little physical activity or a late-afternoon latte are not enough. This, in my experience, is when we need to turn to the forms we value or to new forms we have not yet intimately encountered, to the tools and traditions with which we travel and grapple, and to the occasions that enthral or swallow us.

The goal of the first three chapters of this book has been, of course, to introduce you to the tools and techniques of the trade. One of the desired outcomes of this goal is to reveal the rich range of what is possible—imaginatively, emotionally, intellectually, and so on—within the limits of the many dynamic parts and practices of poetry and the poem. For, as Slavoj Žižek reminds us, "Our intellectual creativity can be 'set free' only within the confines of some imposed notional framework in which, precisely, we are able to 'move freely'—the lack of this imposed framework is necessarily experienced as an unbearable burden" (25). Put another way, only the page faced blankly is truly blank. What is never blank is the page we approach in the company of our occasions, tools, traditions, and forms. This page is a sort of ghost soil enriched with the nutrients of the secret and the dead, seeded with vision and song. This page is a skyline into which invisible girders rise, half-constructed, primed for us to complete or tear down.

So if you get stuck, return to this book. Do the work you did and do it again: each attempt is new. Discover the poems that set you aflame each time and return to those, too (for example, Ashbery's "Syringa" and Plath's "Ariel" never fail to spark me). Seek out new companions and new forms. One step taken on a just-discovered planet in a distant system can sometimes carry you further than a thousand miles treaded in circles around your home.

And, of course, while indulging the limits I have outlined for you, do not be constrained by them: the fixed page and word count, my gaps and lacks and preferences in terms of poems, poets, traditions, histories, communities, forms, and figures. On the subject of other mediums, for example, a future resides in the present, one that I have no access to. More specifically, I have absolutely no handle on computer programming or app design, but these areas very productively interface with poetic creation. To see a very apt example in action, one that shows this meeting between the traditional and the cutting edge, visit pentametron.com. The site description puts it best: "With algorithms subtle and discrete / I seek iambic writings to retweet." In other words, pentametron culls from the oozing sludge of Twitter rhyming couplets of perfectly composed iambic pentameter. For example, when I visited pentametron just now, it had "written" (by extracting excerpts from the tweets of six separate users):

> I have a normal person voice again!
> I have a #weakness for #jamaican men ♥
> I do appreciate a suit and tie
> I leave the past behind, and say goodbye.
> I've never even seen a mistletoe
> Mariah singing Christmas music though

I am not holding this up as an earth-shattering poem, but instead as a brilliant endeavour, the sort of reworking of the work of poetry that makes us rethink our very understandings of poet and poem, of creation and originality. (Also, this example should serve as another reminder that, yes, you do need to know how to write an iambic pentameter line. If you don't, the robots will have won!)

In the context of this question of the limits of my limits, let me borrow the old Zen adage and say that this book and the books I recommend are only fingers pointing at the moon of the poems you are capable of. Or, better, all these books are fingers pointing at the finger only you can build, the digit you will shape to draw the attention of those who turn to you, to point them to the moon of your truths or wonder or lunacy or awe.

With this analogy in mind, let us now turn to Chapter 4: Revising, Reworking, and Wrapping Up. We will focus in on that pointing finger and the hand to which it is joined as we delve deeper into structures of order, thought, and voice, the poem's distal phalanges, palmar arteries, and lifelines. So prepare to build up tougher calluses and do not be surprised if you come away with dirty nails.

Recommended Resources

- *Books on Metrical (and Traditional) Forms*: Books of this kind provide descriptions of a wide range of metrical stanzas and fixed forms (accentual, syllabic, and accentual syllabic). Stephen Adams' *Poetic Designs*, which I recommended last chapter, discusses these types of forms.

- A much more extensive work is the aptly titled *The Book of Forms: A Handbook of Poetics* by Lewis Turco. With this book, you will never be without a form to prompt you to write. Finally, it is worth repeating my previous recommendation: visit the website "For Better For Verse" at prosody.lib.virginia.edu. You will be rewarded (and instantly addicted).

- *Twentieth-Century Forms*: An excellent twentieth century-focused anthology is *20th-Century Poetry and Poetics*, edited by Gary Geddes. Geddes' anthology stands out for two reasons: it gathers together a healthy selection of work from a diverse range of great poets and it includes essays by these poets, works in which they outline their views on everything from the practice to the meaning to the value of poetry.

- *A Companion to Twentieth-Century Poetry*, edited by Neil Roberts, gathers together more than 45 insightful essays in five categories: "Topics and Debates," "Poetic Movements," "International and Postcolonial Poetry in English," "Readings," and "The Contemporary Scene." This book is both a great primer and a means of digging deep into the history, theory, and craft of poetry. For those who wish to learn more about experimental traditions, ubuweb.com is a massive repository of avant-garde texts, visuals, audio recordings, and films created by international sound poets, filmmakers, dancers, and electronic musicians, to name a few of the artistic fields represented. (Make sure your calendar is clear for a good six weeks before visiting this site.)

CHAPTER 4

Revising, Reworking, and Wrapping Up

Introduction: The Goldilocks Approach to Revising Poems

> "[I] [r]evise a lot. Move, cadence, check, read aloud, set aside, read again, move. Read a lot of good poetry while I am working and then cut where mine falls short . . . no mercy, but lots of fun."
>
> —Erín Moure

How do you know when a poem is finished? What is it that tells you a poem is done? Is it an emotional standard of some kind, a conceptual model? Or does the force take the form of a tingling gut or interior voice? Whatever your approach, it seems to me that Erín Moure captures perfectly the spirit of the revision process: in revising, remain as active and energetic as you were when jotting down those first words, and, while undertaking this work, show no mercy.

These general remarks about the revision process, of course, raise more specific practical questions. How exactly do we move and check in this process of reworking? What is it we cut and show no mercy to?

One answer to these questions is that, in the context of your personal writing process and artistic goals, you address the set of related problems that can occur in early drafts of works by writers of every ilk. I have found this method is an effective way of engaging the range of poets with whom I have the opportunity to work, whether philosophical or confessional, spoken word or page bound. I like to pitch this as the Goldilocks approach, due to its reliance on the "too." These problems can be figured variously as too predictable or too incomprehensible, too cliché or too abstract, or, most simply, too far, too far, too far (in other words, too distant from the language, from the figures, sentences, words, rhythms, etc.).

The premise of the following chapter is that a poem is done, or closer to being done, when these problems have been addressed. To continue immersing you in the practice of creating poems, the writing moments and exercises will still prompt you to compose new work. However, each section will engage one of the pairs of problems noted above with the practice that addresses it: getting close with your tools, adding lift and drag, and nurturing tensions and turns. We will, in other words, follow Moure's lead and "[i]nhabit language and let it inhabit [us]" ("Rusty Talk with Erín Moure"). I hope this will encourage you to reflect on what, for you, constitutes a problem, flaw, or fault in a poem, and, in turn, to consider when a poem is complete.

For our artistic motivation, we will also take a page out of Moure's book. She concludes her comment on her writing and revising process by saying, "I think. Thinking is a kind of writing too" ("Rusty Talk with Erín Moure"). We will nurture this idea in our processes by turning to the subject of knowing, since the quest to know—as well as the quest to question, trouble, overturn, and renew ways of knowing—links so many poets, communities, and traditions. Our specific motivations will be received wisdom, the unknown, and other thinkers.

Once you have completed this chapter, I encourage you to consult the appendix, Strategies for Revision. In the appendix, you will find more information about the topics and strategies detailed in the following chapter, including two sample revisions and more specific tips for improving your poems.

Let us begin by considering the poems that result when we remain too far (or, as I wrote earlier, too far, too far, too far) from the world of the poem and the materials that compose it, from the music of vowels to the world-buoying voice. The solution, thankfully, is a simple one: move in close.

Getting Close with Your Tools: Perspective, Sentences, Words, and Rhythms

Poets work with many wisdom-communicating forms and methods, such as aphorisms, adages, proverbs, maxims, and epigrams. Each of these may act as a part of a poem, as a poem in itself, and even as a genre of poetry. For example, the *carpe diem* poem, or "seize the day" poem, started with a line from an ode by Horace. Few remember the ode, but this aphorism continues to inspire.

These wisdom-related forms, due to their brevity, also suit our purposes as we turn to reworking voice. Their terseness permits us to more easily get intimate with our tools and materials. Let us begin, then, by returning to where we began, the position from which I hope we have not strayed too far: the thoroughly inhabited meeting between you and the world and words.

Getting Close with Perspective

Whether your writing process is a totally unself-conscious flow, as though spirit writing, or the meticulous assembling of morally complex dramatic personae, you will need to attend with care to your sentences, words, and rhythms. In undertaking that work, a poem about as riveting as a photocopy of a facsimile of a poorly scanned duplicate can be transformed into a wondrous or challenging or soothing or beautiful or viscous or pop-the-top-of-your-head-off-awesome thing in itself (or, if you are a fan of photocopies, the poem closely tended to is the equivalent of having a front-row seat at the photocopier as its bright eye whirs, shines, and captures, its guts excreting copy after copy after copy as the room fills with that distinctive aroma of the machine-heated page).

The following writing moment will get you started on this intimate turn by inviting you to inhabit a speaker for whom a specific piece of received wisdom does not add up. In choosing your perspective, you may select your own voice, the voice in which you always write, or a voice in which you want to write but have not. You may also choose to inhabit a specific persona or an alter ego. Whatever your choice, be sure to put into practice the adage from the second chapter: perspective shapes voice.

Writing Moment 4.1

- Choose and inhabit your perspective.
- Choose a well-known adage, maxim, aphorism, etc., with which you (i.e., the voice or perspective you have chosen) disagree or about which you are apprehensive. For example, "time heals all wounds."

Getting Close with Sentences

The first element we will engage with is the sentence, the mechanism with which we string these words and sounds together. Remain in the shoes (and skin and soul and so on) of your chosen perspective and undertake the following writing moment, which will introduce two approaches to considering and constructing sentences.

Writing Moment 4.2

- Open your poem by stating the adage with which you take issue. In stating the adage, compose using one of the following two options:
    - Option 1: Write three short sentences, and begin each of these sentences with the same word or words. For example, "Time heals all [insert particular example for a particular type of wound]" (x 3).
    - Option 2: First, rewrite your adage as two more specific parallel phrases. For example, "time heals all wounds" could become "Minutes fix injuries and years patch sores." Now, invert the order of the two parallel phrases according to the pattern ABBA. For example, our "time heals all wounds" rewrite becomes "Minutes [A] fix injuries [B] and sores [B] are patched by years [A]."

- For the first turn in your poem, state your opposition to the adage. In stating this opposition, compose using one of the following two options:
    - Option 1: Question.
    - Option 2: Refuse.

In composing the adage and your opposition to it, you have practiced with two different ways of working with sentences: figures of order (a type of figure of speech), which determine the structure of sentences and the order of words, and speech acts, which characterize the action of sentences.

There are many figures of order, each with its own structure, purpose, and effect. For example, if you chose Option 1, the repetition of the same opening word or words, you employed **anaphora**. If you chose Option 2, the inverted grammatical structure, you employed **chiasmus**. One of the benefits of learning more about figures of order is that you will be encouraged to write a great variety of sentences, and, in turn, break out of habitual forms and compose more dynamic poems. Furthermore, as you become familiar with the different effects of these figures of order, you will be better equipped to produce the effects, inspire the ideas, and/or stir the feelings you wish with your poems.

Speech acts are a method for categorizing the intentions and functions behind our many linguistic expressions. There is a rich and complex theory, one from which you could gain great insights into language. However, for a poet, this turn to the theory is not necessary. What is essential is nurturing your awareness of the different types of possible speech acts—from the question and the refusal to the thanks, complaint, invitation, celebration, and protest—and the directness and subtlety with which they can be rendered. As with figures of order, the benefits are a deeper understanding of your craft and an increased ability to realize your goals.

In the context of these figures of order and speech acts, consider too the rhythm of the poem as a whole. Just as the poem has a sonic rhythm, one that results from the patterning of syllables, so too does the poem itself contain a rhythm that originates in the patterning of the types of sentences and types of speech acts. Consider, for example, the difference between a poem in which every line is an anaphoric question and a poem in which every sentence is a different form and speech act.

Getting Close with Words

In getting intimate with words, particularly in terms of the words you choose, you make gains in terms of the substance and force of your voice and in terms of the energy and animation of your lines.

Diction is the name for this, the manner of speaking and writing as related to the choice of words. That is to say: diction is word choice and also more than word choice, the manner—the larger voice or logic—that informs word choice. As we discussed in Chapter 2, word choice and diction are the most basic ways that perspective shapes voice and, in turn, the most basic ways you construct an authentic, effective perspective, a voice that enthrals, subsumes, or seduces your reader.

As with many of the tools and techniques we have worked with together, the importance of diction is heightened for poets, but it is, of course, necessary for all writers to consider. Even in the case of this book, for example, I maintain a specific diction. I would tempt a commination from the puissant, un-precipitous lightning-precipitator who dost crown Olympus if I were to exercise, nay, execute an elocution at once high and antiquated. Similarly, you would perhaps take my advice less seriously if I were to say like, dude, extending metaphors is like the most totally badass razor thing since caffeinated bread (though, on the topic of being taken seriously, I will admit that, yes, I sometimes do let my enthusiasm get the best of me).

Regarding diction and the energy or pace of the line, both syllables and specificity should be taken into consideration. Here, for example, is a monosyllabic line that names as simply as possible the objects of its attention: "the seed we stuck in the dirt needs rain." Here, by contrast, is the same line rewritten using polysyllabic words and a more complicated rendering of the objects of its attention: "The vegetable-generating particle Savannah and I implanted in the terra firma requires a downpour."

Though as a poet you need to attend with care to every word, you want to give extra attention to verbs. Verbs are the line's engine, activating the poem's objects and agents and insights and impressions. As with metaphoric vehicles, the work is to choose verbs that are both apt and surprising. This does not mean that every verb should be what my elementary school English teacher used to call a "$99 word" (or, I guess, with inflation a $300 word). However, you do not want every agent in your poem simply standing and sitting and reaching and standing and sitting. Aside from avoiding standing/sitting (especially as the opening line—and never ever "standing/sitting there/here"), you want, for the most part, to avoid "starting" actions. The crowd does not "start to depart the spectacle," the crowd simply departs; the "starting" is implied.

Verbs are important too because they are a subtle way to insinuate everything from personality to mood to a field of symbolic imagery. For example, does a baseball player "fall asleep" or does he "snag some Zs," the same way he would snag pop flies? Imagine a poem that draws on the cinema for its symbolic imagery: does the "sun shine" or does it "project"? In a work of mourning for a deceased retriever, does grief "haunt" and "cry" or does it "howl" and "paw, scratching at the other side of the door to the other side"?

Use the following writing moment to expand on your adage response poem, and as you expand pay close attention to your diction and verbs.

Writing Moment 4.3

- Building on the work you did in Writing Moment 4.2, put yourself in the shoes of a specific individual or type of person (type in terms personality, occupation, belief system, and so on) who believes in the adage you have chosen to critique. Compose a defence of the adage employing the diction of this specific individual or type of person. You can put this passage in quotes, and attribute it, for the sake of clarity.
- Returning to your own perspective, propose an alternate adage, one in which you believe and that counters the adage you critique. Pay close attention to verbs (and feel free to revise the section you wrote previously in light of our discussion of word choice). Also, for the purposes of our current undertaking, this will be the last line of this poem, so take this into consideration as you compose.

Getting Close with Rhythm

We create rhythm in a poem, rhythm as measured flow, through careful patterning, whether in terms of the patterning of sound, cadence, or line breaks.

In the case of sound, the problem of straying "too far" from pleasing or effective sound is not necessarily the lack of alliteration, assonance, consonance, or rhyme. Instead, the issue is most often the lack of careful patterning. An abundance of alliteration might not be the proper patterning of sound for every subject or voice. Forcing these musical elements can also cause problems. The cliché rhyme jars readers, knocking them out of the poem with a sonic slap in the face. Similarly, avoid the practice of always settling on the first rhyme that pops into your head, leading you to mangle syntax, flow, and meaning to make the rhyme fit.

The lack of these sonic elements, then, is not necessarily an instance of keeping "too far" from sound. At the very least, though, be aware of the many subtle opportunities available to you. Consider, for example, a short poem that transitions from plosive consonant sounds (such as pepper, tattoo, and babe) to nasal consonant sounds (money, moan, and name). Consider, too, how short vowels and long vowels can be manipulated to affect sensation and pace. If you wish to slow your reader slightly, you might be able to work in some long vowels in lieu of punctuation.

With cadence, like sound, the issue is again not necessarily the lack of cadence (there is often a certain rhythmic flow to conversational chatter). Instead, the problem is poor patterning. There is, for example, the danger of **doggerel**, or verse with an irregular measure. Many poets just starting out end up in this funny middle ground between free verse and metred verse: inconsistent rhythm, uneven line lengths, and a varying rhyme scheme. As I have mentioned throughout, you do not have to choose free or metrical as a poet, but, more often than not, you do have to pick one in each individual poem.

I will say it again, as I say often in my classes, that even free verse poets should master blank verse (and, like some of my students, you can roll your eyes—though I do hope that like them you will come around). There are many benefits to practicing with iambs and **anapests** (the other form of rising rhythm), as well as **dactyls** and **trochees** (the two falling rhythms) and **spondees** and **pyrrhics** (different stress patterns). Possessing a working knowledge of these rhythms will allow you to more easily achieve the cadence you are after in your free verse work. It will also allow you to spot potential problems. Recently, I met with a student who could not figure out why the ending of what was otherwise a very fine poem seemed off. The issue: she had slipped into perfect iambic tetrameter in the last three lines and a slant rhyme linked the end of the last and third to last line. This sudden burst of music did not fit with the rest of poem and particularly grated against the dark turn at the end.

Line breaks, finally, also affect the rhythm and pace of the reading, and, particularly in terms of enjambment, can stimulate a number of outcomes through that microsecond of a pause that occurs between reaching the end of one line and travelling to the start of the next.

There are some excellent examples of these types of line breaks in the Poems in Process below. Alice Stancu, in "Livejasmin.com," effectively employs line breaks to produce a certain expectation before subverting it. A state that begins with promise, that "you will be famous," deteriorates break by break: "on the Internet / for about 5 minutes."

Another strategy is to punctuate with a single word before turning, heightening that pause and the significance of the word. Kate Fewster-Yan realizes this in "Abracadabra, and Other Magic Words." To heighten the shift in her meditation, Katie ends one line with the first word of a new sentence, "Science," before continuing in this new direction with "taught me all I know of optimism."

You can also stir a sense of anticipation at the end of an enjambed line, an anticipation you then satisfy at the start of the next line. In "*Nosce Te Ipsum*," Suzanne Fernando states, "From far away I must look," stirring the question, "like what?" She then answers the question, "like progress," stimulating a subtle dialogue between her poem and the reader.

The following writing moment will give you the chance to get close to rhythm, seeing your work with (and against) wisdom with new eyes.

Writing Moment 4.4

- Return to the material you wrote for Writing Moments 4.2 and 4.3.
- How have you patterned sound, cadence, and line breaks?
- How can you improve on this patterning?

The conclusion of this section marks the beginning, not the end, of the work of getting close with our tools. In the next two sections—adding lift and drag, and nurturing tensions and turns—we will seek a similar intimacy with the materials of our craft. I hope you will continue to develop poems from the materials you composed during your writing moments, and dig further with (and into) your tools through the ensuing exercises.

Writing Exercises

1. Return to the material you created during your writing moments and compose one or two new poems. Revise your adage poem or compose a poem on any topic or occasion that tests out my comments regarding long and short vowels, falling rhythms, and the effects of different line breaks.
2. Compose an adage poem on the topic of adages.
3. The perspective that encompasses all other perspectives—from the very personal "I" to the detached observer, from the unconscious alter ego to the highly refined persona—is the choir. The choral poem is the poem that contains many, potentially differing, voices (for example, the balladeer mixed with the master of graphic poems). Compose a poem that disproves my earlier assertion that the middle ground between free verse and metrical verse is impossible to occupy. Alternately, compose a poem with the choir of your choosing.
4. Locate a print or online resource that discusses figures of order. Compose a two-stanza poem in which you utilize multiple figures of order in the first stanza and the same figure of order repeatedly in the second stanza. Alternatively, figures of order can also be used to shape the larger "sentence" of the poem. Compose a poem that possesses a **chiastic** structure by ordering its attention (literal, conceptual, figurative, etc.) based on the ABBA pattern.
5. Choose a finished poem, whether one of your own or one by a favourite poet. Rewrite this poem a few times according to different registers of diction, for example a high and antiquated diction or a modern, slang-filled diction. Other possible registers include advertising, science, and the schoolyard (middle or late childhood). You could also think in terms of dichotomies: the clinical versus the crass, the serious versus the irreverent, or the general versus the particular.
6. Throughout this book, you have been invited to attend to and pattern with rhythm. However, most of this work has dealt with the iamb

(unstressed-stressed). Compose three couplets on the topic of wisdom. Write the first couplet in trochaic tetrameter, the second couplet in dactylic pentameter, and the final couplet in anapaestic hexameter. (See the glossary entry on "metrical verse" for full details regarding these terms.)

Poems in Progress

We have already looked at some of Alice Stancu's effective work with line breaks in "Livejasmin.com." This piece also struck me for its provocative content: an adult website and the cruel (and popular) act of talking a model into putting a shoe on her head (often for promised funds that never come). In such a short poem, Alice manages to pull off some sophisticated work with perspective: the shift from "we" (which seduces the reader) to "you" (which isolates the reader) and the ironic speaker (who claims to discuss "innocence" and yet reveals exploitation). I also love how Alice's poem hinges upon, again with great irony, our era's ultimate adage: "There's no shame."

Livejasmin.com

It's an innocent game;
we've all played it.
"Put shoe on head!"

If she obeys your request,
you will be famous
on the Internet
for about 5 minutes.

There's no shame
in it. It's not like
you're paying
to watch.

Suzanne Fernando undertakes a contemporary exploration of the aphorism: "know thyself" (or, as her title puts it in Latin, "*Nosce Te Ipsum*"). Here, the song of the self becomes the song of technology as Suzanne's speaker, seeing herself literally reflected in the microwave, reflects upon the substance of her selfhood in relationship to the microwave. In Suzanne's placement of the word "apparition," we see a great example of ambiguity: this "apparition" could refer to her reflection in the microwave's glass or to the microwave as the apparition of a (false) song.

Nosce Te Ipsum

Technology echoes a song.
I watch myself in a microwave,
abhorring this apparition.

The fingerprinted glass
has asked why and who
and why for days; the myth
of efficiency persists.

From far away I must look
like progress,
a smattering of molecules
rearrangable, rearranging,
rearranged.

Katie Fewster-Yan's "Abracadabra, and Other Magic Words" is a sophisticated and moving meditation on that which "still hurts," and that which her speaker has been unable to heal or name or wave (magically and miraculously) away. Her meditative structure is estimable for managing such complex turns with precision. The rhythm of the speech acts is notable, too: the repeated assertions (broken up by a question) are counterpointed by the two extended pleas that compose the poem's second half. Finally, in light of our previous discussion of extending metaphor, note how far Katie extends the "magic" vehicle and how she renders it with such richness and force.

Abracadabra, and Other Magic Words

It still hurts. Everything. After years
of attention: friendships, turning points,
epiphanies, therapy—it's all still there.
Have I been expecting miracles? Like

the wand that waves and vanishes
the apple that is not hidden or tipped
from the table, but gone. Science
taught me all I know of optimism.
Reason maps and can aptly describe
the machine. I have no mechanical
parts, only flesh whose wet slaps
against itself can be approximated
by equation. Somebody, please: sketch
an X on that mound in my head where
the variable needs changing. No more
pills, or pain. Discover me a shovel
to unbury from that spot the flagrant
rabbit, who someday sparked herself
suddenly in my brain, aflame, that white
hot thing I have stroked and fed and fed,
whom I wish and will and wave and wave
away, who isn't, wasn't ever, meant to stay.

Adding Lift and Drag: The Poet's Perception and the Reader's Perception

The cliché-riddled poem turns readers away with red roses, concrete jungles, and the longing to be free like the birds (which, as someone who grew up watching swallows fall prey to barn cats, is a type of freedom I have never viewed as too desirable). The overly abstract poem takes many forms, though all are linked by the quality of being abstracted—detached and distanced—from concrete or conceivable (on the part of the reader, I mean) experience. Such poems can be too tangled with a swirl of metaphors, too general and vague, or too conceptual.

Another way to grasp these problems is to turn to the flight analogy that Don McKay shares with the poets he mentors. Like a plane, McKay notes, a poem requires both lift and drag. The cliché poem is beset by so much drag that it remains ground-bound, the plane half-sunk into the tarmac and unable to get its propellers spinning. The overly abstract poem, by contrast, lacks drag and lifts through the layers of the atmosphere into outer space, but in the form of a craft not equipped to carry passengers.

This is particularly the case when we, as poets, encounter the unknown, whether emotional, moral, intellectual, natural, spiritual, and so on. In these moments—sick with grief or desperate for an answer—we may fall back on the expected, the cliché, or we may reach too far and get lost in the abstraction of ungrounded figures or big ideas.

In our work with the unknown, we will look at perception in two senses: the perception of the poet and the perception of the reader. The goal is to explore how these tools of poetic vision can maintain a balance between the familiar and the new, allowing the reader to enter our craft and rise, surviving the heights we lift them to without wanting to abandon ship because they are running out of air.

The unknown, as we experienced in many of our writing moments, is a fertile region for poets. We experienced this when we turned to the forbidden and lost, and when we endeavoured to make the strange familiar and the familiar strange. As poets, in our encounters with the unknown we do not seek to efface the absence or solve the mystery; instead, we seek to sketch their ripples and edges and hollows, to give our acts of searching form. Since this process so often involves attempts to express the inexpressible, or to make sense of that which defies sense, we turn again and again to one of our core tools to accomplish this: metaphor. We draw on a legible, sensible, palpable figure (the vehicle) to give form to the unknown (tenor).

In Chapter 1, we worked extensively with metaphor, looking at different forms and testing out different approaches. For example, in Writing Moment 1.9, we tried out strategies for exercising our imaginations in the quest for original metaphors. These strategies were: conceiving of the different use (our question: how would a gardener use a stethoscope?), misperception, and the revelation of the hidden.

In our exploration of the unknown and poetic perception, let us undertake a similar writing moment, choosing an unknown as our metaphoric tenor and creating an apt and original metaphoric vehicle.

Writing Moment 4.5

- Choose an unknown: a feeling (joy, anxiety, pain, boredom, etc.) that resists expression, an experience (death, fate, selfhood, the past, etc.) that defies understanding, or a phenomenon (aurora borealis, thundersnow, "zombie ant" fungus, etc.) the scientific explanation of which does not do it justice.

- Conceive of a metaphoric vehicle for your unknown, selecting a concrete object, entity, or activity. Choose something that, in being compared to the unknown, will help your reader grasp the unknown.
- Utilize some of the methods we worked with in Chapter 1. Get your brain going with an uncensored list. Write, "[Your Unknown Here] is _______," and fill the blank with everything that comes to you. Draw on your surroundings (the objects and the words), squint and mis-hear if needed. Ask a friend for suggestions and force yourself to use one of the options your friend names.

Extending Metaphors and Lift

One of the most effective ways to add this element of lift to your poem—to add originality, particularity, and artfulness—is to extend your metaphors. This is what you attempted on a large scale with the conceit in Writing Moment 1.11. Think of the metaphoric vehicle as a sort of lens through which you re-see not only the tenor, but also all objects, entities, and activities that stand in relation to the tenor, in other words, to the rest of the world of the poem. The vehicle—extended—is a sheet you cast over things, giving new shape to both the sheet and the things.

The techniques discussed below can be used at any stage of creation (a way to start out or a method for revising) or as any aspect of the poem (as an entire poem or three lines in a poem that otherwise lacks metaphor).

The first technique of extension is to explore the tenor. Take for example the metaphor: death is a song. Exploring the tenor involves expanding on the ways in which death is a song. In this example, you can take both a negative and a positive approach. In the case of the former, death is a song without notes, bars, clefs, melody, instruments, players, or voice; in this negative example, the lack of these physical, sensory elements is used to materialize the ineffability of death. The positive approach might figure death as the world's lone, endless song, its one global tune, sung for every people and species without acknowledging the conductor, no pause for applause.

The second technique of extension is to explore the vehicle's relations. For example, if death is a song then the body is an ear, always perked and listening for that first note, or the body is an instrument plucked by seconds, drummed by years, or each body is a unique musical score performed by the instruments of sickness and decay and the chance wrong turn.

With both of these techniques, there are two points worth noting. First, these techniques can, of course, work in concert with one another. In fact, as was made evident in my positive example of extending the tenor, this often happens without much effort, a natural outcome of the imaginative voyage. Second, remember that these extensions of the metaphor do not need to be 10-page epics. Sometimes the subtle half-line to two-line extension is all that is necessary. These more subtle adjustments work better with a less abstract tenor so allow me to revise my example accordingly.

The topic of barn cats (which, as you might recall, came up in connection to—not so free—swallows) reminded me of the time I had to put one of our barn cats down. I must have been around 12 and the bus driver, pulling out of our yard, accidently shattered the rear half of a tabby. There was no one else home, and so it was left to me to wait with the cat while it died or until I worked up the guts to put it out of its misery. I can write, "The cat, yowling, wanted my help, but I did not know how to help." Or I can add a metaphor and write, "The cat, yowling, was an outstretched hand, but I did not know how to help." Or, finally, I can extend my metaphor further and write, "The cat, yowling, was an outstretched hand, but I suddenly lacked a hand to reach back."

If you want to extend your work with a metaphor for the length of a stanza or an entire poem, you may explore multiple vehicles for the same tenor. You may stay within the same range (death is a song, a painting, a film, etc.) or shift into different ranges (death is a song, a hotel, a mushroom, etc.). Considering these examples, remember that, for the purposes of our encounter with the unknown, I have chosen an abstract tenor (death) and a concrete vehicle (song). However, you also want to explore concrete tenors and concrete vehicles (as with my cat and hand example) and concrete tenors and abstract vehicles (for example, a song is death, justice, an idea, etc.).

With these new techniques in hand, return to the metaphor you composed in Writing Moment 4.5 and give them a try.

Writing Moment 4.6

- Extend your metaphor by exploring the tenor.
- Extend your metaphor by exploring the vehicle's relations.
- Compose a line without a metaphor (as I did in relation to my memory of my cat), revise this line by adding a metaphor, and then revise it further by extending this metaphor.

Simile, Metonymy, Synecdoche, and Lift

Simile, **metonymy**, and **synecdoche** are three other figures well suited to adding originality, particularity, and artfulness to your poem.

I bring up simile first to make sure that it does not get forgotten following an extended discussion of extending metaphors. In many instances, the looseness of the simile's connection, a looseness generated by the mediating "like," is more suitable than a metaphor. The simile, for example, puts less pressure on the reader's faculty of comprehension, often a desired effect in lighter works. Also, with its more casual quality, the simile can also lend authenticity to a first-person speaker, where a metaphor might seem out of place.

I also bring up simile because it is central to a discussion of the rendering of figurative comparisons in a poem. There are three points on a scale, with a range of variations existing between each point. The simile is at one end of the scale: a comparison mediated by "like" or "as," for example, "love is like a fire." In the middle of the scale sits the metaphor stated outright: "love is a fire." At the top of the scale sits the couched, implied, or partially stated metaphor. These are instances where the tenor or vehicle is not stated outright, only implied. For example, "her love burned her," "her love left her skin smoking," or "ash is what his love made of him." These are by no means masterful lines, but notice how this subtler rendering can take a cliché like "love is a fire" and renew it slightly, adding an element of particularity and vibrancy.

This same sort of subtle and powerful shift is achieved through metonymy and synecdoche. Yet whereas a metaphor makes a comparison, reaching across the divide of the two things it compares and creating a bond, metonymy and synecdoche draw attention to a different aspect or quality of the objects to which they are connected.

Arp and Johnson define metonymy as "the use of something closely related for the thing actually meant" (79). Perhaps the most famous example is the adage, "The pen is mightier than the sword." The pen here stands in for writing, while the sword stands in for war. Metonyms offer many benefits. There is the particularizing quality. Composing a metonym often means drawing attention to a surprising feature of "the thing actually meant," and, in turn, stimulating readers, stirring them to bring this thing to mind. For example, in that adage the pen stands in for writing/knowledge as a contrast to violence, but framing the idea this way using metonyms also brings to mind another aspect of this idea. A fountain pen is very pointy. Knowledge, too, like violence, can wound.

Arp and Johnson characterize synecdoche as a type of metonymy and define it as "the use of the part for the whole" (79). An everyday example is the practice of using a political capital, for example, Ottawa, to stand in for the whole country, in this case, Canada. The benefits of metonymy again apply here. For example, birds can become the "wind-snapping wings" and the cars stuck in a traffic jam can be "the slow-rolling tires and almost necking bumpers."

Use the following writing moment as an opportunity to try out these new techniques as a means of adding more lift to your extended metaphor.

Writing Moment 4.7

- Select one of the overtly stated metaphors you composed for Writing Moment 4.5 and rewrite it as an implied metaphor.
- Return to the material you wrote for Writing Moment 4.6 and see if there is an opportunity to work in a metonym or synecdoche.

The Reader's Perception and Drag

This discussion of extending metaphors and rendering metonyms and synecdoches was designed to help you avoid cliché and to add an element of lift to your poems. However, these techniques also address the question of the reader's perception, the reader's engagement with and comprehension of your poems. Gaining a better handle on the specific mechanics of these techniques will help you add a little productive drag to those poems with too much lift—a means, in other words, of reining in abstraction.

This turn to the topic of drag, of grounding the reader in your poem, of course raises an important question: what if the goal of your work is this lift? What if you want to craft the metaphorical and sonic and perceptual flight, to challenge and destabilize your reader? I recently attended an exhibition of the works of sculptor Evan Penny. He creates very "realistic" human busts. I say "realistic" because while the busts look as though they are made of real skin and hair, they are slightly oversized and warped in the same manner as images hit with the stretch and skew function in Photoshop. These sculptures are so distorted, and, in turn, so perception-bending, that as I navigated the work I fell over on two separate occasions, as though I were drunk.

I bring up my experience with Penny's sculpture in the context of the poem that is too cliché or too abstract, in the context of our conversation about lift and drag, to point out that it is good—and, for many poets, necessary—to compose poems that warp your reader's perspective, that challenge and puzzle and even (pardon my French) piss off. Jericho Brown sums up the point well: "I've never believed that what attracts us to poems is knowing what's going on in them. As a matter of fact, I think just the opposite" ("One Whole Voice").

In the end, even in the most extreme experimental cases, your reader will still need some sort of ground. This "lack of knowing" that Brown describes still requires a certain immersion in the world of the poem so the work is not reduced to words passing emptily before the eye. For example, experimental poets who compose in the "anti-I" tradition, which we discussed in Chapter 3, will often signal their intention and tradition with an epigraph or they will open the book with a detailed introduction that describes the genesis and nature of the project.

Beginnings, Endings, and Drag

You can attend to different aspects of the opening in order to ground your reader: the first line, the epigraph, and the title (which I will discuss in further detail in the next subsection). Think of each of these opening elements as a fence that places a productive limit on your readers, shaping their attention in advance of all the different ways you are about to shape their attention. These elements are signs that let your readers know when, where, and why they are as they enter the bleak forest or buzzing funhouse or dew-spritzed meadow of your poem.

Obviously, there are an infinite number of ways to begin a poem. However, in the context of poems that need a little drag, there is one simple piece of advice to keep in mind: you can be straightforward. Use that first line as the handle the reader grabs hold of before you blast off. Take, for example, the opening of William Shakespeare's "Sonnet 18": "Shall I compare thee to a summer's day?" (1). Shakespeare cleanly establishes the act of comparison he is about to undertake and then commences his intellectual and artistic acrobatics. Another excellent example comes from Audre Lorde. She begins her poem "Stations" as follows: "Some women love / to wait / for life" (1–3). In this excellent opening (what line breaks!), Lorde establishes her poem's central subject, "some women," and the act of turn-filled comparison she undertakes throughout.

The epigraph can also work as a handle for the reader, though I would recommend using them sparingly. To my mind, there are three scenarios: when the epigraph will give your reader needed direction, when your poem responds to a specific passage or adage, or when you explore a concept with which your reader may not be familiar (as you will see at the end of this chapter with Mattieu Ramsawak's "Schumpeter's Gale"). There will be many cases where you will write a poem inspired by a quote you first take as your epigraph; however, when you finish the poem you will find that it has truly become an entity of its own and the epigraph can be cut.

Now, if these opening elements are a limiting fence, you can think of the ending elements as summative seals, as signs that signal to your reader where they have been (as, hopefully, they return again to reread what you have written). The simplest option, which echoes my comments regarding opening lines, is the succinct summary or epigrammatic statement. This, as we discussed in Chapter 3, often occurs in the closing couplet of the Shakespearean sonnet. If you are apprehensive about the outright statement, you can place this statement in the "mouth" of the poem's surroundings, for example, on a billboard or in an overheard conversation.

The second and more restrained technique is the crystallizing image or figure. This is an image or figure that symbolizes the core tension or thrust of the poem. See, for example, the statue at the end of Robert Browning's "My Last Duchess": a bronze sculpture of "Neptune [. . .] / Taming a sea-horse" (54–5). The duke, who has just unwittingly admitted to murdering his last duchess for not remaining completely obedient to him, closes the poem by pointing out an object that sums up his belief in male authority ("Neptune") and female subservience (the wild "sea-horse").

Once again, I want to re-state that these comments on beginnings and endings apply to poems that require a little drag. There are innumerable ways to open and close poems, and your choices will depend on larger questions of order, development, and intention. You may wish to begin out of balance, or *in medias res*, or by asking a question that never gets answered. You may end a poem with a climax or anti-climax, with reconciliation or conflict, with resolution or the reader left on the cusp.

You now have several strategies to add a little drag to your poem (without, of course, making your poem a drag). In the following writing moment, try out some of these techniques for grounding your reader.

Writing Moment 4.8

- Return to the material you composed for the previous three writing moments and choose a section that could serve as a potential poem.
- Compose an epigraph and opening line that give your reader a handle as they enter your poem.
- Compose either a summative epigram (which is couched in the poem's environs) or a crystallizing image.

Titles and Drag

What I wrote about openings and endings applies equally to titles. A catalogue of conventions and styles of titling could fill the pages of this book. Titles can range from the completely straightforward (the topic, event, dedication, etc.) to total nonsense. Lengthwise, all is possible, too. I have written a poem titled, "Poem," and a title that ended up running on for five lines on the printed page.

Rather than provide you with a catalogue of title conventions, I would instead like to share a productive (and quite fun) method for brainstorming titles: using a **semiotic** square. The semiotic square, according to Louis Hébert, was developed as "a means of refining oppositional analyses" ("The Semiotic Square"). In order to get beyond the binary of "Term A" and "Term B" (for example, via Hébert, living and dead), you map "Term A" and "Term B" at the top of a square and add "Term Not-B" (thus, not dead, i.e., zombies) to the bottom left-hand corner of the square and "Term Not-A" (thus, not life, i.e., an anthropomorphized chair) to the bottom right-hand corner. Though this is only the first step, you can see how this basic move begins to generate new relations beyond the binary.

In terms of titles, you can set up a semiotic square as follows:

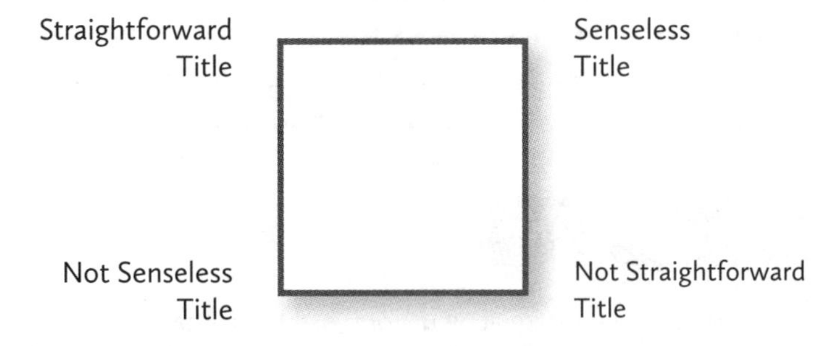

To take a specific example, in the upcoming Poems in Process you will have the chance to read an excellent poem by Daniele Hopkins in which she extends the metaphor: cicadas are aliens. In choosing the title, "Cicadas," she took the straightforward route. Another straightforward option would have been to select a phrase or line from the poem, for example, "Abducting Us with Decibels." Both of these are top-notch titles, so understand that I am mapping “Cicadas” on the semiotic square only as a means of showing you the range of possibilities. Here are some of Daniele’s other options:

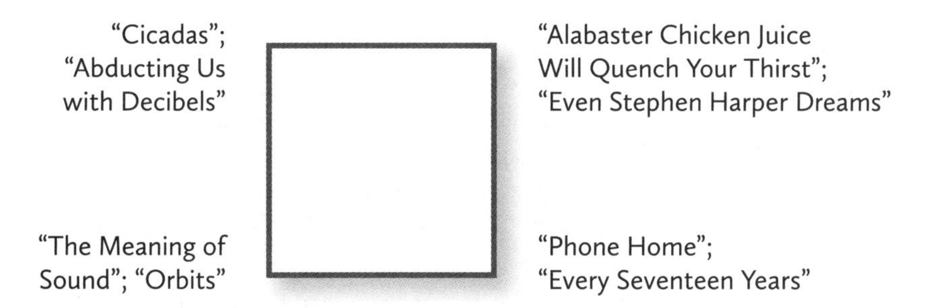

There is no right or wrong way to generate titles with the semiotic square. For example, “not straightforward,” for me, suggested titles that are one step removed from the topic (hence the allusion to *E.T.* and the use of the *magicicada* cicada’s life cycle, which emerges every 13 to 17 years). I used “not senseless” to generate titles that illuminated thematic aspects of the poem. Note, too, how the senseless title at once challenges and proves the power of the imagination. The power of the imagination is challenged insofar as it is really hard to come up with a title (that retains the form and appearance of a title) that is truly senseless. The power of the imagination is proved in that the mind can make these senseless titles make sense in relation to the poem. For example, after properly enjoying Daniele’s poem, reread it with the title “Even Stephen Harper Dreams.”

Writing Moment 4.9

- Return to the material you composed for Writing Moment 4.8.
- Compose a straightforward title.
- Brainstorm other potential titles by employing the semiotic square.

In the next section we will turn from the too cliché and the too abstract to the related issues of predictability and incomprehensibility.

In an attempt to nurture tensions and turns, we will explore the power of difference as subject and practice.

Writing Exercises

1. Return to the material you created during your writing moments and compose one or two new poems. Complete your extended metaphor by situating it within a meditative structure (for example, providing different metaphoric takes on the unknown) or a narrative structure (for example, beginning or ending a quest-like story with your metaphor).
2. Write a poem so mind-bending it makes your readers fall over (if they dare stand up having finished it).
3. Compose an extended metaphor poem in which you reverse the tenor–vehicle relationship we explored above. Instead of giving form to an abstract tenor with a concrete vehicle, illuminate a concrete tenor with a series of abstract vehicles. For example, the bicycle is justice and illusion, or the construction crane is freedom and patriotism.
4. A great way to practice thinking in the "parts" that characterize metonymy and synecdoche is to compose a chimera poem. A chimera is a mythological creature that is part-lion, part-serpent, and part-goat. A chimera poem is a poem that gives form to the unknown by naming its (metaphorical) concrete parts. Death, for example, might have an ashtray for a head, maggot-filled veins, and the husks of dried up cocoons for toenails. Create a chimera poem for a concept, topic, or event of your choosing.
5. Reread a handful of your favourite poems by your favourite poet. Pay particular attention to how the poems begin and end. Can you isolate the strategies the poet employs to add drag to the beginnings and endings of his or her poems? Compose a poem, on the topic of flight (in any or all of its varied manifestations), in which you try out your favourite poet's "dragging" strategies.
6. Generate a poem using a semiotic square. For your "Term A" and "Term B," choose a binary pair such as True–False or Beautiful–Ugly, and then add the "Term Not-B" and "Term Not-A," in these examples either Not False and Not True or Not Ugly and Not Beautiful. One possible approach is to create four-line stanzas by writing a line based on Term A and then rewriting this line in relation to the other three terms. For each ensuing stanza, you can write a new Term A–inspired first line and repeat the process.

Poems in Process

I have included two poems by Daniele Hopkins, "Cicadas" and "Eyemoebic Floaters." These poems undertake the same process: an extended metaphor for a biological body (cicadas and eye floaters, respectively). And yet, despite this shared process, these are two very different poems. "Cicadas" is an excellent example of the simply rendered metaphor. Attending carefully to word choice and line breaks, Daniele manages to both renew our perception of the cicada and yet express this creature's eerie sound so aptly.

Cicadas

The arrival of the aliens
can be heard resonating above.
Not everyone notices,
but it has been said:
they are abducting us with decibels
into their world, penetrating a depth
they never asked to breach. They take
a moment from us and leave
us changed, haunting us with their plight,
their short visit to Earth.

Daniele's "Eyemoebic Floaters," in contrast to "Cicadas," lifts us higher. She stretches our perception as she uses these perceived "particle people" to explore many different registers of looking (looking as seeing, as receiving, as appearing to be). Flight-wise, has she gone too far for your liking or not far enough? Either way, you have got to appreciate the particularity of image and the way the somewhat stilted voice of the opening gives way to the nicely popping, alliteration-flecked language of the second stanza.

Eyemoebic Floaters

Set amidst inherently always-looking
machinery, the vitreous particle people
perform their realism in stop-motion poses
between blinks. Microscopic emulation
of life patterns reveals a community of receptors,
recipients of refracted awareness—feed
a hungry child; buy ethical engagement

rings; receive life insurance up to 90; purchase
a human leather mask.

Lensed shut and often lidded closed,
most photoreceptors only know to convert
image to electrical signal, glazing over gods
and monsters with hot-potato passion, blind
to the few who hooked the radius round to bowed
and built a hole to enter. Suspended within,
they dance on the desiccated tongues of deities past,
positioning their cast of shadows against
the retinal scape for a perpetual play.

Stephanie Kazan employs a simple vehicle, "the edge," in her thoughtful yet disturbing encounter with one of the ultimate unknowns: what some label chance, others fate. Note the effective jumps Stephanie makes in her meditative "takes" as she moves from stanza to stanza. Also worth comment is her work with scale. Stephanie nicely mixes particular detail with precise reflection and then she explodes this intimacy with that gut-tuggingly abyssal final turn.

The Edge

The stagnant sky hovers as I leave the hospital,
its dingy pontoons blot all the green
and turn every car sepia. The smiles
when she opened her presents, the rattles,
the little sleepers, the teddy bears. Now tears.
With one torn open package everything changes,
the future is re-wrapped, the building blocks crash.

There is no such thing as a gradual cliff.
You test positive for cancer,
the train derails, noxious chemicals poison,
the phone rings and he is gone. No warning signs.
No glimpse. You blink, and in a shimmer
you have been transported.

Who says alternate realities are not possible?
A subtle shift and we wake up
in a new universe, a deviant atom wobbles too far,
reroutes the chain, and an event unlikely breathes.

I wander the streets, the cement sidewalk no comfort
as each step brings me closer. It could be
this minute or the rest. Who knows when you're at
the edge—the black hole always on the move.

Nurturing Tensions and Turns: Juxtaposition, Reclamation, Refusal, and Irony

As I compose this book, the thirtieth Olympiad is underway in London, and everyone from athletes to talking heads to politicians to advertisers are unified in promoting the ideal of the global village, asking us at once to celebrate our differences and to recognize that we are all, in the end, united by the Olympic spirit, which has something to do with our shared humanity and the thrill of high-level competition (and, perhaps, an unappeasable appetite for McDonald's).

Yet, despite this united front, the reality of the games undercut this laudable ideal at every turn: the London streets are militarized, participating nations wage wars (aimed at erasing difference) against other participating nations, and athletes take to Twitter to post racist tweets.

What, you might be asking, does this have to do with poetry? For one, this is a prime example of the tension between the ideal and the real, which we discussed in Chapter 1 as one of the conflicts at the core of our experience as people and as poets. And it was while reflecting on this tension exemplified in the Olympic enterprise that I saw how nurturing tensions and turns in our poems might help us address issues of both predictability and incomprehensibility.

The predictable poem that plods along, shuffling from statement to statement, is obviously very different from the poem that manifests as an incomprehensible explosion of impressions and figures, the poetry equivalent of the stars that sting the eyes when you get knocked on the nose. However, what often links these very different types of early draft is a lack of tension or turns, whether in terms of attention or form. The predictable poem does not turn or tense because it proceeds down the safe, expected path, while the incomprehensible poem lacks a sustained detail, figure, or form to be in tension with or to turn from.

One very generative way to nurture tensions and turns in your poems is to encounter the power of difference. We will encounter difference in two ways in the following section: as experience and practice.

Difference as Experience and Practice

Let us begin with the experience of difference. Consider how the global example of the Olympics brings into relief the same conflict that manifests daily on the local, individual level.

The ideals of equality, tolerance for difference, and the recognition of the rights we share—all of these hopes are opposed by acts of discrimination and harassment committed with relentlessness and regularity against individuals due to their respective gender, race, sexual orientation, religion, class, ability, age, weight, intellect, and on and on and on.

Have you been a witness to or the target of this kind of discrimination? Does this abuse ring true for you? Was there a moment when you were singled-out as different and attacked verbally, emotionally, or physically? Is there a trait, experience, or activity that is central to your identity for which you have been distinguished for ridicule and isolation?

With these questions in mind, undertake the following writing moment.

Writing Moment 4.10

- Choose a moment when you were the target of, or witness to, difference-based discrimination and abuse.
- As you did early in your work with the image, return to this memory and situate yourself deeply in it. Draw on all of your senses, while also reflecting on the dynamics of identity—the dynamics of knowledge, power, and desire—that characterize this particular manifestation of difference-based discrimination and abuse.
- Jot down all of the insights and sense memories that you retrieve from that memory, doing so without filtering or editing.

If the challenge of recalling this experience of abuse seems too great, consider the benefits of undertaking this work. For one, those who discriminate crave silence and dread particularity, the lived life that explodes their assumptions; your work undercuts them in both regards. Furthermore, your work is supported by a vibrant and enduring tradition of marginalized poets, protest poets, and political poets, who speak out against injustice. At the same time, your poem, completed, would sustain this tradition, empowering future readers who have been in your shoes and enlightening those who have not.

In the following section, we will take this experience of social difference, difference as the subject for a poem, and render it through two ways of practicing with difference. The first is turning to different (i.e., non-poetic) thinkers. The second is with tools for crafting difference: juxtaposition, reclamation, refusal, and irony. These thinkers and these tools will provide you with the means of transforming your first quiet dissent into a persuasive protest or an all-out, revolutionary howl. By their very structure, they will also encourage you to nurture tensions and turns in your work, addressing issues of predictably and incomprehensibility.

On the topic of other thinkers, there is one key point to note. I have chosen to work with philosophers (quite broadly defined, as you will see). However, this is only one of many possibilities. Explore your own interests: history, biology, anthropology, psychology, and so on. The value of doing so, of travelling with these companions, is that this type of reading inspires a greater breadth of vision, a penetrating depth of insight, and a more generous imagination. What Dylan Thomas says about the poem applies to these other works at their best, too: "A good poem helps to change the shape and significance of the universe, helps to extend everyone's knowledge of himself and the world around him" (61).

Philosophy and Juxtaposition

Poetry and philosophy have been in conversation, or, according to some, conflict, since well before the foundational works of the ancient Greeks. Plato, writing 2500 years ago, described the relationship between poetry and philosophy as the "ancient war."

However, despite Plato's characterization, and his accusation that poets lie, corrupt, and create imperfect imitations (more on this later), poetry finds great sympathy with the roots of philosophy's name, the Greek *philosophia*, "love of wisdom," as, for centuries, thinkers of every ilk chose verse as the means of composing medical texts and political treatises.

Where poetry most obviously diverges from philosophy is in method. Poetry, unlike philosophy, does not seek to reason out the fundamental inner workings of metaphysics, knowledge, ethics, existence, and so on. In one of the earliest defences of poetry, Sir Philip Sidney argued that "the poet, he nothing affirms, and therefore never lieth" (52), and poetry is therefore best considered, as Helen Vendler interprets Sidney, to be "proffered hypothesis" (309). More recently, Gilles Deleuze and Felix Guattari have put the difference succinctly by contending that philosophers build concepts, while artists compose with feelings and perceptions (24).

Two of the most common views of the relationship between poetry and philosophy are distinguished by their different opinions about the originality of poetry's ideas, or, put another way, the type of originality in thought that poetry is best able to achieve. For one school, poets are communicators. The goal is not to undertake innovative, groundbreaking, intellectual inquiry. Instead, as Alexander Pope put it, poetry conveys "What oft was *Thought*, but ne'er so well *Exprest*" (298). For the other school, poets are visionaries. Percy Bysshe Shelley argued that the metaphorical quality of poetry allowed poets to "[mark] the before unapprehended relations of things" (123), making them "the unacknowledged legislators of the world" (159).

The easiest and most popular way for us to engage both philosophy and this debate as poets is through the poetic elaboration. In these poems, the poet works with a selection from a philosophical text, whether a specific line or a particular concept, and elaborates on it in any number of ways. A poet may compose an allegory that promotes or troubles a chosen concept. Working from a striking line of philosophy, a poet may present actual examples from the world, or imagined figures, that show this line "in action" or that contrast its assertion.

For the following writing moment, return to the experience of difference-based discrimination you just explored. The goal will be to elaborate one of Plato's attacks on poetry, and prove him wrong with your counter-experience and the help of one of the most basic techniques for figuring difference: juxtaposition.

Writing Moment 4.11

- Compose a draft of (or the beginnings of) a short two-stanza poem.
- In the first stanza, articulate one of Plato's attacks on poets (and perhaps while you are composing, keep in mind Pope's adage regarding the "ne'er so well expressed"):

    - Poets lie. They present false representations of the gods, revelling in the shocking and sinister, rather than the good and ideal.
    - Poets corrupt. Rather than teaching us to let our reason guide us, poets stir our emotions and subvert our capacity to reason.
    - Poets make imperfect work. There are ideal forms, of which the objects of the world are imitations. Poets merely give us imitations of imitations.
- In the second stanza, explore your experience of difference-based discrimination. Do not comment on or reference the previous stanza. Instead, show your reader, through your rendering of your experience, how poets tell the truth, how they use emotion to enlighten us, or how the imperfect work is better than no work at all.

Regarding the rendering of difference, note how juxtaposition is an effective technique for two reasons. First, it establishes an easily perceived moment of comparison. Second, it leaves much of the work to your readers, stirring them to actively seek out and reflect on the difference (and overlap) rather than just receive the information. This is a much more gratifying and moving aesthetic and intellectual experience.

Identity-Based Philosophers, Reclamation, and Refusal

Many contemporary poets have turned to identity-based philosophers for inspiration. This particular branch of philosophy was one of the major intellectual developments in the second half of the twentieth century. It is most simply characterized by the blossoming of philosophers, theorists, and critics who advocate for the rights of all those who have been oppressed and marginalized in the past for differing from Western culture's ruling norm: white, male, rational, and heterosexual.

These identity-focused inquiries did not aim to obliterate difference but, instead, to distinguish it further with an empowered voice. They salvaged their traditions from the margins of the past, and promoted the critical study of everything from gender, race, post-colonial experience, queerness, class, mental health, and so on. In a philosophical context, those who had once been defined as outsiders, as the other, sought to re-locate the centre from which the terms of truth, good, beauty, and justice were determined.

One particular historical tendency these thinkers take issue with is the oppression of a group through prescribed and fixed identities. These may be social duties (for example, women must only perform *this* kind of work) or stereotyping identities (for example, *this* race is lazy). Two processes these philosophers often undertake, and two processes you can utilize in your poetic practice, are the work of refusal and the work of reclamation.

Works of refusal quite simply repudiate the prescribed duties and stereotyping identities by constructing an alternative self, the self whose experience, insights, vision, figures, and images not only shatter the oppressive stereotype but found an empowered position from which to speak. Works of reclamation take two forms. The first method involves locating a historical figure (real or fictional, local or global) who was outcast for reasons of class, race, or gender, etc., and to reclaim this individual, to explore her or his life as a means of formulating an alternate (in many cases, truer) history. The second and more provocative method involves accepting the suppressing identity, but reconstructing it into a position of power. The goal is to take a word, symbol, or concept used to deform, humiliate, and silence—such as "slut" or "queer"—and to reclaim it for purposes of empowerment and liberation. For a potent example of this, see Hélène Cixous' feminist reclamation of the figure of the snake-haired, monstrous Medusa in her essay "The Laugh of the Medusa."

For the following writing moment, return to your experience of difference-based discrimination and carry out your own work of reclamation.

Writing Moment 4.12

- For your assailant or assailants, their abuse is justified by a set of baseless, wilfully blind assumptions. These assumptions are often sustained by historical, pop cultural, or stereotyping figures.
- Which figure or figures—whether overtly or unconsciously—did your assailant or assailants deploy against you? Which figures have you encountered in the past?
- How might a poem attempt a reclamation of these figures or concepts?

"Philosophy" and Irony

It is not only philosophy proper that makes for an invigorating companion. Any guiding principle, in other words, philosophy more colloquially considered, is equally suited for inspiring new modes of expression and understanding. The "philosophies" of service-selling corporations are a unique candidate, particularly when considered in the context of difference. One of the chief representational goals of a service-selling corporation is to conceal its difference, the two facts that distinguish it from the individuals who consume its service: the fact that profit precedes service, and the fact that it is a corporate, rather than an individual, entity. The goal is to create a human face.

The most obvious way a service-selling corporation constructs this face is through advertisements. Another means is the corporate mission statement, the formal summary of the aims and values of the corporate entity. The mission statement is, in a certain sense, more intriguing than advertisements because mission statements have multiple audiences. Ads are designed for consumer seduction; the company itself does not need swaying. The mission statement, on the other hand, is addressed to the consumer and the company, and in the case of publically traded businesses to the shareholder, as well. The consumer is assured that more than profits drive the corporation, while the corporation's employees are united under the watchful eye of the mission statement's tenets, a sort of occupational ethics that assert how and why to sell, sell, sell.

Let us take the McDonald's mission statement as our particular example. It deserves this place of honour, having successfully inundated me while I cheer Canada on to bronze:

> McDonald's brand mission is to be our customers' favorite place and way to eat. Our worldwide operations are aligned around a global strategy called the Plan to Win, which center on an exceptional customer experience—People, Products, Place, Price and Promotion. We are committed to continuously improving our operations and enhancing customer experience ("Mission & Values").

There are a number of ways to compose in concert with the corporate mission statement. Translation and transformation are two of the most productive.

Two types of translation can be performed to humorous or poignant ends. The first involves translating the mission statement's goals and values in poetic form (for example, as composed by Emily Dickinson or Frank O'Hara). The second entails presenting a mundane task (for example, making toast) or a significant relationship (for example, asking someone out on a date) in the high-minded, abstract, and peppy corporate language of the mission statement.

There are also two types of possible transformation. Both of these approaches possess a more critical bent. As with any set of ideal goals, the real results often conflict, and one form of transformation addresses this fact by replacing the abstract statements of the mission statement with real world wrongs (for example, clear cutting rainforests, spreading heart disease, and underpaying workers). The second type of transformation, the cut up, is a sort of quest for the mission statement's hidden message. The cut up, as we have discussed, entails physically (or digitally) cutting the words into individual units and rearranging them into a new mission statement.

One of the benefits of testing out any one of these methods is that each, to varying degrees, produces an ironic poem. Whereas our three other techniques for rendering difference—juxtaposition, refusal, and reclamation—are much more straightforward in their application, irony can be more challenging to grasp and require greater care to handle effectively. In all four of these cases, the contrast between the content (what is said) and the form (how it is said) produces an immediate ironic discrepancy.

For this section's final writing moment, explore your experience of difference-based discrimination in the context of the ironically transformed corporate mission statement. Work from our sample, along with other mission statements you know or can track down, and try one of the following.

Writing Moment 4.13

- Compose a corporate-style mission statement in which you (ironically) outline how you will remove from yourself (externally and internally) all signs of difference.

- Compose a corporate-style mission statement in which you (ironically) outline the motivations and values that you speculate might drive those who have discriminated against you. To heighten the irony, create a voice that is as upbeat and cheerful as possible.

Difference, as this section demonstrates, takes many different forms in poetry: difference as social experience, difference as compositional tool, and difference as way of knowing. Each of these incarnations of difference addresses issues of predictability, by instigating turns, and incomprehensibility, by providing solid experiences, figures, and thinkers from which to turn.

I encourage you to engage further with these various forms of difference, developing poems from the materials you composed during your writing moments and continuing to test out these new insights with the aid of the exercises listed below.

Writing Exercises

1. Return to the material you created during your writing moments and compose one or two new poems. For example, complete your Plato-centred piece, your reclamation poem, or return to the initial writing moment and head in a completely different direction.
2. You have reflected on your experience as a victim of difference-based discrimination. Switch positions in this relationship and compose a poem about a moment when you were the perpetrator of discrimination.
3. Compose a poem titled "The Same" in which you imagine a world without difference. Employ all three of the techniques for figuring difference that we looked at in this section: juxtaposition, reclamation, and irony. Note that one of the ways to effectively render the irony would be to present this undesirable world of sameness in an upbeat or seductive voice that presents this sameness as desirable.
4. In the same speculative vein as the previous writing exercise, compose a **faux-ccasional** poem. Designed to enact both reclamation and refusal, the faux-ccasional poem is an occasional poem written in honour of an historical event that did not happen. For example, you could write a poem marking the seventieth anniversary of the Enola Gay's

refusal to drop an atomic bomb on Hiroshima or an elegy for Dr Martin Luther King Jr who passed away in his sleep at the age of 86.

5. Write a mission statement for an individual, entity, or group that you would not expect to have a mission statement. Alternately, compose a mission statement for a feeling or an abstract idea.
6. Which field or area of knowledge do you have a strong interest in? This could be an academic field, an area of knowledge connected to a job, or something more related to entertainment. Employ a persona who is an expert in your field (for example, the mathematician, the mechanic, the Trekkie). Choosing a common poetic theme (such as love, loss, death, etc.), write about this theme from the perspective of your knowledgeable persona.

Poems in Process

Sam Burton bravely and vigorously delves into the experience of not only struggling with obsessive-compulsive disorder (OCD), but also struggling with its diagnosis and treatment. *The Diagnostic and Statistical Manual of Mental Disorders* (*DSM*) serves, in a sense, as her counter-companion, a methodology she questions and critiques. Sam powerfully captures both the desperation of her quest for answers and the sense of being trapped by so many of the answers. She accomplishes this effect through a number of strategies: the intermixing of multiple past memories with the present moment, surprising shifts in thought, and a multi-vocal, almost choral text (the *DSM* is joined by everything from Wikipedia to the work of psychiatrist and Holocaust survivor Viktor Frankl). Due to space constraints, I am not able to include "Freedom Is Not in the *DSM*" in its entirety. The following excerpt opens the poem.

excerpt from **Freedom Is Not in the *DSM***

"If you have any urge to check the locks," the doctor
yawns, "or wash your hands . . ." (The first hand to raise
back in my Grade 11 Anthropology/Sociology/Psychology course
could have diagnosed me just as well ("OH! ISN'T OCD
WHEN YOU WASH YOUR HANDS A LOT AND KEEP
THINKING YOU LEFT THE STOVE ON?").) I don't
tell the doctor that I haven't worried about the locks

since I was ten, or that my sister's the one who tells me
not to slide my hands down the public banister.
        I see that mom can feel my grief
on the inside. Doctors are not Gods
anymore. (I want to tell her to shut up, ask,
"Will Celexa get rid of my shame?" (I've hunted
the shame-transmitter from psych course to psych course,
only managed to glimpse its shadow, always trailing me,
skirting all attempts to stop it from slipping back
into the dark as I turn and reach out my hand.))

When I asked Mattieu Ramsawak which non-poetic thinkers inspired "Schumpeter's Gale, or The Joker Must Have Read Marx," he listed an article in *Nature*, two superhero movies, ad copy for the latest smart phones, and his economics class. I love how Mattieu draws on these diverse sources to give a range of imaginative and mind-bending forms to economist Joseph Schumpeter's statements about the "creative destruction" that defines capitalism. This poem does not so much develop in a linear progression as a circular one, repeating with a sort of fierce, almost Joker-esque glee, the same act of potentially apocalyptic destructive renewal.

Schumpeter's Gale, or The Joker Must Have Read Marx

"incessantly creating a new"
—Joseph Schumpeter

I heard they're making jellyfish from rats' hearts;
somewhere, a stung surfer dies from Leptospirosis.
The corpse turns into cheddar for black-suited rodents
who earn their livings by razing the dead.

My first economics lesson came from Mufasa.
He taught me that sooner or later my ass
would be grass to feed the world's antelope,
or, at least, to make space for the lions to roam.

The Joker was an economist, too; he wasn't mad.
He read Marx while mixing Smilex cocktails
and figured out why Rome was too big not to fail:
everything must burn in the name of aggressive expansion.

> I burn my iPod in anticipation. Long ago, I used to burn
> CDs for these occasions. Wal-Mart will eventually put itself
> out of business, make space for the mega-factories
> that will mass-produce low-cost entrepreneurs.

Conclusion: The Three Bears Approach to Revising for a Self-Revising Reader

I opened this chapter with the figure of Goldilocks providing the model for how to revise. By taking up her "too" in the context of our poetic processes and products, we can work to complete poems that are, to borrow her words again, "just right." However, while we do need to keep Goldilocks' guidance in mind, we also need to remember that we each remain—to further extend the figures of this fairy tale—bears: the porridge, chair, and bed are created in accordance with our bodies and tastes and techniques.

In other words, as we have experienced throughout this book, there are many motivations for writing poetry and an array of schools that foster very different views on what a poem can do. Each of these schools in particular generates new mechanisms for confirming the work is done, and invokes new standards for what qualifies as a finished—and good—poem. One poet's spontaneously achieved masterpiece appears to another poet as notes for the poem still to come, while another poet's thoroughly revised tour de force appears to others as pure craft drained of all recognizable life.

The key, then, is to know what kind of "bear" you are both in terms of the finished work and how you get there. Another important step is to gain a more intimate understanding of your reader, living, dead or yet to come, a stouter bond with the ones or one for whom you compose. Reflection on how you revise should lead you to ask: for whom do I revise?

If you are still sceptical about the prospect of revision, the idea of changing what you made for the sake of someone else, consider this: we self-reflect on our practice, critique our own work, for the sake of the reader's own reflection and self-critique. We craft as carefully and originally as we can with the hope that our reader will bring the same originality and care to the act of reading. We wrangle with our craft, with our tools and turns, because the more we can address issues with cliché or incomprehensibility or distance the more the reader can experience, in the words of Ian McEwan, that element of "self-annihilation" ("Ian McEwan: By the Book") that is part of the pleasure of reading, the experience of being "so engrossed that you barely know you exist" ("Ian McEwan: By the Book").

This experience of being engrossed in the poem, in the work of art, as McEwan suggests, is not solipsistic or self-sustaining, but self-transcending, liberating. "Poetry is not only dream and vision," Audre Lorde writes, "it is the skeleton architecture of our lives. It lays the foundation for a future of change, a bridge across our fears of what has never been before" (38). And it is this feeling of self-overcoming that transforms "my fears" into "our fears," "my life" into "our lives." It is what opens us up, as Lorde puts it, to "what has never been before."

This connection, this act of reaching out to another who reaches back, characterizes our work in the next chapter as we turn to the venues of poetry. To enter these venues means not only to share our poems, but also to share the processes and practices of their creation.

Recommended Resources

- *Structures and Tools*: Mary Kinzie's *A Poet's Guide to Poetry* is a nearly 600-page compendium of all things poetry. Kinzie provides an in-depth look at every essential element of traditional form. For those interested in a more focused turn to the basics, Stanley Fish's *How to Write a Sentence and How to Read One* is the ideal book. Fish has composed both a great primer for new writers and an inspiring refresher for old pros.

- *Revision*: Edited by Robert Burr and Barry Wallenstein, *Visions and Revisions: The Poet's Process*, is the perfect resource for anyone interested in learning more about how poets as diverse as William Shakespeare, Emily Dickinson, and Marianne Moore undertook revisions. Each poem is accompanied by an older original (or originals) that illuminate what a wide range of canonical and contemporary poets viewed as problems and demonstrates how they sought to address these problems.

- *Rhetoric*: Weighing in at less than 100 pages, *The Essential Guide to Rhetoric*, by William M. Keith and Christian O. Lundberg, is an accessible and straightforward general introduction to the history and tools of the rhetorician. Though a book aimed at teachers of poetry, Tom C. Hunley's *Teaching Poetry Writing: A Five-Canon Approach* is still one of the most practical poet-centred discussions of rhetoric.

- *Other Thinkers*: Continue to explore the wide range of non-poetic thinkers in your field of interest or in an area in which you have only, until now, dabbled. Anthologies or readers (on a specific topic or gathering together selections of one thinker) are invaluable in this context, too. For example, *The Norton Anthology of Theory and Criticism* was for me, as the saying goes, a real game changer.

CHAPTER 5

Sharing Process and Sharing Poems

Introduction: Gaining through Losing

> "For one must be able at times to lose oneself
> if one wants to learn something from things
> that we ourselves are not."
>
> —Friedrich Nietzsche

We lose ourselves, as the multiple variations on the phrase suggest, in many things: work, love, a favourite book or song. As Nietzsche observes, losing ourselves can also have a larger, interpersonal end, freeing us to commune with, to come to know, that which we do not know and that which we are not.

In a certain sense, we have experienced this "learning through losing" throughout this book. The best poetry is always so much more than the sum of one self, and each chapter, every writing moment, has asked you to lose yourself in the subjects, traditions, and practices of poetry, to become acquainted with familiar terrain in a new way or to enter unfamiliar territory altogether.

Nietzsche's advice that we must lose ourselves in order "to learn something from things that we ourselves are not" is perhaps most relevant to our fifth and final chapter, "Sharing Process and Sharing Poems." For it is in relation to these acts of sharing that we truly encounter—in the flesh—the practices, opinions, and poetry of other living poets, and it is in these acts that we are able to form the poetry communities that buoy us to new horizons of the past, present, and future.

In the following chapter, we will explore two ways of sharing process: the sharing of practice and the sharing of feedback. These are the opportunities for co-creation and co-critique that arise in the creative writing classroom or when you form a writer's group. With the sharing of poems, we will look at the different ways in which you can share both your own particular poems and poetry as a living tradition.

Much of what follows involves projects to be undertaken with a writing group, so, if you have not done so already, I highly recommend you join or form one. A writing group may consist only of you and a close friend or it might involve a writing class or a group of literary-minded neighbours. I also encourage you to take advantage of continuing developments in web forums and social networks as a way of keeping connected with your writing group and meeting new writers.

Let us begin by losing ourselves in new, collaborative creative processes, processes that ask us to share the act of writing, to find new ways of seeing, singing, and scavenging our topics, traditions, and tools.

Sharing Process

It was in high school that I first shared the writing process. My best friend came up with the idea. He held the notebook and asked me for a first line. He wrote it down and then added a line of his own, a line that I was not allowed to read. He asked me for another line. He wrote it down, added another of his own. We repeated the process, back and forth, until we had what he felt was a finished poem. He read the poem to me. I do not remember if it was any good, but I do remember being exhilarated by the experience.

The qualities that made this specific experience of sharing the writing process valuable are many, and they are common to the various strategies for sharing process. This practice broke my friend and I out of our respective individual routines of thought and language as we wrote in concert (and conflict) with the other's mind and voice. We were also shown how far we could push figures and sense and still achieve any number of ends, from truth to shock to beauty. Furthermore, when you were the recorder, this challenge posed by the other's always-surprising contribution demanded a response that was at once quick and careful.

Use the following writing moment to give collaborative practice a try.

Writing Moment 5.1

- If you are in the company of a friend, invite her or him to compose a poem with you based on the collaborative practice I undertook with my friend. Remember, one poet holds the notebook, contributing every other line and recording, while the other poet adds every other line, with no knowledge of what is happening on the page.
- If you are not in the presence of a friend, you can undertake this process in the e-verse (for example, texting a friend for contributions) or the universe (for example, taking your surroundings as your co-poet and drawing lines from phrases you overhear).

Sharing Limits and Sharing Composition

The sharing of the poetic process takes two basic, often interrelated forms: the sharing of limits and the sharing of composition.

To share limits means to create and share a specific set of compositional coordinates—restrictions or directions related to form and/or subject matter—but to undertake on your own the act of writing the poem. For example, you and a pair of friends may each come up with one restriction each, and then individually compose poems that follow these three restrictions. By contrast, sharing composition involves creating a work collectively. For example, you and a friend writing a sonnet together by composing alternating lines.

In the rest of this section, we will explore how these two forms of collective composition can be undertaken separately as well as in relation to the writing event.

Collaboration and Many from One

"Many from one" is my way of naming one of the two general approaches to collaborative creation. "Many from one" processes are those in which each participating writer produces a work (hence the "many") from one shared set of directions. The conception of these directions involves two steps.

First, decide on the subject(s), tradition(s), and/or tool(s) from which your directions will be derived. In other words, your directions may connect to both topic and form, and may involve determining the genre of the poem (a love poem, for example), the tradition (for example, a type of fixed form), and the tools used (a conceit, maybe, or a certain type of rhythm). Ideally, your choices will be surprising, inspiring your fellow writers to compose in a manner with which they are not familiar.

The second step is to decide how specific, and, in turn, how "directing," you want your directions to be. In the case of the most general instructions, you may simply ask for the following: a regional poem that a) is about the place where the writer was raised and b) includes a metaphor. I do a variation of the same exercise in which I give extremely specific instructions for the poem's title (the name of the region) and each of its five lines (even, in some cases, providing a skeleton for the sentence structure).

The following writing moment will give you the opportunity to conceive of your own "many from one" collaborative undertakings.

Writing Moment 5.2

- For yourself and at least one companion, choose at least one topic and one tool.
- Create two versions of the same collaborative undertaking. For the first, provide general goals, while for the second, offer very detailed instructions.

Collaboration and One from Many

"One from many" processes, in contrast to "many from one" processes, are those in which many writers work together to produce one work. As with the "many from one," the conception of the directions involves the same two steps: choosing your directions and determining specificity. However, since in this instance many writers are creating one work, you must also decide how the actual act of writing will take place.

There are a wide range of options. You may assign one person to record, as in my introductory example, or you may pass the notebook around in a circle, with each writer adding a line at a time or a word at a time. If separated by distance, you and your co-writers could take turns adding your contributions in a discussion thread or in a shared document. Each writer, as in our previous writing moment, can compose in isolation and then you all combine your pieces together, or you may work with a more fixed document, as in a Mad Lib or N+7, where you add a few specifics to a half-finished piece.

A popular and simple collaborative practice is to compose an "exquisite corpse." This practice, invented by **surrealist** artists, involves either following a set and repeated pattern (for example, "The adjective noun adverb verb the adjective noun") or composing on the basis of knowing only a part of what the previous writer wrote (for example, by folding the page over and revealing only a few words). You can also create modified and more involved versions of the exquisite corpse. For example, Figure 5.1 shows one that I have found to be a lot of fun titled, "A Manual for the Machine that Doesn't Exist."

When I undertake this collaboration with other writers, I always hand out one copy for each person to keep everyone active and involved. You proceed by filling in the first blank and passing your paper to the left. After you have filled out the second blank (drawing the image of the machine), you fold over the machine's name and pass the paper to the left. You should never be able to see more than the most recent entry. The results, I promise, range from hilarious to mind-bending to moving.

The following writing moment will give you the opportunity to conceive of your own "one from many" collaborative undertakings.

The Machine's Name: ______________________________

Image of the Machine

FOLD HERE - FOLD HERE

How to Operate the Machine

Step 1: ____

FOLD HERE - FOLD HERE

Step 2: ____

FOLD HERE - FOLD HERE

Step 3: ____

FOLD HERE - FOLD HERE

In case of _____________,

FOLD HERE - FOLD HERE

____.

FIGURE 5.1 A Manual for the Machine that Doesn't Exist

Writing Moment 5.3

- Invent a modified exquisite corpse.
- Encourage the integration of words and image, and solicit different types of language.
- If you would like a title to inspire you, feel free to work with one of the following: "Instructions for Ending the End of the World" or "The List of Things that Quicken the Heart."

Collaboration and Writing Events

In the context of the sharing of the poetic process, there are, essentially, two common sites in which writing events are undertaken: sites of your daily routines and sites of special distinction. Sites of daily routine are your everyday locations, the places where you live, work, regularly unwind, or frequently get wound up. A site of special distinction is any site that organizes a specific type of unique cultural experience, such as an art gallery, the abandoned factory of a defunct business, or a zoo. These sites could also include those that are essential to your experience (a religious event, for example), but distinct to many of your writing group's potential readers. The reverse is also fertile: a site that is common to mainstream culture, but foreign to your writing group's beliefs. For example, a political rally for a party whose platform you all deeply disagree with.

One strategy is to plan a poetry scavenger hunt. Make a list of "items" that a group of poets must find and document in their words. This is a great way to see a familiar place in a new way, to see the spectacular that hides behind the mundane. I have started doing this with students new to university as a means of getting them to explore our campus. I give them a title, "On Education," and four items to find and write about in one sentence each. The students work in pairs, finding the items together, composing their sentences separately, and then combining their sentences in any order they see fit.

When it comes to conceiving of the compositional directions that will guide you around your site of special distinction, I highly recommend you let the form and/or content of the site shape the form and/or content of your poems. For example, when our university's writing group learned that scenes for the remake of *Total Recall* (a nineties sci-fi, action classic starring Arnold Schwarzenegger) would be filmed on our campus, we knew immediately that we needed to plan a writing event. Since the film was a remake we decided to go with the theme and compose remakes about remakes. Each of us randomly selected a poem from a book of poems selected from the shelf in my office. We then "remade" that poem—mimicking its formal rules, style, voice, figures, etc.—while writing about the remake of *Total Recall*.

The following writing moment will give you the opportunity to conceive of your own potential writing events.

Writing Moment 5.4

- What is a site that you consider a part of your daily routine, but that would be considered distinctive by your writing friends? Compose the directions for a collaboration undertaken at this site.
- If money (and, perhaps, technology) were not an object, what would be the site of special distinction that you would like to visit with your friends? Compose the directions for your collaboration. Be sure to let the form and/or content of the site shape the form and/or content of your poems.

The act of writing—despite the legend of the suffering and lonely genius—is never a wholly solitary act. Both the page-facing mind of the poet and the paper-bound pen are always joined by so many only seemingly invisible listeners, so many contributing delegates of the world: the angels, ghosts, and monsters of our experience in general and, in particular, of our experience of the topics, traditions, and tools of poetry.

The plenitude that populates the moment of writing is brought most fully into relief when we share the process with other writers. Most obviously, this occurs due to the mere fact of another embodied consciousness with which to collaborate and contend. More importantly, though, this occurs because the presence of your collaborator's invisible choir forces you to more fully reflect on your own choir, to question some members, re-train others, and welcome new vocalists.

In the next section we will turn to the place where this experience of questioning the self through the questions of others is even stronger: the writing workshop.

1. Grab a friend (in the physical or digital flesh) and undertake the collaborative practice I described in my opening remarks.
2. The *renga* is a Japanese form of collaborative poetry that requires a group of three or more poets. The first poet composes the *hokku* (three lines with a syllable count 5, 7, and 5). The second poet composes the *waki* (two lines with a syllable count 7 and 7). The next poet composes another *hokku*, while the next poet composes a *waki*. Repeat the pattern until you reach your desired length.
3. Plan a creative collaboration dedicated to working with the musical tools of poetry. Each participant needs to bring one line written in any musically dedicated tradition (whether metrical, rap, or spoken word). Have the participants, first, write their respective lines on separate pieces of paper and, second, write at the top that page the "limits" of their line (stress pattern, rhythm, length, and, even, desired rhyme). The papers are then passed to the right and each poet, following the prescribed rules, composes the second line. Pass the pages again and write the third line. Repeat until you reach your desired length.
4. Organize a collaborative writing event. However, do not choose a physical, spatial site. Instead, you could choose a temporal site, for example, a specific time and duration. You could also choose a physical state: exhaustion, hunger, or the state of being overheated.
5. Create your writing group's joint poet persona, the fictional identity through which you share works written individually or collectively. You could seek commissions, compose works in honour of an important event, or offer to be the poet laureate for a group or venue (for example, a festival, gallery, or street corner).

Sharing Feedback

Who am I to tell another poet what to do?

This is most likely one of the questions—if not *the* question—you ask yourself when you read the title "Sharing Feedback" and hear me mention the creative writing workshop. Each semester, many poets new to my class, after learning that they will have to provide critiques of the works of their peers, quite understandably ask a variation on this question.

What I tell my students, and what, indeed, I would have said to my younger self who felt very much the same, is that this is not quite the right question to ask.

For one, "who you are" is a poet. That is all the authority you need. To provide helpful feedback, you do not need to be a half-century into your journey with decades of training under your belt. You have read and written poetry, and you have thought deeply about what you have read and written.

Secondly, having undertaken this work, you have the grounds and ability to "do what we do" when sharing feedback, which does not involve telling other poets what to do. Your feedback is one perspective on a particular set of poems, which, in turn, gives the author a new perspective on these poems.

In this sense, the first question to ask is: what is my perspective? This self-assessment allows you to grasp the range of your strengths as a reader, as well as your potential blind spots. Admittedly, then, I was wrong when I said the initial question is off the mark. The first half is spot on: who am I?

Writing Moment 5.5

- As a means of reflecting on your tendencies as a poet, jot down two or three responses to each of the following questions. Which occasions most often inspire your work? Who are your most common poetic companions? Which tools are you most gifted at crafting with?
- What is the aim of your work? How does your work achieve this aim?
- Who is your favourite poet? Which occasions inspire her or his work? Who are her or his companions? Which tools has she or he mastered?
- What is the aim of her or his work? How does her or his work achieve this aim?

Who Is the Poet That Only You Can Become?

Regarding the basic end of sharing feedback, the goal is simple: to help your fellow poets write better poems. I like to think of this as helping a poet become the poet that only she or he can become.

In the context of your own development as a poet, the imperative "become the poet that only you can become" reminds us to compose with courage and imagination, to write authentically and sincerely. This imperative stirs us to commence the self-reflection we undertook in the previous writing moment.

In terms of sharing feedback, this imperative should be kept in mind both when we give feedback and when we receive it. Regarding the latter, this imperative usefully checks us against trying to turn every poet into ourselves. Yes, we want our fellow poets to write the best poems, but these are their best poems, not our best poems. On the flipside, this imperative reminds us to receive feedback with attentiveness and genuineness; a new, generative direction may be hidden in a remark we initially wish to dismiss.

Now, more practically speaking, there are three essential steps to the sharing of feedback: identify, assess, and reply. If possible, truly turn to the work of others by undertaking the ensuing writing moments with a friend's poem and preparing some feedback on it. However, if you do not have a friend's poem handy, one of your older poems or one you are not happy with will more than suffice.

Identify: What Is It?

Think of a poem as a window. It frames a specific section of the world. Some poems seek to shatter the window and immerse us in the world beyond the glass. Other poems want to be windows at the far end of a long hall, revealing, if we stare hard enough, spots of blue and the odd flash of colour, an alighting bird, perhaps, or the sun reflected in the window of a passing car.

The first step to providing feedback is to read the poem three or four times, and, as you read, to begin to identify both the poem's scope and its parts. To return to the window analogy, this is the equivalent of determining both what, in general, the window frames, and, in particular, the parts that compose this framed world.

First, you want to note what you see as the poem's occasions: an occasion of feeling (a central experience), an occasion of encounter (a central topic), and/or an occasion of language (a central tool). Once you have completed this, the second step is to firm up your grip on the poem's most basic happenings. To do so, come up with a short summary of the events of the poem and/or the event of the poem.

The next step is to identify the tools with which the poet works. On the one hand, you want to cast your net as widely as possible and consider imagery, voice, music, figures, structure, line breaks, words, and so on. On the other hand, you also want to make effective use of your time, while also providing useful and focused feedback. Thus, note the elements that strike you, the ones that leave a strong impression because you were moved or confused, because the language flowed or tripped you up.

The last step is to identify the poem's companions or forms. As with your identification of the poem's occasions, the goal is to note the obvious (for example, a fixed form) and the perhaps not so obvious (a thinker with whom you feel the poem's thought resonates).

With these remarks in mind, take up your friend's poem, grab a pen and piece of paper, and answer the following questions. I encourage you to circle, underline, star, and otherwise mark parts of the poem that strike you. For now, however, you should make your identification notes on a separate piece of paper.

Writing Moment 5.6

- What are the poem's occasions?
- What tools are employed?
- Who are the poem's companions?

Assess: How Does It Work?

Think of a poem as a machine, a mechanism for producing meanings, feelings, and/or perceptions. It is a vehicle for bearing these meanings, feelings, and/or perceptions from the writer and world to the reader. When assessing a poem, we return to the scope and parts we identified and determine both how they work and whether they work.

To begin our assessment of the poem, of how the poetic machine works, we return to the occasions we identified and at once refine and expand on our initial insights. This is what June Jordan succinctly and effectively names the poem's purpose (36).

Thus, the potential questions now are: what, in relation to the occasions, is the poem's purpose? How does the poem treat the occasion? What sorts of speaking, seeing, being, becoming, etc., is the occasion an opportunity to undertake? Connected to these questions, there are three potential areas to consider when undertaking this first step of the assessment: the mode (meditation, story, monologue, perception, perception of perception, etc.), the motivation (strange, familiar, fidelity, difference, etc.), and specific speech acts (to celebrate, pray, disavow, question, etc.).

In the end, the goal is to compose a succinct statement about what you view as the poem's purpose. The forms your statements take will vary poem to poem. However, in every instance, aspire to the short and sweet. For example, "the purpose of this poem is to celebrate a lover," or "this poem aims to capture autumn in its many growing and deteriorating forms."

Once you have determined the purpose of the poem, or, to return to our analogy, the function of the machine, you can return to the tools and companions you identified and assess how these parts work to realize the poem's purpose. Undertaking this assessment is simply a process of observing what, in relation to the poem's purpose, works—is coherent, striking, genuinely moving, jaw-droppingly awesome, etc.—and what does not work—is incoherent, dull, maudlin, head-scratchingly clichéd, etc.

The goal once again, as was the case when identifying these parts, is to be thorough but not exhaustive. The "rule of three," which so often holds in fairy tales, also holds here: three remarks on what works and three remarks on what does not work. This gives the poet substantial material to think about without overwhelming her or him, and it encourages you to keep your remarks focused.

For the following writing moment, return to your notes and your friend's poem and answer the following questions.

Writing Moment 5.7

- What is the purpose of the poem?
- Note three sections and/or tools that effectively realize this purpose? How do they do so?

- Note three sections and/or tools that inhibit the realization of this purpose? How do they do so?

Reply: Providing Feedback

The final step in this process is, based on your process of identifying and assessing, to provide a precise, sensitive, astute, and, hopefully, inspiring reply to the poem. This, of course, is no easy task. In a way, the poem seeking feedback is something whispered in a hushed hall or shouted to you in a storm, and your response is a very detailed, "This is what I heard."

As for the form your feedback takes, you will, with practice, develop your own approach. I tend to prefer a sort of letter (handwritten or typed) that begins and ends by thanking the poet and signs off with my warmest regards. Others prefer a spare and formal list. What is most important is to be generous and sensitive in composing your reply; the poet, in seeking feedback, will not gain from an assault. At the same time, though, compose your remarks with confidence, rigour, and authority; the poet will not gain from empty praise and will greatly gain from a unique and well-wrought response to her or his poem.

Answer the following questions as a means of composing your reply. This is the feedback you want to write directly on your friend's poem (or type and attach to her or his poem).

Writing Moment 5.8

- Return to the feedback you generated during Writing Moments 5.5 through 5.7.
- Compose a letter or a list (or combination of the two) in which you share your feedback.

Before concluding, I would like to add that when it comes to receiving feedback, you want to approach the process with the same attentiveness, openness, and rigour. I can testify based on my personal experience, the experience of my poet friends, and the experience of my students, that the workshop environment, however formal or informal, will expose tendencies and bad habits, and reveal paths and practices you would not have otherwise discovered. How you actually work with the feedback will be completely up to you. The key is to not get overwhelmed by the need to heed everything, or the defensive desire to shut it all out. Take the opportunity to share another poet's pair of eyes, and see what she saw in what you saw, and, quite simply, see where this takes you.

Writing Exercises

1. Practice the process of sharing feedback on published poems (though do not forward your comments to the author).
2. Once you have performed a few workshops with your writing group, vary your methods. If you have been meeting in person, shift the workshop online. If you have been sharing the work with your names on the poems, submit the work anonymously. Try a session in which the authors of the work being discussed are not allowed to talk.
3. This section used metaphors for the poem (the window and the machine) as a means of explaining the composition of critical feedback. Conceive of your own metaphors for the poem and reflect on how they help us understand not only the poem but how we read it, judge it, and provide feedback.
4. The persona is a great way to bring focus and range to your feedback. Create two critical personas. Name them and decide their views on poetry. What do they admire and value? What do they dread and lament? Provide feedback to a friend from your two personas.

Sharing Poetry

Why do poems composed hundreds or thousands of years ago remain with us today? Why do I still have a copy of the poem my brother wrote for me (titled "The Man", about, you guessed it, a man) when he was eight? Why can my friend, at three a.m., recite his favourite lines by Yeats? It is the same reason we have so many ancient and ever-changing poetic forms at our fingertips. Someone in some distant time cared for them, valued each one of these forms enough to compose within their restrictions, or teach them to a student, or write down those instructions and pass them on. It is the same reason previously unknown poets, past and present, come to our attention, and why poets who we thought we knew inside and out take on new shape under the influence of an original interpretation. Someone felt passionate enough to think deeply about their words, to celebrate their significance and argue for their worth.

Acts of celebration and interpretation, of preservation and propagation, are a central experience in the life of every human being. There are many ways, as a poet, to contribute to poetry's part in this conversation, to sustain poetry's past, enliven its present, and ensure its future fertile endurance. We will explore four general areas of possibility, though by no means is this list exhaustive: sharing your work, sustaining companions, poetry outreach, and (trust me) reading poems to crickets.

Sharing Your Work

No matter who you are as a writer, or which stage you are at in your career, you already have a circle of people with whom to share your poems. This circle may include your family, friends, classmates, a writing group, co-workers, fellow members of a religious, cultural, or recreational group, and on and on and on.

Even though distant from the professional business and public scene, your circle is still your most valuable "audience" because it is more than an audience. You share with them routines and a region, a way of life, the passing of the same days and nights, and what you share with them in your poems is the artful preservation of this local, collective experience, the rendering of these days and nights in well-chosen words and original visions. I can say with great confidence, as someone who has both received and shared such work, that the significance of this simple gesture cannot be overstated.

I say simple gesture not because the composition of your poems was simple, but because the act of sharing them is. The most basic vehicle—a few poems, handwritten or printed, and bound with a staple—will do the trick. If you are more artistically inclined, and willing to make the investment of time and money, you can also make a more visually appealing and carefully crafted **chapbook**. These same remarks apply to your creative writing class or writer's group. You could, for example, create a chapbook from any one of the collaborative practices recommended in this chapter.

Beyond this more personal act, sharing your work at a public reading and publishing your poems in print form are two very important goals. However, I will not go into great detail here on these topics but instead direct you to the recommended resources at the end of this chapter for further information. Why? First, both public reading and publication venues vary too much from region to region and community to community for me to offer guidance that is succinct and relevant. Second, with the rise of electronic means of dissemination, everything is in flux; what I advise now may not be true in a month (or may not have been true as of five years ago).

Instead, I will offer three basic but essential pieces of advice. First, research, research, research, and research some more, whether online, in print, or in person. This is the best way to discover all of the opportunities and venues for sharing your work. Second, rejection, put simply, is inevitable and plentiful, so prepare to have your poetry turned down left, right, and centre, up and down, diagonally, and, more than likely, in directions that you did not know existed. Finally, you should never have to pay someone to publish your work; publishers are the ones who pay you. Beware the many and varied schemes that prey on the desires of people who long only to see their names in print.

Writing Moment 5.9

- Choose a group from your circle (family, friends, etc.) for whom you will create a small chapbook.
- Decide which poems (between three and seven) you will include.
- When you have completed this chapter, create your chapbook.

Sustaining Companions

The most obvious way to share poetry is to sustain the work of the poets you most admire and the traditions through which you first found and continue to discover your voice. The goal, of course, is to promote these poets and traditions, and to do so in a way that conveys their richness and originality, that signals to readers the textures and depths of the poetry that awaits them.

Three of the most common methods for doing this are the interview, the essay, and the review. The interview is particularly suited to providing the intimate and candid portrait of the poet. The strength of the essay is deep and rigorous analysis of a subject, while the review, due to its short length, allows for greater breadth, leaving you time to write on multiple poets or movements in succession.

Though major print and online venues do not tend to accept unsolicited materials, many magazines and **literary journals** accept queries for interviews and reviews especially. If you are truly committed, you can follow the lead of the many writers who start blogs or dedicate pages on their websites to regularly posting interviews, reviews, or reflections on poetry, in particular, and culture in general.

In terms of your local community, there are also a number of avenues to pursue. Visit schools and public libraries and make sure they have copies of books by these authors. Libraries will often seek feedback from their communities regarding future acquisitions. If you are involved in a writing course or group of some kind, take the opportunity to present the work of these poets. Another rewarding and community-building strategy is to hold an event dedicated to the poet, poets, or tradition of your choice. This can take many forms, ranging from the themed private party (encouraging costumes and impromptu performances) to a public, more formal group performance. The key in all cases is to organize an event that captures the energy of the work or the vibrancy of the tradition.

The most obvious way that you sustain these companions, of course, is in your poetry; you can make this influence more overt, and your celebration more personal, by writing a poem in praise of one of them. The following writing moment will give you the opportunity to begin this piece.

Writing Moment 5.10

- Which poet influenced you most deeply? What, in terms of the poet's life, subject, and/or form do you most admire?
- With these remarks in mind, begin a poem that celebrates this poet, a poem that is composed in the poet's form and style.

Poetry Outreach

Once you have gained more confidence and experience as a writer, and established a strong writing circle, one of the most rewarding steps you can undertake is poetry outreach. This involves visiting groups, communities, and institutions that are not equipped to offer the opportunity to write poetry, but whose members would gain from the chance to explore their experiences in poetic form.

Over the past few decades, more and more writing groups and university creative writing programs have been sharing their creative writing expertise with high schools, eldercare facilities, prisons, mental health organizations, homeless shelters, and many other communities and institutions. These writers run free writing courses, plan stimulating exercises, and hold writing workshops, teaching, in some cases, basic literacy, and, in all cases, giving a unique voice the chance to speak. Chapbooks, blogs, or readings will often be planned to provide the new writers the opportunity to share their work, encouraging them to continue writing and giving them a new presence within the community.

Use the following writing moment to reflect on how you and your writing circle might undertake this sort of outreach.

Writing Moment 5.11

- What is a group, community, or institution in your area that would benefit from poetry outreach?
- How would you undertake this work? What types of opportunities would you offer?

Reading Poems to Crickets

I once read a poem to some crickets. It was one of Shakespeare's sonnets, though I do not remember which one. Our old farmhouse, a few years from being torn down, had been infested, and I felt like welcoming our multiplying guests. I read Roethke and Rich to a campfire. In high school, my friend and I found an out-of-the-way spot in the stairwell windowsills and read aloud our favourite poems from English class as well as our own strange creations. More than a decade later, I read one of my own poems to strangers at a simulated UFO crash site. (There is photo evidence online if you do not believe me.)

I have had poems read or recited to me out of the blue, by strangers and friends, in pubs, in parks, in water, in transit (the subway car clattering beneath the city's unfelt weight), on street corners, and from overturned milk crates. We used to write poems in chalk on the murky walls hidden in alleys and the sides of abandoned buildings, just to leave an unexplainable prize for anyone else who ventured there. Others, I discovered, use paint for the same purposes. I know poets who read all of their work to trees. An acquaintance claimed to have wasted her work on human ears; her true audience, she believed, was the static-filled screen of an outdated, unreceptive TV.

This is all to say: be the USS *Enterprise* of bards and read where no poet has read before. Mark your favourite poems by your favourite poets on the surfaces that have never held them. Read aloud and leave these words wherever you feel they are needed. Just as you must remember to listen to all and see all, remember that all things see and listen back. Take for example the fire hydrant outside the window, which I watch as I write this to you. In its muteness, its shadow-bending and shadow-casting solidity, its yellow, it is another, unending eye and ear.

Writing Moment 5.12

- Grab your favourite poem and then "Enterprise."
- Which poem did you choose? Where and how and when did you share it?

A book the length of the book you now hold could be written on the topic of sharing poetry, outlining the various practices, strategies, and benefits. I hope this discussion of these four general areas of opportunity have inspired you to explore the full range of possibilities regarding poetry preservation, promotion, activism, and celebration. I encourage you to develop this side of your creative life in concert with your individual poetic growth; each will fuel the other as you explore the poets and traditions you admire, promote them in particular, and poetry in general, and, inevitably, add your own contribution.

Writing Exercises

1. There are numerous electronic resources dedicated to sharing free, collaboratively created, user-generated knowledge. Wikipedia is, currently, the most popular example. Visit one of these resources and either improve or add an entry for your favourite poet.
2. Choose a popular communication technology or medium that allows for the creation of avatars. Create an avatar based on your favourite (preferably long dead) poet. For example, Emily Dickinson could become @e_dickinson on a micro-blog, while, on a social network, Eddie P. Oe could start friending folks. Use the avatar as a means of exploring the poet's work, promoting it, and creating something new.
3. Organize a themed poetry night. Choose a theme that is suitable for festive celebration, such as drink or food. Invite your guests to read one of their favourite poems on the topic.
4. Buy a box of chalk. Start spreading the words.

Conclusion: In Praise of Losing

Poetry, as Helen Vendler reminds us, is born out of moments of disequilibrium (14), a feeling of plenitude or vacuity, an encounter with that which is more than us or that which is lacking, or, just as often, an experience of being that very thing that is more or that lacks. Thus, note by note, figure by figure, line by line, broken here then broken there, we (to return to Nietzsche) lose ourselves to learn from that which "we ourselves are not." We lose ourselves in our efforts to give lyrical form to our immersion in the world, to the connections and disconnections, to the resonances and deadlocks, to the successes and failures, the embraces and the beating fists.

This same experience, as this chapter demonstrated, is repeated at the level of your poetry community, both the local and the global, both the present and the past. These venues of composition and dissemination are another avenue through which to explore these connections and disconnections, these deadlocks and resonances. Most importantly, they expand and extend the conversation that takes place between you and the page, adding new voices with which to converse, more attentive ears perked for your well-formed accounts of your travels and your just-forming replies.

Recommended Resources

- *Publishing*: Poetry publishing, for the most part, works like baseball: first, you prove yourself in the minor leagues (publish in literary journals), then, once you have done so, you are called up to the majors (your own full-length book). All of the information you need to navigate the ins and outs of this process can be found in *Poet's Market*, which is the best print resource, or at placesforwriters.com, which is the best online resource.

- *Public Readings*: Readings, reading series, and literary festivals provide a great opportunity for you to discover new poets and, if you are lucky, to see your favourites perform in person. You will be able to find out about such events in everything from local and regional newspapers to culture blogs. You should also consider attending (or, if you are feeling adventurous, organizing) an open-mic event. Like readings and reading series, open mics often take place at coffee shops or pubs and they give new poets the chance to share their work. The benefit of all of these venues is that they give you the chance to meet like-minded folks and start all-night conversations that can turn into lifetime arguments and dialogues and exchanges.

- *Writer Organizations*: Once you have begun to publish your work, and, in some cases, even before you have, you may want to join a writer's organization. These are poetry-specific organizations (for example, the League of Canadian Poets), national organizations (such as the Writer's Union of Canada), and provincial organizations (such as the Saskatchewan Writer's Guild). These organizations undertake crucial advocacy work on behalf of writers, and they provide a wealth of resources and knowledge. Most organizations hold a yearly conference, a great opportunity to meet like-minded poetry folk.

CONCLUSION

The Writing Moment without End

> "Nothing is a mistake. There's no win and no fail, there's only make."
>
> —Rule 6 of the Immaculate Heart College Art Department

I have wrapped up this guide to writing poetry by turning to publication not only because publication is a satisfying accomplishment but because, as I noted earlier, publication is also a means of sustaining the practice. Publication frees you up to begin something new, and it can earn you the opportunities and confidence that will allow you more time to lose yourself in this meeting of world and language, our times and your mind.

Expecting anything more than this from publishing your work is to risk losing sight of what is good in this practice, in the moment of writing. It is to tempt getting caught up in the dangers Sister Corita Kent warns against in the rules she composed for her art department at the Immaculate Heart College: the muse-mangling mentality of worrying about making a mistake, the creativity-killing culture of winning and losing and failing. "There's only make," is Sister Corita's reminder. She brings the point home with her ensuing and definitive rule: "The only rule is work."

With her warnings against the "win or go home" mindset, and her imperatives to make and to work, it is not surprising to find that Sister Kent further advises, "Consider everything an experiment." What does it mean to experiment when we, as poets, make and work? It means fully embracing a practice whose outcome is uncertain. And why, when we make and work, do we experiment? In order to discover—to give form to—what we do not know: what we have glimpsed or want to glimpse, what we have lost or cannot lose, what we believe could be possible and what we want to take the first step toward making so.

This is the process of experimentation with which I hope this book has stirred you to work as you explored the life in art and the art in life. This is the process of experimentation I hope this book has inspired you to undertake in your encounters with the tools and techniques of our practice, in your travels with our various companions and forms. And, just as importantly, this is the process of experimentation that I hope you see also underpins this book. This book also experiments. It seeks the unknown that is the meeting of my life and art with your life and art, hoping that in all of the uncertainties of this encounter you will discover something of worth: the poems you have composed, a passion for the practice, and the impetus to join the communities and conversations through which poetry, poets, and poems have and will endure.

On the occasion of our encounter, I would like to dedicate one final writing moment to these processes of experimentation, to all our fellow practitioners, to all the poets who even for a moment have written. I will number this writing moment in tribute to all of these moments, and I will leave the page beneath it blank for you to fill (again and again) with poems, with proposals for practice, with methods you extend to your friends or strangers or back to me.

So, in the following writing moment: work, make, and do. Figure, turn, leap, and swerve. Revel in making real all these ways of naming our acts of naming: form and shape and craft and, as they holler back where I'm from, get to it.

Writing Moment ∞

Appendix

Strategies for Revision

The following section supplements this book in general, and Chapter 4 in particular, with a few more specific remarks on revising, reworking, and wrapping up. The goal of this appendix is simply stated: to help you, as a poet, improve your skills of self-critique and self-refinement. These improvements will, ideally, lead you to write better poems and allow you to aid others in their respective revision processes.

We will accomplish this goal with a three-part method. First, we will explore two particular and very different examples of student revision, highlighting elements of the Goldilocks approach covered in Chapter 4. Second, I will share a few reflections on how we, as poets, revise not only poems but also our poetic practice. Finally, in place of a series of writing moments or exercises, each section will conclude with a list of relevant revision strategies and advice for reworking to help you both undertake particular revisions and reflect on your larger process.

Let us begin with one such list. This list covers the basics—you should always address the following points as you finalize your finished drafts.

Strategies and Advice for Revising

- Read your poem out loud a few times to ensure it sounds right. Depending on the poem, this could mean checking for tongue twister-esque constructions, jarring sound patterns, or overly melodious arrangements.

- Weed out any clichés.

- Go to work on your verbs one last time. Verbs serve as the poem's engine, animating the agents and elements of your poem and, in turn, activating the reader.

- Ensure that point-of-view and tense are consistent (or, if your poem makes wild leaps in point-of-view and tense, ensure these leaps are bounding how you please).

- Check grammar. Common errors include sentence fragments, subject-verb agreement, misplaced or dangling modifiers, and unclear pronoun reference.

- Check punctuation. Common errors include comma splices, missing commas, misused semi-colons, and missing and misused apostrophes.

- Check spelling. Spell check will catch most spelling errors; however, you still need to watch out for properly spelled words in the wrong spot (for example, "hole" instead of "whole") or for common errors such as your/you're, there/their/they're, and its/it's.

- When checking grammar, punctuation, and spelling, there is a key point to keep in mind. This checking may be undertaken in relation to standard rules of usage or in relation to your own rules. In the case of the latter, the goal is to remain consistent, so the reader recognizes your work as innovation and not as error. For example, if sitting down to workshop with bill bisset you would not advise he change the line, "discovr / a mountin sliding in2 th sand," to "discover / a mountain sliding into the sand."

Revising Poems: Two Examples

For our particular examples of the revision process, let us turn to two poems on the same topic (the fairy tale), but poems that are nonetheless different in an important way: they require different approaches to revision. These are two poems we looked at already, at the end of the section on "Voice and Developmental Structure" in Chapter 2, Novelette Munro's "A Real Fairy Tale" and Safa Minhas's "Frog Prince."

To turn to the terminology of the Goldilocks approach to revision, while Novelette needed to address issues with incomprehensibility and abstraction, Safa needed to address predictability and drag. Furthermore,

Novelette shared a very raw first draft. Thus, her poem was in need of a major revision. Safa's more polished draft only needed minor refinement.

Example 1: Major Revision

Here, to begin, is the first draft Novelette shared with our creative writing class:

A Real Fairy Tale

Ever had a memory, of a memory, of a memory of a memory?
It happens so interchangeably that you can't really remember
  the texture,
Or the width or lick of its essential features.
Then you wonder if it was all some great fairy tale.
But you could swear it smelled like a whispered promise
And it gripped so infinitely that trusting it became an ordinary
  frequency
So you pause in that strip of air and realize,
that the longing is more tangible than the birth of its cheer.
And then that's when you remember that the dream was all that
  was there.

The class was grabbed by the paradox of Novelette's title and the stimulating accumulation of layers of memory in the opening line. However, the students agreed that Novelette did not deliver on the promise of this opening. Put simply, we came away from the poem without a deeper understanding or experience of the "real fairy tale."

A number of students noted issues with incomprehensibility and clarity. For example, what exactly is the "it" that happens so interchangeably in line two and what exactly is being interchanged? The multiple ambiguous "its," too, with their indeterminate referents, amplified this problem.

The other major critique was that Novelette remained too abstract. The poem did not delve into the rich, particular imagery suggested by the metaphor "memory is a fairy tale." Nor did it give us a whiff of either the particular memory or the particular act of remembering.

Novelette visited with me after class and we discussed the class critique in relation to her purpose. She wanted to show how, in moments of important personal transition or transformation, fantasy often precedes (even replaces) reality. Memory, in other words, is not always the culprit; fantasy can herald the so-called real experience itself.

We decided on three goals to her revision: first, particularize the memory or the process of remembering; second, explore some of the metaphoric vehicles suggested by "memory as fairy tale"; and, third, avoid falling down the "rabbit hole" of repeated "its." As we discussed reworking the beginning, we took the always-helpful step of outlining. We sketched out a skeleton for the opening line and the first two turns, categorizing the segments by how they rendered and related to the particular memory that was the poem's core.

Over the next few weeks, Novelette completed six different drafts of the poem, working at building ground in the particular experience and crafting lift through figures. This is the final version she shared outside of class with the creative writing group:

A Real Fairy Tale

Ever had a memory of a memory of a memory of a memory?
As a child I believed in talking teenage turtles
who ninja-ed under the New York city streets
and half-scaled humans who breathed
through gills and sang under the sea.
My grandmother told me once that as a child
she saw a mermaid on the beach. And that
confirmed it all for me. She said
she was told stories about how mermaids were lonely
but did not want to be disturbed by us land geeks.
When a memory becomes a fantasy
the fantasy becomes the memory. I have
a memory of a memory of a memory of a memory
that my soul fell in love once for it reached out
and touched the nose of another. But that's
when I sneezed. It's hard to depend
on a memory to know what's true

when the longing for what used to be there
is more tangible than the birth of its cheer.
It reminds you that the fairy tale is all
that was there. My grandmother's right:
mermaids do live under the sea.

Note first how Novelette addressed the issue of clarity and abstraction by particularizing her perception through different memories—of her childhood, of her grandmother's childhood, and of falling in love. Just as significantly, she used these first two memories to establish the pull of fancy and fantasy, effectively setting up the poem's final turn: "the fairy tale is all / that was there." She also worked with a more dynamic blend of not only abstract reflection and concrete imagery but figurative rendering ("the birth of [what used to be's] cheer") and surprising turns (the sneeze that absurdly undercuts the moment of body-transcending love).

Novelette also followed that other piece of core advice given in Chapter 4: get closer to your tools. In lines two through five, she undertook her work of particularizing memory through an allusion (to the *Teenage Mutant Ninja Turtles* and *The Little Mermaid*) and she very cleverly allowed the *TMNT* allusion to shape her verbs: the turtles do not just "live" in the sewers but "ninja" there. Working with a shorter line also allowed her to nurture a number of fertile line breaks. Some leave us wanting to know what happens next (for example, "when a memory becomes a fantasy") while others create a pausing sense of resolution (for example, "the fairy tale is all"). Do you recognize the figure of order Novelette fruitfully employs in completing "when a memory becomes a fantasy" with "the fantasy becomes a memory"? Chiasmus, which we discussed in Chapter 4.

Example 2: Minor Refinement

Let us turn now from Novelette's revised poem to the first draft of a very different poem, Safa Minhas' "Frog Prince":

Frog Prince

There once was a time
Once upon a time

There was once upon a time
A rock existed
A stone?
That perhaps was
Man made or woman made
And there was a frog
A frog prince
And a peasant woman
She was pretty
By human standards anyway
So the frog lived on the rock
Not that it was comfortable
But it was his rock see
And the woman lived in her hut
Not that it was charming
But it was her hut see
Oh! And she fell in love with the frog
Some sort of fetish I guess
And the frog fell in love with the woman
Another sort of fetish I've heard
The frog kissed the woman
And the woman kissed the frog
They both transformed.
There were also some villagers
With pitchforks
And the end lived happily ever after.

In contrast to Novelette's first draft, which her classmates found had issues with clarity and abstractness, Safa's first draft was critiqued for lacking lift and being too predictable. Most simply, it lacked turns, whether the thought-provoking shift in action, the surprising leap in attention, or the mind-bending metaphor. The obvious suggestion was for Safa to work with figures of thought or to make bigger leaps in attention from line to line, but this did not suit her sensibility or her goal for the piece.

The more we discussed the poem, the more we realized it was not as predictable or lacking in lift as we thought. The turns were, in fact, already happening at two levels: in the teller and in the tale. The fix, then, was not wholesale change to the poem or Safa's approach to writing poetry. Instead, she needed to attend with greater care to the basics: punctuation and line breaks. Safa's lack of punctuation weakened the substance and force of the self-subverting voice of her tale-subverting teller; in other words, by abandoning punctuation in this particular poem, Safa underplayed the turns in voice that are the poem's crux. Her lack of enjambment also underplayed these turns and, furthermore, created repetitive, predictable line breaks that lulled rather than stimulated.

Here is the revised version of the poem, with the words left the same, but punctuation added and the lines re-broken:

Frog Prince

There once was a time, once
upon a time, where once
upon a time a rock existed
(a stone?), which perhaps
was man-made (or woman-made)
and there was a frog (a frog
prince!) and a peasant
woman who was pretty
pretty (by human standards
anyway). So the frog lived
on the rock (not that the rock
was comfortable (but it was
his rock, see)), and the woman
lived in her hut (not that it was
charming (but it was her hut,
see)). Oh! The woman fell
in love with the frog (some
sort of fetish, I guess),
and the frog fell in love with
the woman (another sort of fetish,
I've heard). The frog kissed
the woman and the woman
kissed the frog. They both

> transformed. There were also
> some villagers with pitchforks
> and flaming torches. The end
> (lived happily ever after).

This is, in terms of words, the exact same poem; and yet, through this close work with line breaks and punctuation, we have an entirely different and much more engaging and effective poem. The added enjambments snap the lulling, repetitive quality of the first draft, and achieve a number of different ends, at once pulling the reader forward (for example, the lines that end with verbs) and giving pause (for example, the double-meaning "fall" takes on in the line "The woman fell / in love"). The punctuation heightens the turns in the teller and the tale by more clearly demarcating them, upping the humour and foregrounding the complexity of the speaker. The bracketed bits can be read (as I suggested earlier) as the declarations of a self-subverting speaker or as different voices piping up, adding what they feel is missing from the primary teller's tale.

This more fully realized voice allows Safa's dark conclusion—the idea of the end living happily ever after—to really resonate in a way that it did not in the first draft. With the poem's overall humour sharpened, the ending marks a greater shift in tone in that, so to speak, it has "further to fall." The ending, too, is an excellent example of a general strategy that has many applications: the nurturing of repetition with a difference. In this example, we see the same strategy repeated (brackets), but with a different end (in terms of tone and mood). One of the effects, in a sense, is to reflect this darker tone onto the rest of the bracketed statements, separating the bracketed voice even further from the un-bracketed voice.

To conclude, then, these two examples of revision demonstrate how we can practically apply the Goldilocks approach to our own respective revision processes. The initial drafts of these two sample poems were marked by different issues, and, in turn, required different approaches to revision. We thus saw that the work of revision can involve large-scale re-visioning, as in the case of Novelette, or, as in Safa's case, it can involve addressing one or two elements of form.

We also saw in Novelette's and Safa's efforts that whatever type of revision is called for certain traits should always underpin your process: first, you need to get intimate with your tools and with the experience, idea, and world you seek to render, and, second, you need to be keen to test and experiment, eager to venture into alleys and caves, up fire escapes and down valleys, and willing at all times to abandon your results, tramp back from dead-ends, or wander farther, leaving behind the spark that lit you as you search for a new flame.

The following list of strategies and advice for revising will help you apply these insights as you revise your own poems. In the next section, I will conclude this appendix with a few reflections on revising the writing process.

Strategies and Advice for Revising

- Mark for cutting or rewriting parts of the poem that are too predictable or too incomprehensible, too cliché or too abstract, or where, as a poet, you remain too distant from the language, from the figures, sentences, words, rhythms, etc. As I wrote in Chapter 4: get close, get close, get close.

- Remember that the etymological root of the word "text" is "web." Like a web, all the parts of the poem connect. In this regard, employing "repetition with a difference" (whether in terms of image, sound, statement, or line break) is an indispensable technique.

- Remember, too, that the etymological root of "verse" is "turn." This "turning" can occur in every aspect of the poem: opinion, action, perspective, perception, tone, rhythm, diction, layout, and so on. If your poem sounds one note, counterpoint it with a surprising image, change in speech acts, or variation in tone. (Alternately, if your poem is a dissonant mess, cut away every element and feature that crowds out the raw note you wish to sound.)

- Cut, cut, and cut some more. No matter how much you love a line for its flow, sound, image, or figure, if it does not fit the poem, it has to go. As William Faulkner famously observed, "in writing, you must kill your darlings." (Though you can keep these dead darlings in a file and reanimate them in other poems.)

- There are a number of ways to add lift to your poem. Work in a metaphor and extend it. Shift agency by letting another entity or object speak and/or act for a line or two. Vary your forms of address and speech acts. Rewrite questions as speculations, speculations as definitive assessments, or definitive assessments as questions.

- The easiest way to add drag to your poem is to be specific in terms of idea or experience. The mystery should not be: "what is this poem about?" Instead, the mystery is the paradoxes, gaps, or transformations you reveal as characterizing the subject of your poem.

- Attend to the many rhythms that constitute a poem. For metrical verse, obviously, ensure you have not composed doggerel but also ensure that you are not being too metronomic. Work in rhythmical variations. There is also the rhythm that develops between concrete and abstract language, between straightforward sensory experience and metaphorically rendered vision. Consider sentence length, too. Are all your sentences the same length? Is this suitable? Would the poem work better as a single sentence or as five short sentences followed by a long sentence?

- When you get stuck, and you seriously doubt a poem's worth, step away from the poem with a part of the poem. Take the best line and start again. Choose an individual, entity, or object from the poem and rewrite the poem from this individual, entity, or object's perspective. In Chapter 2, I mentioned the techniques my professor, Andy Stubbs, taught me for enlivening stale poems: reverse the poem's order, randomize the order, or cut every flat line and word. Another popular technique is to replace your verbs with nouns and your nouns with verbs.

- If you are lacking "oomph" in your revision process, but need to keep working (for example, this is your one writing night of the week), return to your favourite poems. I also like to flip through a book of paintings or crank up a favourite song.

- If you remain dissatisfied with a poem, do not be afraid to set it aside for a few days, weeks, or months. The poem will benefit from your renewed (and refreshed) perspective.

Revising Process: Three Approaches

While reading (and reading and reading) and writing (and writing and writing), it is important to pause and reflect on your writing practice, on its traits and aims, on its repetitions and results, on your poems and your process. By reflecting on what and how and when you write, you, in effect, open yourself up to revising your writing practice. This revision takes the form of a whole range of productive questions. What are your habits—both in terms of the day-to-day practice and at the level of the line? What topics, tropes, and tools are you drawn to? Where, in terms of design and idea, have you not ventured?

When it comes to our tendencies as poets, then, there are many areas to explore. For example, throughout this book we have, in a sense, explored how different poets, schools, traditions, and artistic motivations can inspire us to revise our practice. Rather than retrace those tracks, I instead want to draw your attention to a few general possibilities regarding poems, revision, and artistic impulses, and share some personal examples. My hope is that these remarks will aid you in refining, renewing, or even revolutionizing not only the poems you compose but also the process by which you write them.

Revising Writing

Most obviously, you can reflect on and revise your writing process. You may need to work at developing better writing habits and committing to a consistent writing routine. Alternately, a set routine may be leaving you stuck in a writing rut. Change up where and when you write. Write at a different time of day or day of the week. If you normally write in solitary silence, spend a few writing sessions at a coffee shop or pub, or, if you feel like breaking further with the norm, at a shopping mall or sporting event. Attend a talk or panel on a topic you know nothing about. The number of fertile phrases, images, and potential metaphors that will bombard you will amaze you.

You should also experiment with how you write. Screen-bound folks should pick up a notebook every now and then, and paper-dedicated poets should try composing entirely at the computer. And do not underestimate the size of your canvas, whether it is an electronic document on a monitor or a paper document in your hands. These dimensions will influence the length of your lines and the length of your poem.

When it comes to revising the types of poems you compose, you can consider everything from tools and topics to origins and goals. The key is to reflect on the what, the how, and the why. For example, in the context of tools: what tools do you gravitate toward, how do you use them, and why (or, better, to what end)?

To turn to a personal instance, in high school, when I was first getting a handle on metaphor, I became obsessed with it. My practice changed: I composed metaphors for metaphors for metaphors and compiled them with lists of tenor-less vehicles. The results, at best, elicited an enthusiastic "that's a trip" from my best bud, but, at worst (and more often then not), they left my friends and teachers scratching their heads. This response in turn influenced my practice insofar as it made me reassess my goals: was that the reaction I was after?

While reflecting on the types of poems you write, you also want to think about the what, the how, and the why of the tools you do not gravitate toward, the topics you do not explore, the origins and goals by which you are not immediately occupied.

I am, for example, currently at work on some poems through which I am swerving from my tendencies and habits in terms of topic and practice. First, my first book was half-elegies and my second book was all elegies, so this time: no elegies. Second, I am a real "early to bed, early to riser," and I do the majority of my writing in the morning, rarely writing at night. For this new project, I write each poem over the course of 24 hours, staying awake the whole time.

Revising Revision

You can also revise the way in which you revise. Consider, for example, the two poles we have encountered in this book. There is the method I promoted in Chapter 4 and outlined above through the student examples, and there is the alternative process we tested out while exploring the work of Frank O'Hara in Chapter 2.

This first approach to revision is the process of finishing a draft, returning to the draft to revise, rework, and refine until you have a new draft, a draft that in turn may be open to this same process of revising days, weeks, months, or years later. Marianne Moore famously worked on her poem "Poetry" from 1924 to 1967, making a number of revisions throughout the decades and cutting the poem from more than 30 lines to 3.

The O'Hara approach, by contrast, is best summed up by returning to John Ashbery's remarks about his friend: first, that for O'Hara the poem is "the chronicle of the creative act that produces it," and, second, that this belief moved him to "constantly [experiment] in his poetry in different ways without particularly caring whether the result looked like a finished poem" (viii). Such a process might involve doing a series of poetic sketches of an object, activity, or scene, or creating poetic studies by attending to a single tool, or writing the same poem again and again from memory.

If you tend to favour one approach to revision, try out the other strategy. The key point to note is that both poles involve revising, refining, and reworking. The difference is that where for a poet like Moore the refining and reworking occurs part by part (in each poem), a poet like O'Hara refines and reworks poem by poem, the way a monk attempting to paint a perfect circle will start again each time, leaving the imperfectly completed shape be and painting a new one, adjusting his stroke, the way he dips the brush into the paint.

Revising Artistic Impulse

Beyond the two poles of revision, you can also consider the impulses that shape process. Two impulses you have probably encountered before are the minimalist impulse and the maximalist impulse. For a visual contrast between the two, compare a painting from Agnes Martin's series "The Island" to Joe Coleman's "Faith, 1996." (I will leave it for you to decide—both are available online—which is minimalist and which is maximalist.)

Minimalist poets come in many different forms, ranging from the haiku masters to the lyric minimalists like Joy Kogawa to the more concrete (and uber-) minimalists like Aram Saroyan (who, before the category's delisting, held the Guinness World Record for the world's shortest poem, which consisted of a single character: an "m" with an extra leg). Minimalists, more than any other poets, craft with silence, the unsaid, the blank—these foundations of speech and writing are foregrounded, treated overtly as materials of composition. The minimalist writing process involves, most obviously, paring the poem down to its purest, elemental features. This work may take the form of a reduced set of tools, such as short line length and limited figuration (in terms of sound and image). It may also involve attempts to reduce the world or experience to its surface, as a way of pointing to a yawning abyss or revealing a lack of authentic depth.

The maximalist, by contrast, sprawls, stretches, stuffs, stacks, and swells the line, the figure, the poem, and the page. The contemporary maximalist tradition stretches from Walt Whitman's "Song of Myself" to Allen Ginsberg's "Howl," from William Carlos Williams' multi-book (and multi-form, multi-vocal, multi-medial) *Patterson* to Kenneth Goldsmith's *The Weather*, a one 100-plus-page transcription of weather reports transcribed over the course of a year.

For me personally, the maximalist impulse manifests quite simply as this desire to expand, the sense that something more needs to be added, and, depending on the poem, it materializes as a counterpointing turn or perspective, a mix of styles (or mediums), a packed page, framed poems, and/or a nurturing of the choral.

To give you a specific example, a few years back my dad and I were cleaning out the barn and we discovered an old photo album. It was filled with black-and-white photos from the 1950s, documenting the daily life and vacations of an unknown family. A boy of about four or five years dominated the frames. I started writing a more conventional lyric poem about my dad and I discovering the album and speculating on its origin, meaning, and purpose.

Two things happened: first, I did not feel that this poem was doing justice to the images, and, second, one of my speculations—that the boy was a Cold War–esque spy assigned to murder the moon—sparked the maximalist in me and I started expanding. By the time the poem was published as "Last Flight of Sergeant Deadhead, the Astronut! (A Message in a Bottle)," the poem was framed by a fictional story about a made-up great-uncle and the poems themselves were a combo of my fictional great-uncle's cowboy poet ballads and his paranoid comic book-collage poem. (You read a sample of his work in Chapter 2.)

In taking this approach to revising your process, you can draw on any other popular approaches, schools, or movements: for example, absurdist, expressionist, surrealist, realist, and so on. You can also take any verb of your choosing as a defining impulse: drift, stutter, glow, deface, save, and so on. Alternately, forget any kind of reflection altogether and let your body take over; follow the impulse that seems to be the most inherent in the meeting of body and process and world. For example, even though I end up with poems that will never see the light of day, I still, every now and then, let the maximalist in me maximize, and fill all the white space, compile piled voices, manufacture a noise that aims to silence silence and blank out all the blanks.

To conclude the appendix, here is a final list of strategies and advice for revising.

Strategies and Advice for Revising

- Shake up your writing routine: new place (private or public), new time (morning or night), and new method (page or screen).

- Write a type of poem you have never written. What is a tool you rarely use? What is a subject about which you have never written? What is a fixed form you have never test run? Where is a venue from which you have never drawn inspiration? For whom have you never written a poem? You could compose five poems in response to these questions, or you could combine your responses and compose a single poem.

- Try out a different revision process. If you are more like Marianne Moore, make yourself a Frank O'Hara for a week. If you are an O'Hara, become a Moore.

- While visiting our poetry workshop, Stewart Cole recommended the following practice. Fill a notebook, bag, or drawer with the scraps of paper that contain your random notes, nighttime ramblings, and half-remembered dreams (and even the darlings you cut while revising). Compose a poem from these scraps, or, if you get stuck revising, pull out one of these scraps and see if you can work it into your poem.

- In this same vein, you could borrow a technique from the composer Brian Eno. Write the names of different poetic tools and different possible events or turns in a poem on scraps of paper and shake them up in a bag. Pull out a scrap and write a line using that tool. Repeat until you finish a first draft.

- Based on the above description of minimalism, compose a minimalist poem. You could also return to one of your completed poems and revise it while guided by the minimalist impulse.

- Based on the above description of maximalism, compose a maximalist poem. You could also return to one of your completed poems and revise it while guided by the maximalist impulse.

- Compose under the influence of a new impulse: drift, stutter, glow, deface, or whatever other verb moves you.

- What do you want your poem to do in the world? Write (and revise) accordingly.

Glossary

Accentual and accentual-syllabic verse These are two types of metrical verse. An accentual verse poem is composed according to a limit placed on the number of stressed syllables per line. Lines of accentual verse may vary in terms of syllable number, but each line will possess the same number of stressed syllables. By contrast, each line of an accentual-syllabic verse poem possesses the same number of stressed syllables and the same number of syllables per line.

Aesthetic Aesthetics is the branch of philosophy dedicated to the study of art. These philosophers ask questions about the nature, substance, value, and experience of the work of art. Aesthetic experiences are the sensations produced by the work of art, the sensations the work is often created to produce.

Aleatory Aleatory artistic practices are those that try to work an element of chance into the composition, presentation, or consumption of the work. For example, a number of aleatory artists have used the flip of a coin, throw of a die, or flip of a card to determine everything from which notes to compose to which order to screen the reels of a film. An aleatory poet may randomly draw words from the dictionary or borrow sentences from a newspaper, keeping the syntax but changing all the nouns.

Alliteration The repetition of the first consonant sound of words, as in "sleep soberly snaky state" and "church chimneys chime, 'achoo!'"

Ambiguity A word, phrase, sentence, symbol, etc. that is composed to have a double meaning is considered to be (effectively) ambiguous.

Anapests See metrical verse.

Anaphora A figure of order that involves repeating the same word or words at the start of successive verses, clauses, or sentences. For example, and perhaps most famously, "I have a dream" in Martin Luther King's "I Have a Dream" speech. A related figure of order is epistrophe, the repetition of the same word or words at the end of successive verses, clauses, or sentences.

Apostrophe A figure of speech through which the poet addresses a thing, abstract idea, or person (dead or alive).

Askew A productive perspective to maintain when composing poems: the askance, slant, awry, the unexpected angle.

Assonance The repetition of vowel sounds in words, as in "see Pacino bleed on screens" and "a bowl of awful coals."

Ballad stanza The ballad, one of the oldest forms of English-language poetry, was a popular oral form. These songs would celebrate love or tell bawdy, allegorical, or darker tales (sometimes about incest or infanticide). The ballad stanza is the metrical codification of this folk form. It is a quatrain that consists of two iambic tetrameter lines alternating with two iambic trimiter lines with an *abcb* rhyme scheme.

Beat poetry The essence of the Beat movement, which flourished in San Francisco and New York throughout the 1950s, is summed up in the double-meaning of the name: "beat" as in down-trodden and countercultural and "beat" as in beatific. Poets such as Jack Kerouac, Allen Ginsberg, and William S. Burroughs were as experimental and adventurous in their poetry as they were in their drug use, sexuality, and politics. Start with Ginsberg's *Howl* (1955), the movement's battle cry, and then explore the writings and recordings of Kerouac, Ginsberg, Burroughs, Gary Snyder, Diane di Prima, and Gregory Corso.

Black Mountain School A convention-spurning Black Mountain poet like Charles Olson, Robert Duncan, or Denise Levertov might guide me to write the school's definition like so: I, Daniel the Glosser, to you / write on this page of page-changing (so / present to presence) Yankee (doodle / not / always / dandy) poets who carefully re-carved verse / at Black Mountain College / in North Carolina / in the 1940s and '50s.The central move in this school is the turn to the body to redefine practice: the breath determines line length and rhythm, the location of the writing act determines content and form, and the poem is less an object than a process.

Chapbook A book of poems shorter than 40 pages. Very small, independent presses (micro-presses) tend to publish these, often with a low print run and in a well-designed edition.

Chiasmus A figure of order in which a potentially parallel order is presented in an inverted manner. For example, "the first will be last, and the last first." Chiasmus is often represented as ABBA (i.e., [A] first, [B] last, [B] last, [A] first) or an X (foregrounding the word's Greek root *chi* or X).

Chiastic See chiasmus.

Conceptual poets A type of avant-garde poetry popularized in the 1960s. A pair of poets, Katie Fewster-Yan and Novelette Munroe, summed up the school well in a recent class presentation: conceptual poets are anti-self-expression, privilege the idea, and (as Katie and Novelette put it, adding extra quotation marks for effect) appropriate! "appropriate!" ""appropriate!"" In other words, to rewrite Pound, don't "make it new," but "borrow, steal, cite, remix, etc., and make what you've borrowed, stolen, cited, remixed, etc. new."

Concrete poets Concrete poets explore the graphic and material quality of language, taking a wide range of approaches. A concrete poem may be an "unreadable" poem that manipulates typography or it may be a hybrid between a concrete, iconic shape and a conventionally readable poem.

Confessional poetry Beginning most prominently with Robert Lowell's *Life Studies* (1959), a number of poets in the late 1950s and early '60s took a deeply personal turn toward the self, exploring both a more individual language and private topics—suicide, alcoholism, mental illness—than had been encountered before with such intimacy and honesty. After finishing Lowell's *Life Studies*, move on to Sylvia Plath's *Ariel* (1965), Anne Sexton's *Live or Die* (1968), and John Berryman's *The Dream Songs* (1969).

Consonance The repetition of internal or end consonant sounds in words, as in "some alumnus amble" and "caricatures of Tricky Dick."

Cut-up This avant-garde technique, invented by Dadaists in the 1920s, involves cutting the individual words from a source text and rearranging them into a new text. You could, for example, cut out the words of this glossary and reorder them into a new (absurd) definition.

Dactyls See metrical verse.

Dadaist An early twentieth-century European artistic movement that sought to shock the established order with spontaneous, transgressive, and often hilarious creations. If writing this entry, a Dadaist would probably add: dadadadadadadadadadadadadadadada dadadadadadadadadadadadadadadadada-dadadadadadadadadadadadadadadadada-dadadadadadadadadadadadadadadadada-dadadadadadadadadadadadadadadadada-dadadadadadadadadadadadada.

Defamiliarize The ability of a poem (or any work of art) to overthrow our perceptual habits and routines of thought, and to thrust us into seeing our world and ourselves anew.

Doggerel Irregular, crude, and poorly crafted verse. Or, to let the doggerelist speak for itself about itself: Rhythms so irregular, that grate, / is how the doggerel-makers most basically make, / though bawdy burlesque verses they might wick / and light with drink and merkin and with—sick!

Draft A poem in its preliminary stages. It might be ready for a reader, but it is still in need of further work.

Duende Spanish for "ghost" or "evil spirit," the *duende*, in art, names the arising of the violent, unconscious, irrational, primal, and so on. Federico García Lorca, one of the great thinkers of *duende*, writes: "With idea, sound, or gesture, the *duende* enjoys fighting the creator on the very rim of the well. Angel and muse escape with violin, meter and compass; the *duende* wounds. In the healing of that wound, which never closes, lie the strange, invented qualities of man's work."

Ekphrastic Works of ekphrasis are verbal works (whether poetry or prose) that attempt to represent a work of visual art. The original Greek word meant "description," and, initially, "ekphrasis" was the rhetorical term for presenting a very detailed description of an object.

Envoi A three-line stanza that often ends French fixed-form poems. Traditionally, the function of the envoi is to reflect upon the preceding poem or to address someone (real or invented).

Epigram A pithy, piercing saying.

Faux-ccasional Occasional poems are poems composed on or for a particular, significant occasion, and they are often intended for public reading (at or after the event). There are many types of occasional poem: epithalamion (wedding poems), elegy (a work of mourning), paean (song of triumph), war poems (protesting or celebrating), birthday poems, and so on. A faux-occasional poem is an occasional poem with a speculative slant in that it is composed for an invented occasion (an imagined wedding, for example, or the birthday an historically significant individual never reached).

Figure When writing poetry, we use the word "figure" in a number of different ways. The figure can refer to an example of a figure of speech. The figure as a sort of symbol (as, for example, in case of the ideal image) can be any form (word, picture, etc.), object (tree, car, etc.), or entity (a person, cat, etc.) that embodies or represents a certain idea. Figure as a verb (to figure) describes our act of composing with a figure of speech, the work of manipulating language with a figure of speech.

Figure of speech Figures of speech (also referred to as figurative language) are, as Chris Baldick states, forms of expression that swerve from conventions of literal meaning (figures of thought), attend to the patterning of sound (figures of sound), or depart from normal order (figures of order).

Fixed forms Forms of poems (also known as closed forms) in which the metre and rhyme scheme are determined by a set of rules.

Found poem Composing with "found" material is an avant-garde technique invented by Dadaists in the 1920s. It involves finding objects of literary or visual art in the everyday world. A found poem is composed of text found by the author in a book or film, on an advertisement or passport, graffitied in an alley or bathroom stall, and so on. There are a number of different ways to compose a found poem: present the found text as is, combine it with other bits of found text or original words, or erase words from the found text to create new sentences and phrases.

Free verse Forms of poems (also known as open forms) in which the poet does not follow a set metrical pattern or rhyme scheme. The basic unit is the line, and work with line breaks, line lengths, layout, and rhythmic patterns varies poet to poet.

Futurist Do you agree with the following? 1. War is the world's only hygiene. 2. We need to murder the moonshine. 3. I am sick of pensive immobility's inability to love (and become) the airplane. If so, then this early twentieth-century Italian and Russian movement, which demanded the abandonment of old forms and "feminine" sentiment for "masculine" aggression and modern industry and technology, is just the thing for you.

Genre A genre is a kind, species, style, or type. For example, poetry, prose fiction, and drama are all literary genres. Poetry itself is composed of a range of genres. These genres are often linked by a shared topic and a shared set of (ever-changing) conventions. Genres of poetry include elegy (a work of mourning), ekphrasis (poems about works of art), aubade (a love poem in which the speaker laments the arrival of morning because the speaker now has to leave her or his lover's bed), and the angry love poem.

Harlem Renaissance A cultural movement that flourished in New York's African American community (and beyond). These musicians, writers, visual artists, and thinkers explored African American experience in all its forms—racial pride, rage, language, and future potential. Significant poets include Langston Hughes, Countee Cullen, and Gwendolyn Bennett. For an insightful primer on some of the movement's concerns, read Hughes' essay, "The Negro Artist and the Racial Mountain" (1926). For an excellent selection of essays, poems, stories, and plays pick up *Double-Take: A Revisionist Harlem Renaissance Anthology* edited by Venetria K. Patton and Maureen Honey.

Hybrid works See mixed media poetry.

Iambs See metrical verse.

Imagery Imagery is the material of our senses moved into language. A poetic image may serve a solely sensory function. More often than not, though, an image possesses a figurative or symbolic element as well. Imagery can also be considered in terms of what it is not—as Chris Baldick observes, it is "distinct from the language of abstract argument or exposition."

Imagist Here is a definition of Imagism that the Imagists would agree with in content but not in form: With apparitions imaged, beats unbound, / these poets would have scorned this metered sound. Why? The content addresses the key ideas these English and American poets developed beginning in 1908—a practice based on precise attention to things (objective and subjective) and the unbound beat of a newer, looser rhythm—and yet, form-wise, the couplet is written in iambic pentameter.

Interlocking rhyme A rhyme scheme that alternates (e.g., *abab*).

Internet comment thread The comment thread is one of the many communicational mediums to replace IRL conversation and one of the many communicational mediums that will be replaced by Apple's techno-psychic implant, iLink.

Irony This figure of speech creates a contrast between intended meaning and implied meaning, or between content (what is said) and form (how it is said). Irony produces a kind of doubling and is thus often described in terms of an ironic discrepancy, incongruity, inconsistency, and difference.

Language poetry A politically engaged and avant-garde poetry movement that arose in America in the late 1960s. Poets such as Ron Silliman, Lyn Hejinian, Susan Howe, and Bob Perelman turn from the self to language insofar as they are interested less in making meaning and more in meaning making, in the codes and contexts, the politics and conventions, the relationships and repressions that determine meaning making. An excellent place to start, if you can get your hands on a copy, is Silliman's Language poetry anthology, *In the American Tree*.

Leap Concerning the structure or development of a poem, the leap describes a surprising, illuminating, defamiliarizing, stirring, and/or unbalancing shift in attention from one sentence to the next.

Line break A line of poetry is the combination of words and punctuation points that appear on the same horizontal row. Thus a line is distinct from a sentence. The point where this line ends is the line break.

Literary journals Periodicals that tend to publish poetry, short stories, creative non-fiction, and often reviews and visual art. Journals may be run independently or affiliated with a university. They are a great way to stay abreast of developing trends and cutting-edge work, and they also offer you the chance to share your own poems.

Lyric poetry The lyric (in Ancient Greece) was originally a song performed on a lyre. The lyric poem has since become most commonly characterized as a short first-person poem dedicated to more personal meditations.

Lyrical What we describe as lyrical is often that which manifests some of the (ideal) qualities of the lyric poem: an experience of self-transcendence or beauty, the manifestation of formal ingenuity or precision, or the figuring of—the making present of—something fleeting, impossible, or lost. This is why many awe-inspiring acts—from Lebron James throwing down a slam dunk to Jiro Ono preparing sushi—are described as poetry. These acts manifest this lyrical experience, embodying the edge of what is possible in the meeting of craft and life.

Mediums Any intermediary forms that enable the shaping and sharing of expression, gesture, thought, etc.

Metaphor A figure of speech that makes a connection between two things, puts an equals sign between them, without using "like" or "as." A metaphor is composed of two parts: a tenor (the literal term) and a vehicle (the figurative term). For example, in the everyday metaphor, "love is a sickness," love is the tenor and sickness is the vehicle.

Metonymy Arp and Johnson succinctly define metonymy as "the use of something closely related for the thing actually meant" (79). Helen Vendler echoes Arp and Johnson with her definition, "assemblage by parts" (682), as does Stephen Adams, defining metonymy as the use of "one object (or concept) to stand for another to which it is closely or customarily related" (137). For example, you could state, "two boxers fought in a championship fight," or you could describe "gloved fists trading blows for the sake of the belt."

Metrical verse Metre is the patterning of stressed and unstressed syllables. The two main types of metrical verse (accentual and accentual-syllabic) are the foundations of fixed poetic forms. There are four main types of rhythm (also known as metrical feet). The two rising rhythms are the iamb (unstressed-stressed) and the anapest (unstressed-unstressed-stressed). The two falling rhythms are the trochee (stressed-unstressed) and the dactyl (stressed-unstressed-unstressed). Spondees (stressed-stressed) and pyrrhics (unstressed-unstressed) may also be used as substitutions for a line's dominant rhythm. The number of stressed syllables (or metrical feet) determines the length of the metrical line. For example, the trimter line possesses three stressed syllables (three feet), the tetrameter line four stressed syllables (four feet), and the pentameter line five stressed syllables (five feet).

Mixed media poetry Like mixed media visual art, this poetry employs more than one medium. Poetry (as written word) can combine with painting, photography, film, comics, and so on.

New pen A burgeoning or yet-to-be utilized means of (or medium for) composing (mostly mixed media) poetry. The typewriter once fell into this category. Photoshop and Twitter are ideal right now. Home-brew pharma and cyber-combining may one day pass from possible to real.

Non-hegemonic identities The hegemonic identity is the dominant, ruling identity. The position that aims to define what is normal, right, good, etc., and, through this, proliferate. Non-hegemonic identities are those that resist a specific hegemony and those that try not to reproduce hegemony as such.

Objective Objective statements are stripped of obvious (emotional, figurative, etc.) embellishments, and are aimed at (not always successfully) presenting material facts and truths that can be perceived regardless of personal identity or subjective position.

Pentameter See metrical verse.

Perception Most generally, perception is the act of apprehending with the mind and body. As poets we perceive and shape our perceptions (and, as Helen Vendler notes, our analysis of our perceptions) with our poetic tools.

Perspective There are two possible levels of perspective in a poem. First, perspective is a way of naming the position from which we perceive and compose, or, in other cases, the position from which our poem's speaker perceives and composes (for example, a persona's recollection of a day at the beach). Second, perspective refers to the perceiving positions of the different agents within our poems (for example, the different people and creatures whom the persona recalls, imagining what they saw and remember).

Plot structure Whether Aristotle's whole, with its beginning, middle, and end, or Freytag's triangle or dramatic arc (which I outline in my Orpheus example), plot structures are the strategies by which stories are outlined and planned before being executed. The assumption is that there are patterns that produce, for example, a more entertaining work, and that these patterns should be abstracted and obeyed.

Prosopopeia A figure of speech through which an inanimate object, non-human entity, or abstract idea is endowed with the ability to speak.

Pyrrhics See metrical verse.

Quatrain A four-line stanza.

Rhyme The repetition of the same sound (vowel and/or consonant) at end of words, as in "owl-fowl" and "explicate-speculate."

Rhyme scheme The method for patterning end-rhymes. The convention is to document this scheme with the letters of the alphabet. For example, if you have a quatrain in which the first two lines rhyme, and the third and fourth lines rhyme, your rhyme scheme would be: *aabb*.

Satirical Satires are works that critique, ridicule, and/or expose hypocrisy, often through the use of irony. A poem can be entirely satirical or simply possess a moment of satire.

Scansion The act of determining a poem's metre. There are three steps: mark the stressed and unstressed syllables, divide the lines into feet, and note both the dominant rhythm (for example, iambs) and the divergences from this dominant rhythm.

Semiotic Semiotics is the study of signs and systems of signs. Semioticians may study language as such or they may study a specific realm or activity (for example, wrestling) as a system of signs.

Simile Like a metaphor, a simile makes a comparison. However, a simile differs in that it makes its comparison using "like" or "as." Due to the mediating "like" or "as," the connection the simile draws can seem less intense, more tentative, and/or more personal than a metaphor's connection.

Sound poetry A type of avant-garde poetry popularized in the 1910s. Sound poets, as the name suggest, take the sounds of words as their basic compositional material.

Spondees See metrical verse.

Sonnet A fixed form that has flourished since its invention in thirteenth-century Italy. Two of the most popular sonnet forms are the Petrarchan and the Shakespearean. The Petrarchan consists of an eight-line stanza (an octave) with a rhyme scheme of *abbaabba* connected to a six-line stanza (a sestet) with a rhyme scheme of *cdecde* or *cdcdcd*. The Shakespearean consists of three linked quatrains rhymed *abab*, *cdcd*, *efef*, and a closing couplet rhymed *gg*.

Stanza A group of lines of poetry that are identified according the number of lines: couplet (two lines), tercet (three lines), quatrain (four lines), quintain (five lines), sestet (six lines), septet (seven lines), octave (eight lines).

Stimuli The causes, the factors that spur, or inspire.

Stressed and unstressed syllables The core units of metrical verse. Stressed (or accented or heavily stressed) syllables are syllables that receive more emphasis, while unstressed (or unaccented or lightly stressed) syllables are syllables that receive less emphasis. A unit of stressed and unstressed syllables is known as metrical foot.

Subgenre A genre within a genre.

Subjective Thoughts, feelings, perceptions, views, etc., that relate to the individual self. Subjective knowledge is often considered the opposite of (and devalued by) objective knowledge.

Surrealist Originating in the 1920s, surrealism is an artistic movement that values the unconscious and the defamiliarizing, and employs a series of self-transcending/defeating techniques. These techniques include automatic writing, collage, and the expression of a totally free imagination that can lead to Dalí-esque images—seeing the slumbering elephants that are the throbbing of your page-gripping fists.

Syllabic verse A poem composed according to a limit placed on the number of syllables per line.

Symbolic A symbol is a figure of speech through which a word, thing, person, event, etc. expresses a meaning beyond its literal meaning. For example, light has both a literal meaning (for example, the dictionary definition: "electromagnetic radiation from about 390 to 740 nm in wavelength that stimulates sight and makes things visible") and a variety of symbolic meanings (for example, life, knowledge, salvation, or home).

Synecdoche For Arp and Johnson (79), and for Helen Vendler (682), a type of metonymy defined as "the use of the part for the whole." Another common way to think of synecdoche is genus for species (or the reverse). For example, if a knife-wielding maniac threatens you with "his steel," he is making a synecdoche: steel (genus) for species (knife blade).

Tense The grammatical means by which we mark different times.

Thematic A theme is the abstract idea (for example, ideal love or justice) a work of art explores. This is not to be confused with topic.

Tools Anything we use to shape language and compose poems: figures of speech, conventions, traditions, methods, styles, strategies, and techniques.

Trochees See metrical verse.

Troubadour A specific type of lyric poet, prominent from the eleventh to the thirteenth centuries, who sang songs of chivalry and gallantry. A female troubadour was called a trobairitz.

Visual poets A type of avant-garde poetry popularized in the 1910s. Visual poets take the graphic aspect of words as their basic compositional material.

References

Adams, Stephen. *Poetic Designs: An Introduction to Meters, Verse Forms, and Figures of Speech*. Peterborough: Broadview, 1997.

Arp, Thomas R. and Greg Johnson. *Perrine's Sound and Sense: An Introduction to Poetry*. 13th ed. Boston: Wadsworth, 2011. Print.

Ashbery, John. "Introduction." *The Collected Poems of Frank O'Hara*. Ed. Donald Allen. Berkley: U of California P, 1995. vii–xi.

Baldick, Chris. *The Concise Oxford Dictionary of Literary Terms*. New York: Oxford UP, 1990.

Ball, Hugo. "Karawane." *ubu.com*. UbuWeb. n.d. Web. 7 Sept. 2012.

Brown, Jericho. "One Whole Voice." *Poetry Foundation*. Poetry Foundation. 1 Feb. 2012. Web. 22 Oct. 2012.

Browning, Robert. "My Last Duchess." *The Oxford Authors Robert Browning*. Ed. Adam Roberts. Oxford: Oxford UP, 1997. 101–2.

Burke, Edmund. *The Writings and Speeches of Edmund Burke: Volume I: The Early Writings*. Eds. T.O. McLoughlin and James T. Boulton. Oxford: Clarendon, 1997. Print.

Cole, Stewart. "re: textbook." Message to the author. 9 Mar. 2013. E-mail.

Coleridge, Samuel Taylor. *The Complete Works of Samuel Taylor Coleridge*. Vol. 6. Ed. James Marsh. Harper & Brothers, 1884.

Creeley, Robert. "The Language." *The Collected Poems of Robert Creeley, 1945–1975*. Berkeley: U of California P, 1982. 283.

Deleuze, Gilles and Félix Guattari. *What Is Philosophy?* Trans. Graham Burchell and Hugh Tomlinson. London: Verso, 1994.

Dickinson, Emily. "There's a certain Slant of light." *The Complete Poems of Emily Dickinson*. Ed. Thomas H. Johnson. New York: Little, Brown, and Co., 1976. 118–9.

Eliot, T.S. "Reflections on Vers Libre." *To Criticize the Critic and Other Writings*. Lincoln, NB: U of Nebraska P, 1991. 183–8.

Ferguson, Margaret, Mary Jo Salter, and Jon Stallworthy, eds. *The Norton Anthology of Poetry*. 5th ed. New York: Norton, 2004.

Frost, Robert and Louis Untermeyer. *The Letters of Robert Frost to Louis Untermeyer*. New York: Holt, 1963.

Glück, Louise. "Disruption, Hesitation, Silence." *Proofs and Theories: Essays on Poetry*. New York: Ecco, 1994. 73–86. Print.

Hébert, Louis. "The Semiotic Square." *Signo*. Signo. n.d. Web. 2 Dec. 2012.

Heffernan, James A. W. *Museum of Words: The Poetics of Ekphrasis from Homer to Ashbery*. Chicago: U of Chicago P, 2004.

Heighton, Steven. "Given to Inspiration." *Work Book: Memos & Dispatches on Writing*. Toronto: ECW, 2011. 11–9.

Hirsch, Edward and Eavan Boland, eds. *The Making of a Sonnet*. New York: Norton, 2008.

Jordan, June. *June Jordan's Poetry for the People*. Ed. Lauren Muller and the Poetry for the People Collective. New York: Routledge, 1995.

Kunitz, Stanley. "The Portrait." *The Poems of Stanley Kunitz: 1928–1978*. Boston: Little, Brown, 1979. 86. Print.

Lorde, Audre. "Poetry Is Not a Luxury." *Sister Outsider: Essays and Speeches*. Berkeley: Crossing Press, 2007. 36–9.

———. "Stations." *Our Dead Behind Us*. New York: Norton, 1986. 14–15. Print.

Lowell, Amy. "Preface." *Some Imagist Poets: An Anthology*. Ed. Amy Lowell. Boston: Houghton Mifflin, 1915. v–viii.

Marlatt, Daphne. "Imagine: a town." *Steveston*. 1974. Vancouver: Ronsdale, 2001. 11–12.

McCaffery, Steve. "Sound Poetry—A Survey." *ubu.com*. UbuWeb. n.d. Web. 7 Oct. 2009.

McEwan, Ian. "Ian McEwan: By the Book." *The New York Times*. 6 Dec. 2012. Web. 6 Dec. 2012.

"Mission & Values." *aboutmcdonalds.com*. McDonald's, n.d. Web. 9 Aug. 2012.

Moore, Marianne. "England." *Collected Poems*. London: Faber and Faber, 1951. 53. Print.

Moure, Erín. "Rusty Talk with Erín Moure." *The Rusty Toque*. 9 Sept. 2012. Web. 5 Dec. 2012.

O'Hara, Frank. "[The Light Presses Down]." *The Collected Poems of Frank O'Hara*. Ed. Donald Allen. Berkley: U of California P, 1995. 475–6.

Olson, Charles. "Projective Verse." *20th-Century Poetry and Poetics*. 5th ed. Ed. Gary Geddes. Toronto: OUP, 2006. 1027–36.

Pentametron. "I have a normal person voice again!"*pentametron.com*. Pentametron. n.d. Web. 25 Nov. 2012.

Pope, Alexander. "An Essay on Criticism." *The Poems of Alexander Pope*. Ed. John Butt. Chelsea, Michigan: Sheridan, 1963. 143–68.

Pound, Ezra. "A Retrospect." *Literary Essays of Ezra Pound*. New York: New Directions, 1968. 3–14.

Ransom, John Crowe. "Poetry: A Note on Ontology." *Close Reading: The Read*. Eds. Frank Lentricchia and Andrew DuBois. Durham, NC: Duke UP, 2003. 43–60.

———. "Stations." *The Broadview Anthology of Poetry*. 2nd ed. Ed. Herbert Rosengarten and Amanda Goldrick-Jones. Peterborough, ON: Broadview, 2008. 754–5.

Sans Soleil. Dir. Chris Marker. Perf. Alexandra Stewart. Argos Films, 1983. DVD.

Service, Robert W. *Selected Poetry and Prose*. Ed. Michael Gnarowski. Toronto, Dundurn: 2012.

———. "The Cremation of Sam McGee." *Songs of a Sourdough*. 1907. London: Ernest Benn, 1957. 64–70. Print.

Shakespeare, William. "Sonnet 18." *The Broadview Anthology of Poetry*. 2nd ed. Ed. Herbert Rosengarten and Amanda Goldrick-Jones. Peterborough, ON: Broadview, 2008. 18.

Shelley, Percy Bysshe. "A Defence of Poetry." *Shelley's Literary and Philosophical Criticism*. Ed. John Shawcross. London: Henry Frowde, 1909. 120–59. Print.

Sidney, Sir Philip. *A Defence of Poetry*. Ed. J.A. van Dorsten. New York: Oxford, 1971. Print.

Stevens, Wallace. "Modern Poetry." *The Palm at the End of the Mind: Selected Poems and a Play*. New York: Vintage, 1990.

———. "The Idea of Order at Key West." *The Collected Poems of Wallace Stevens*. 1954. New York: Knopf, 1965. 128–30. Print.

Thomas, Dylan. *On the Air with Dylan Thomas: The Broadcasts*. Ed. Ralph Maud. New York: New Directions, 1992.

Vendler, Helen. *Poems, Poets, Poetry: An Introduction and Anthology*. 3rd ed. New York: Bedford/St Martin's, 2009.

Wallace, David Foster. "*E Unibus Pluram*: Television and U.S. Fiction." *A Supposedly Fun Thing I'll Never Do Again*. New York: Little, Brown, and Co., 1997. 21–82.

Wordsworth, William. *Lyrical Ballads: With Pastoral and Other Poems*. London: T.N. Longman and O'Rees, 1802.

Žižek, Slavoj. *The Indivisible Remainder: An Essay on Schelling and Related Matters*. London: Verso, 1996.

Index